The
BEST SPECIMEN
of a TYRANT

The
BEST SPECIMEN
of a TYRANT

The Ambitious Dr. Abraham Van Norstrand
and the Wisconsin Insane Hospital

THOMAS DOHERTY

University of Iowa Press
Iowa City

University of Iowa Press, Iowa City 52242
Copyright © 2007 by Thomas Doherty
First University of Iowa Press edition 2013
www.uiowapress.org
Printed in the United States of America

Design by Jennifer Bottcher

No part of this book may be reproduced or used in any form or by any means without permission in writing from the publisher. All reasonable steps have been taken to contact copyright holders of material used in this book. The publisher would be pleased to make suitable arrangements with any whom it has not been possible to reach.

Photographs of Abraham Van Norstrand and his son courtesy Neville Public Museum of Brown County. All other photographs courtesy the Wisconsin Historical Society.

The University of Iowa Press is a member of Green Press Initiative and is committed to preserving natural resources.

Printed on acid-free paper

Library of Congress Cataloging-in-Publication Data

Doherty, Thomas.
The best specimen of a tyrant: the ambitious Dr. Abraham Van Norstrand and the Wisconsin Insane Hospital / Thomas Doherty.—1st University of Iowa Press ed. 2013.
      p.   cm.
Originally published: Madison, Wis.: Spenser-Hoyt, c2007.
Includes bibliographical references and index.
ISBN-13: 978-1-60938-146-2, ISBN-10: 1-60938-146-7 (pbk)
ISBN-13: 978-1-60938-161-5, ISBN-10: 1-60938-161-0 (e-book)
1. Van Norstrand, Abraham, 1825–1883.   2. Physicians—Wisconsin—Biography.
3. Wisconsin State Hospital for the Insane—History.   4. Psychiatric hospitals—Wisconsin—History—19th century.   5. Businessmen—Wisconsin—Biography.   I. Title.
R154.V356D64   2013
362.2'109775—dc23   2012024073

In democratic times enjoyments are more intense than in the ages of aristocracy, and the number of those who partake in them is vastly greater; but, on the other hand, it must be admitted that man's hopes and desires are oftener blasted, the soul is more stricken and perturbed, and care itself more keen. ... Complaints are made in France that the number of suicides increases; in America suicide is rare, but insanity is said to be more common there than anywhere else.

—ALEXIS DE TOCQUEVILLE, *Democracy in America*

CONTENTS

INTRODUCTION

For those who learned about mental hospitals from *One Flew Over the Cuckoo's Nest* and other popular fare, it may be hard to believe that once upon a time those isolated, mazelike institutions were expected to usher in a kind of golden age. In the early nineteenth century, a group of asylum doctors came together to argue that insanity was not a curse but a curable disease. Build hospitals to our demanding specifications, and, they vowed, we will not only comfort and nourish your suffering loved ones; we will make them whole again. Thus was launched the so-called "Hospital Movement." Over the following decades, huge and breathtakingly expensive facilities went up in virtually every state. So much was invested. So much was expected in return.

It wasn't long before those places were famous mostly for the scandals uncovered there. Later still they were dismissed as "warehouses." What went wrong?

That question was certainly *not* on my mind in 1972, when, as a graduate student, I started a year-long field placement at Mendota Mental Health Institute, on the north shore of the lake in Madison, Wisconsin, for which it is named. What did strike me then was how puny the utilitarian, 1950s-era brick buildings appeared among the great oaks that towered over them and the grassy fields that surrounded them and swept down to the lake. Such a majestic setting deserved architecture to match.

Eventually I went to work at a treatment unit in one of those buildings, and from nursing assistants I learned that in fact a palatial stone presence had once dominated the landscape, although nothing remained but a tunnel to nowhere, a half-buried greenhouse, and a span of stone foundation.

That was my introduction to the Wisconsin Insane Hospital. The fact that it was long-vanished and virtually forgotten made it even more fascinating to me, but decades passed before I could attempt some serious research. At the Wisconsin Historical Society I found early hospital casebooks, applications for admission, minutes of the original trustees, and annual reports of harried superintendents itemizing hardships encountered and crises overcome. From all that accumulated mustiness emerged an endless stream of lost souls, such as a young woman devastated by the deaths of her brothers in a Confederate prison camp: "Conceives that she can feed the portraits of her brothers ... by crumbling up bread and trying to make them eat it," her records say, and I began to comprehend the enormity of the burden shared by the superintendent and his handful of underlings.

But nothing brought the place to life like the document appended to the annual report for 1868. It was thick as a Russian novel and consisted primarily of testimony elicited over months of dramatic hearings. This was spellbinding stuff. From the mouths of teen-aged attendants, feuding doctors, suspicious visitors, and even a patient's widow, came stark accounts of what the Hospital Movement had actually wrought, at least in one state.

Also brought to life was the extraordinary figure at the heart of this book, the ambitious former army surgeon, banker, speculator, and entrepreneur, Dr. Abraham Van Norstrand, the first superintendent of the Wisconsin hospital to truly take command and bend the place to his will—as well as his dogged adversary, the social crusader Samuel Hastings.

Their conflict, played out against a backdrop of scheming employees, brooding patients, and pleading families, was high drama. As for the hospital itself—that incredible leap of faith nearly two football fields long and four massive stories high—it was everything leaders of the movement said it should be, which proved to be a mixed blessing.

To protect the reputation of their young hospital, officials kept this story hidden from the public, and thereafter it was lost in the archives, a footnote to a government document. This book is an attempt to bring those remarkable people and their hospital back into the light of day.

A Locked Room, a Battered Body

Monday, January 23, 1865, was a day to put off errands if you could get away with it, much less a thirty-mile trip to Madison. To the family of Reverend Romulus Oscar Kellogg, yesterday's snowfall had been a godsend, starting before dawn and lingering over Fort Atkinson long enough to compel Kellogg to cancel services at the Methodist Church on South Main Street. If not for the snow, his wife and brother would have had to cancel anyway and then put up with his raving. They could not have let him return to the pulpit, not after all they had been through the past week. Only Romulus knew whether, like John Wesley, he had at long last achieved "a heart so all-flaming with the love of God,"[1] but it was clear to everyone else that he had lost his mind in the quest.[2]

Yesterday's blessing was today's curse, the snow and awful cold making the journey his brother Amherst was about to undertake downright perilous. He could not delay a day or two, not after the crisis this morning. Although he had spent a few years in the lumber business, by his mid-thirties Amherst Willoughby Kellogg had long since settled into city life. An office worker, a numbers man who had found his place as secretary of a young and prospering life insurance company in Milwaukee—for a time he had been its only full-time employee—he would not have been eager to trade a warm hearth for a snowy trail.

Although R. O., as he was known to his many cousins, was older by nearly four years, it was Amherst who played the role of older brother, helping Romulus Oscar through more than one soul-searching career change. In the eyes of family members and parishioners, Romulus was the fragile one. Upon graduation from Wesleyan University in Connecticut he had gone directly to Lawrence Institute, a new Methodist school in Wisconsin, as professor of ancient languages, but left after five years and ended up back home with his parents in Milwaukee.[3]

Through church connections he served briefly at a seminary in Rock County, then launched himself into the business world. Religious fervor apparently translated into impassioned salesmanship, as he proved to be a crackerjack agent for his brother's company. When a competitor in Chicago offered a better commission he moved on, only to anguish through another profound change of heart once he got there.

In his early thirties, with a wife and young son, he took a position as minister to the church in Fort Atkinson, and in the manner of John Wesley he set out zealously recruiting, organizing, and exhorting. The founder's feet seem never to have touched the ground. Methodists look back upon the circuit rider as the abiding symbol of their church's vitality, but to John Wesley circuit riding was more than an act of faith. It was a constitutional necessity. In the age of wind and hoof power he traveled, by one estimate, a quarter million miles and gave 40 thousand sermons. He could not sit still.[4]

Methodism's good news was that through the exercise of free will, man the sinner could redeem himself in God's eye and achieve perfection on earth and salvation in heaven. The flaming cross came later, but Romulus seemed to anticipate it and was drawn to it like a moth.

He simply was not built for such a life. Two years before he had suffered his first breakdown. Exhaustion, his wife felt.[5] He had since taken up a diet of vegetables, fruit, and graham flour, and he abstained from sex with his wife, Caroline. His frailty struck parishioners as a visible manifestation of his faith and sensitivity, and many felt protective. He was no fire-breather, and sometimes when his well of inspiration ran dry he rode out among them in search of a volunteer to deliver the sermon in his place. He was a vulnerable little man on horseback, asking a favor. They could not turn him down.[6]

But watching him at the pulpit last week, they were amazed. Liberated from the crippling burdens of inhibition and doubt, he seemed a new man, passionate and divinely inspired. Back home he continued to pace and lecture throughout the day and into the night. It was the first sustained manifestation of what Amherst was later to call his "exalted state" and what Caroline called "paroxysms [of] violence." Always prone to insomnia, through Sunday night and into Monday morning he remained triumphantly, excitedly wakeful. At two in the morning he was a wild, flailing prophet. In the week since, periods of calm routine had alternated with more frenzied marathons, which usually erupted in the early morning hours. He complained of pains in his head and back, and he suspected that enemies lurked in the house. Caroline exhausted herself bathing his feet in hot water, wrapping him in sheets and blankets kept warm from frequent ironing, and applying ice water or snow to his head. Tormented, sleepless, he rattled on—preaching, praying, and accusing. "Tongue-raving," Amherst called it.[7]

Caroline enlisted the help of friends. A neighbor, Ebenezer Frisell, spent long hours standing guard, at some cost in bruised shins when he fought to confine Reverend Kellogg's inspired outbursts to the family sofa.[8] She also telegraphed Amherst, who soon arrived from Milwaukee.

At three the morning after the snowstorm, Romulus was up fretting over the baby's croupy cough. He told Caroline that he was going downstairs to heat water. She comforted the child and listened in vain for sounds of activity below. Finally she woke Amherst, who followed tracks in the snow left by his brother's slippers, ending up at the Chicago and Northwestern depot. It was open but unattended.

Later he learned that Romulus had attacked the clerk, raging at him for not sending an imagined telegram. The clerk fought back with the only weapon at hand—his own boot. They wrestled, plunged outside, and went at it in the snow. Finally the clerk broke free and ran for help, leaving Romulus sprawled in his nightshirt.

At a nearby house Amherst found his brother spraying threats and prophecies at a circle of men who were in no mood to be lectured. Doctors were summoned and friends consulted, the upshot being Amherst's bleak and dangerous sleigh ride to Madison.

It was nearly midnight when he found the Gorham Street home of John Favill, a Harvard-trained doctor and a founder of the state medical society. Favill had recently served as assistant physician at the insane hospital across the lake. He welcomed Kellogg in spite of the hour and heard his story. The solution was obvious and there was no time to waste. A "speedy recovery" was likely, Favill said, but only if Amherst brought his brother to the hospital without delay.[9]

It was still well below zero Tuesday morning when Amherst Kellogg set out on his sleigh. Guiding him across three miles of frozen Lake Mendota toward a horizon black with oak trees was a pillar of smoke standing over an enormous stone building. Big as it was, the hospital was still a work in progress and had been accepting patients for only four and a half years. In years to come more wings would be added—a skyline of slate shingles and white cupolas stretching nearly two hundred yards and crowning four massive stories of quarried stone and dark, vertical windows. After the capitol building across the lake it was the most expensive public building in the state. Only the iron grillwork over the windows hinted at the building's purpose, although visitors from Jacksonville, Illinois, and Indianapolis, Indiana, and other states as well would have recognized it for what it was. Like hospitals for the insane across the country it was a product of the so-called "Kirkbride Plan," after Dr. Thomas Kirkbride, perhaps the nation's best known hospital leader.[10]

The new superintendent, Dr. Abraham Van Norstrand, had been at his post for only nine months, having spent the preceding three years in the army. Tall and barrel-chested, Van Norstrand carried his 250 pounds with a commander's confidence and sense of privilege. As a former administrator of army hospitals in the east and deep south he was accustomed to moving in a world of subordinates.

But Amherst Kellogg was at home in the company of important

men, and he was apparently at his most persuasive Tuesday morning as Van Norstrand and his assistant, Dr. John Sawyer, patiently sat through a detailed account of his brother's decline into madness.

They were busy men. Like all superintendents, Van Norstrand was an absolute ruler, responsible not only for the 170 patients but for everything that happened at the hospital, from landscaping to the purchase of livestock for the farm, bulk tea for the patients' meals, and coal for the boilers. He hired and disciplined attendants and oversaw the endless process of expansion and repair. He also had a board of trustees to answer to, some of whom might show up at any time.

Maybe he was impressed by the Kellogg name. On one of his first nights in Wisconsin he had stayed in a tavern in the woods run by a Kellogg family. There were Kelloggs in Jefferson where before the war Van Norstrand had been a leader of the Democratic party, a state legislator, and a businessman, in addition to practicing medicine. Years before, Sheriff Austin Kellogg, an uncle of Amherst and Romulus, had helped Van Norstrand rig an election, thereby upsetting the schemes of politicians in Watertown who had set out to hijack the county seat.[11] Besides all that, Amherst Kellogg would have impressed him as a man of substance like himself.

He was wise to listen patiently. Helmont Kellogg, a Revolutionary War veteran, had come west with seven adult sons and their families in the mid-1830s, nearly two hundred years after the first Kelloggs had settled in Connecticut. In Wisconsin they became farmers, blacksmiths, carpenters, evangelists, and hard-headed businessmen. Children of pioneer Kelloggs died of drowning, fire, and poison, and they died for the Union. Helmont had been the first of his family to break from Calvinism and embrace evangelical Methodism, and his westward migration was in part a flight from the oppressiveness of their old faith. The Wisconsin Kelloggs were ambitious, energetic, and intensely dedicated to their church and its expansion.[12]

The hospital and the Northwestern Mutual Insurance Company, as it would be called on its new state charter, were linked in ways that Dr. Van Norstrand probably did not yet fully understand. The hospital was built on one hundred acres donated by its neighbor, former governor Leonard Farwell, one of the founders of the insurance company in which Amherst held high office. Several hospital trustees—Van Norstrand's bosses—also served on the board of trustees of Northwestern Mutual Life.[13]

Years later Amherst would recall how much time the doctors had spent with him and how attentively they had listened. Like Favill, they responded with optimism mixed with urgency. Early admission was crucial. About that, medical science was unequivocal. The deranged subject must be removed from the influences that brought him to his present state. There was "little doubt of a speedy recovery," they told Kellogg, if his brother was brought to the hospital as soon as possible.[14] Rest, sedative medications, nutritious meals, diversions designed to calm the excited, to restore the melancholy, and to orient the deranged; such care was what this monument to the people's faith in the medical arts had been created to provide, at such great public expense, and what Reverend Kellogg desperately needed.

When Amherst arrived back at his brother's house that night he learned from Caroline that there had been more of the dreaded paroxysms. The next day Romulus submitted grudgingly, walking to the depot with Amherst on one side and Ebenezer Frisell on the other. Except for a brief flare-up at some rowdy soldiers in their car he was well-behaved, and the trip was blessedly uneventful. They reached the hospital after dark.

Years later Amherst submitted written testimony to a committee investigating the hospital. Of that first night he wrote: "He [Romulus] warmed himself in the parlor and then went to his room quietly. I handed the superintendent a letter from his wife, stating that he was better when his feet were kept warm and head cool. I also stated that morphine would tend to excite rather than soothe him, and advised against its use. I remained through the night, but was not permitted to stay with him."[15]

Religious excitement had long been recognized as one manifestation of insanity along with its opposite, religious melancholy, and Kellogg seems to have followed the classic path: a long, dark period of doubt and dread followed suddenly by liberation—"a sense of lively joy . . . amounting to rapture and ecstasy. . . . But the strain of excitement is too high, the expressions of happiness too ecstatic to be long mistaken: signs of pride and haughtiness are betrayed, and of a violent and boisterous deportment."[16] The quote is from Bucknill and Tuke's *A Manual of Psychological Medicine*, the authoritative text of the mid-nineteenth century, to which Van Norstrand and Sawyer no doubt had access. Jean Etienne Esquirol, one of the earliest crusaders for humane treatment of the insane, had labeled this type of insanity "theomania."[17]

So from the doctors' point of view there seems to have been nothing out of the ordinary about Kellogg's case. Even Caroline had an enlightened grasp of her husband's condition. Her application of cold towels to his head and warm water to his feet was the treatment for acute mania recommended by Benjamin Rush in his famous *Medical Inquiries and Observations upon the Diseases of the Mind*, a book that might well have been found in the library of an educated, liberal clergyman. Rush believed that cooling the head slowed mental activity, while heat applied to the feet improved circulation and enhanced the effectiveness of the iced towels.[18]

There is nothing in the records to indicate that these measures were continued at the hospital. Maybe they were too labor-intensive given the number of patients each attendant was responsible for. Instead, Doctors Van Norstrand and Sawyer ordered morphine, which the family had specifically warned against. Sawyer noted in the casebook that on that first night Reverend Kellogg ate supper and went to bed, "but at eleven o'clock he became noisy, singing, praying, exhorting, running around his room, pounding at the door, etc. Half a grain of morphine was now administered, but as he did not become quiet at the end of an hour he was removed to a shuttered room in the fourth story. After this he seemed to rest, was quiet in the morning, washed, dressed, ate breakfast regularly and conversed during the forenoon with a good degree of clearness."[19] Lowe, the young attendant who had responsibility for Kellogg, later told Mrs. Kellogg that the medicine had been "forced . . . into his mouth."[20]

Thursday morning Amherst Kellogg was told that his brother had been taken to an isolated room where he could not upset others. He assumed an attendant was on duty nearby. He emphatically reminded the doctors that morphine would only aggravate his brother's mania, and Dr. Sawyer agreed—in the presence of the superintendent—that in Romulus's case morphine did not seem to have the desired effect. Amherst's statement continues: "I asked carefully about the attendance [*sic*] he would have and offered to procure a man to stay with him all the time, but Dr. Van Norstrand said none but regular attendants were allowed in the institution, but promised me that 'he should have all the attendance he needed, even if it required some one to be with him constantly.'"

From Dr. Van Norstrand he learned that his brother was "quiet and rational" that morning, but even so he was advised to leave without saying good-bye.[21]

The "shuttered room" to which Dr. Sawyer referred was known in-house as a "strong room." These were on the fourth floor. The oak shutters were two inches thick and built to survive a pounding.[22]

Romulus remained calm and accommodating well into his second night. Sawyer wrote that when Dr. Van Norstrand visited he was "apparently in the act of prayer. After a time he rose, was assisted into bed and seemed disposed to remain quiet."

Dr. Sawyer's note continues: "Twenty minutes after this [Kellogg] received a half a grain of morphine and was still resting quietly in bed, but he soon became noisy."[23] Sawyer did not record why the medicine was given or which doctor ordered it. A while later Lowe showed up at his office and asked permission to take Kellogg upstairs to a strong room once again. Sawyer gave his consent. Together, Lowe and another attendant were responsible for maintaining order among forty very disturbed men. Attendants lived in rooms on the same floor as their patients. A noisy patient disturbed everyone, patients and attendants alike. Theoretically, attendants were always on call unless excused by one of the doctors. Having to deal with a loud, belligerent patient late into the night made for a long day indeed. Kellogg had turned combative, and so Lowe recruited a notoriously surly supervisor named Guppy to help overpower and drag him upstairs. Dr. Sawyer may have waited in a nearby stairwell until Kellogg calmed down, or he may have remained in his office. The strong room had either been warmed in preparation for Kellogg's return, or it was ice cold. The conflicting opinions elicited about these and other events of that night were never resolved.

The theorizing began when Lowe unlocked the strong room door at five o'clock Friday morning and found Romulus Kellogg face down on the floor, naked, and "quite dead," as Sawyer noted.[24] The shutters had been forced open. A stinging north wind whistled through the broken window panes. The walls were smeared with blood.

Van Norstrand was not easily shaken. As a former army surgeon and hospital administrator he was well acquainted with the havoc that flying metal and roaring infection could inflict upon flesh and bone. He had lived among the wretched smells and fading groans. But here in one of the most up-to-date institutions in the west, under his leadership, sprawled a chilled and mottled specimen that could have flopped off of a battlefield corpse cart.

"The whole frontal region was discolored, puffy, oedematous," Dr. Sawyer wrote. "There was a slight depression 1 1/2 inch above left eye, but it seemed not to be a fracture. The lids of the right eye were much discolored." His jaw was gashed. There were bruises and lacerations on his chest, spine, and shoulders. The backs of both hands were abraded, as were his elbows and feet. The scrotum was "discolored and somewhat excoriated."[25]

Dr. Van Norstrand sent the following telegram to Amherst Kellogg:

"Sir,

Your brother committed suicide last night, we will expect you on the four p.m. train. I have telegraphed his wife."[26]

* * *

While death from contagious disease was a constant worry, the occasional death from other causes was a sad fact of institutional life. At virtually every hospital for the insane a tally of the dead was to be found among the array of statistical tables in the superintendent's annual report. During his four years at the Wisconsin hospital, Van Norstrand recorded a low of seven and a high of seventeen.[27]

One of his first decisions as superintendent had been to move the cemetery. The mental status of melancholy patients urged outside for fresh air was not improved by the presence of headstones.[28]

For most patients the time of greatest risk was the period just after admission. After weeks, and possibly years, of confinement in barns, jails, or poorhouses, they often endured a pounding cross-country ride on the bed of a wagon, the dangerous or maniacal usually trussed up or wrapped in chains. They arrived dehydrated, filthy, and often physically battered. Delia Clancy[29] had to be carried into the hospital's central building, although back home in Crawford County she had been known to "run like a deer." Neighbors used to see her and a sister dart naked through woods and fields, "their sufferings unparalleled and indescribable." Once inside, Delia refused solid food and did not move a muscle or say a word. She died on the sixth day, "her vital powers [having been] thoroughly exhausted when she arrived."[30]

Two others were Robert Peterson and Margaret Smith, each in effect a casualty of the war. Although sick with mumps, Peterson had insisted on accompanying his regiment east to war. He was stunned by a spent bullet, knocked out by sunstroke, sickened by "impure" smallpox vaccine, and finally struck down by chronic diarrhea. Back home, a letter arrived from a chaplain at City Point Hospital in Washington, followed by another from a surgeon at Satterlee Hospital in Philadelphia. Robert was deranged and of no further use to the army. Could someone come and take him home? His father was dead, his only brother off with the First Wisconsin Cavalry. A sister set out from rural Marquette County and found him locked in the guardhouse at Satterlee Hospital—sick, naked, "a raving maniac." Confined with him was another uniformed lunatic. They were like lions in a cage, each venting his rage upon the other. Her desperate letter to the governor ended up on Van Norstrand's desk. He agreed to admit Robert, but he was angry about it. Army doctors were supposed to send insane soldiers to the government hospital in Washington, but too many could not be bothered. It was much easier to simply cut them loose.[31]

Peterson was admitted in mid-January of 1865, shortly before Kellogg—"Quite demented, very untidy." He was treated with whiskey and quinine, plus applications of croton oil to the back of his head and neck, apparently as a so-called "counterirritant."[32] Although he lingered for over a year, he had already, in effect, crossed to the other side. On May 20, 1866, Dr. Sawyer wrote, "Has eaten little and at last the stomach became so irritable that nothing was retained. He continued to sink and died today."[33]

Margaret Smith was a farm wife of sixty. The army had taken her two sons, leaving her and her husband on a farm they could no longer work or pay for. She attacked her husband, tore off her clothes, and stalked field and forest angrily lecturing God. The doctor who filled out her application matter-of-factly attributed her condition to "Trouble and poverty."

"Highly excited, noisy, incoherent and destructive," Sawyer wrote on the day of her death, a month after she arrived at the hospital. "Would not take a sufficient quantity of proper nourishment but would eat any unsuitable thing she could find. Ten days ago she commenced to have diarrhea which grew steadily worse and helped to exhaust her."[34]

* * *

But Kellogg was different. His death was a superintendent's nightmare. He was no demented farmer or maiden aunt long estranged from family and neighbors, nor had he arrived half-dead. Ten days before his death this young man from a well-connected family had excited his congregation with a display of uncharacteristic energy and passion. Thirty-six hours after appearing at the hospital door he was a battered corpse in a blood-smeared room.

Van Norstrand had been on the job for only nine months, and he knew that the position was his by default. A committee of trustees had returned from the East empty-handed, having been turned down by doctors at the Hartford Retreat and a New Jersey asylum. Even then, the board was reluctant to take on someone with no experience in the field of asylum medicine. Of eleven trustees present at the critical meeting, only six had voted to offer the job to Van Norstrand. The last thing he needed was an uproar over the death of a popular clergyman under his care.[35]

The *Milwaukee Sentinel* carried a detailed account of the funeral, the casket born by grieving fellow ministers who tearfully recounted "the virtues and endearing qualities of their deceased brother." Mention was made of his "sorrowing widow [and] two children of tender age."[36]

Over a hundred members of Kellogg's church petitioned the legislature for an investigation. A joint committee was appointed.[37]

Fortunately for him, Abraham Van Norstrand was an old hand at dealing with crises of one sort or another. He was a New Englander who had moved west in 1847 to find, as he put it, "the fortune I desired and expected."[38] He was twenty-one when he settled in Wisconsin Territory and set up practice in the midst of a handful of fledgling Yankee towns with outlying communities of German and Norwegian farmers. Like most who had preceded him he soon learned that riches were not about to fall into his lap. By 1865 he had survived hardships of his own. He had become an experienced businessman, banker, and speculator, and above all a capable physician. His medical and business peers respected him; his employees feared him; his family mostly obeyed him. At intervals the ether around him had sparked and crackled with the prospect of scandal, dishonor, ruination, but these storms did no lasting damage. He was still firmly in charge and as dedicated as ever to the pursuit of a better life. Middling status and middling account balances; that is what life in the West had brought him so far, but his dream of wealth was undiminished, and he was not about to be brought down by a notorious death in his hospital.

After all, his last encounter with Reverend Kellogg, as he described it to Dr. Sawyer and almost certainly to the investigators, was a picture of benevolence. He had watched over a bedside prayer and helped with a cozy tuck-in. Painful as it must have been to find the affair on the front pages, he at least had the satisfaction of seeing himself depicted as a kindly father-figure, the superintendent pausing in his endless, wearisome duties to hover protectively over a troubled soul at bedtime.

After completing his rounds that night he had returned to the family quarters, leaving his assistant in charge. When the legislative committee came around asking questions he could only refer them to Dr. Sawyer, who in turn referred them to the hapless attendant, Mr. Lowe, the buck traveling downhill and stopping with the humblest player. Van Norstrand told the investigators that if only Kellogg's family had informed him that the poor fellow was suicidal he could have taken steps to avoid the tragedy. The implication was clear. By withholding vital information the family shared in the blame.

By mid-April it was all over. The superintendent and his staff had been vindicated: "Your committee therefore report that not only no blame attaches to Dr. Van Norstrand or Dr. Sawyer but entirely exonerates them from all blame. . . . The hospital is in good hands." A suggestion was tactfully volunteered: it might be a good idea to assign a night watchman to each wing of the institution.[39]

By then this local tragedy had been overwhelmed by news of Lee's surrender. Church bells rang. Bonfires flared near the capitol and on the university's Bascom Hill. A crowd had staked out the telegraph office, impatient for more details. Less than a week later, President Lincoln was assassinated. In the chambers of the state capitol and among the public generally, the Kellogg affair was old news. Newspapers ignored the committee's report. Four days after it was read to the senate, Dr. Van Norstrand wrote to the trustees requesting a salary increase.[40]

The committee added insult to the Kellogg family's injury by ignoring their side of the story. Neither Amherst nor R. O.'s widow are mentioned in its report. The death had been tragic but avoidable. If only crucial information had not been withheld by the family. Three years would pass before their version of the events of January 25 and 26 would get an official airing.

Why was the brief report so one-sided? Just as the layout of the Wisconsin hospital was based on a model recommended by eastern experts, so was its system of administration. In 1853, the Association of Medical Superintendents of American Institutions for the Insane—still young, small in number, and feeling its way—attempted to standardize the management of public insane hospitals. The highest authority was to be a board of trustees. Appointed by the governor, the board would oversee the welfare of patients, staff, and physical plant, and stand as a firewall between the hospital and statehouse politics. Trustees selected the superintendent, who in turn hired and supervised staff and took responsibility for day-to-day operations. This model was already in place at most institutions in the East. In theory the chain of command was clear: the superintendent served at the pleasure of the trustees. When friction developed between the two, as it did with painful regularity during the Wisconsin hospital's early decades, the superintendent was sent packing. But when faced with threats to the hospital from the outside, the board of trustees and its superintendent invariably joined in a common defense.

Old New England dominated the board. William Taylor, from Connecticut, would one day be elected governor. David Atwood, from New Hampshire, published the *Wisconsin State Journal* and later went off to Congress. Ephraim W. Young was a Harvard graduate from Maine who had of necessity become a man of many parts in the west—farmer, teacher, judge, legislator. So had Simeon Mills. Born in Connecticut and raised in the Ohio wilderness, Mills built a log hut in the forest when Madison was little more than a real-estate scheme on a fanciful map. The hut became Madison's first store, and Mills, the first storekeeper, became an early booster and developer, and eventually the mail carrier, justice of the peace, territorial treasurer, a state senator, a railroad executive, the paymaster general to state Civil War soldiers, and one of the longest-serving trustees of the state hospital.

Judging from the obituaries of these pioneers, a seat on the hospital's board of trustees was a distinction that lasted a lifetime. They were ambitious, public-spirited, strong-willed Yankees, just like their new superintendent. State legislators were also prone to be defensive about their hospital, preferring to fault critics rather than critically examine the hospital. In time, even some trustees wearied of the cycle of platitudes they and the legislators perpetuated.[41]

By the late 1800s this pattern of denial would have come as no surprise to a public made cynical by widespread hospital scandals or to a medical establishment irked by the aloofness of hospital superintendents. By then, so much had been promised; so little delivered. But in 1865, in Madison, statements from the experts were taken at face value. If trustees and legislators said the hospital was doing just fine, then it must be so. Given his wartime accomplishments and commanding presence—the soft glove of geniality over a firmly guiding hand—Van Norstrand might eventually have stood in the second rank of superintendents behind innovators like Thomas Kirkbride, Samuel Woodward, Pliny Earle, and Isaac Ray, whose names were synonymous with the hospital movement and the conviction that insanity was curable. Or so it might have seemed to him and some of the trustees at the time.

In the short term the committee's report did wipe the slate clean for him, but nothing could erase the awful circumstances of Kellogg's death or the family's bitterness over the one-sided investigation. And the fate of his predecessors was a constant reminder of how abruptly things could change. The hospital's first superintendent was gone before the central building was completed, fired by trustees upset that money and space designated for much-needed isolation rooms had been wasted on nonessentials. The next man was cast out after three years—exhausted, hounded by employees, and abandoned by the board.[42]

Van Norstrand knew that a superintendent was a lightning rod—at the mercy of busybodies crying abuse where realists saw prudent care, of outside doctors second-guessing him and forever extolling the latest fads from Europe, of angry ex-patients and their disappointed families, and above all, of embittered former employees polluting watering holes and statehouse corridors with poisonous gossip about what *really* goes on in the hospital.

Even a man as vigilant as Abraham Van Norstrand could not put out every fire or discredit every grudge-holder. From time to time, in the comfort of his family's elegant quarters on the second story of the central building, he might have stood at one of the towering windows overlooking Lake Mendota, his gaze fixed on the skyline of the distant city, and brooded upon his fate should some eminent figure rise out of that feverish undercurrent of rumor and resentment to point an accusing finger at him.

Standing at a high point in the city, the capitol building was visible from the superintendent's quarters. From time to time state treasurer Samuel Dexter Hastings may have lifted his eyes from the wartime flood of paper crossing his desk to gaze over the lake and seek a kind of serenity in the blur of distant trees and the white cupolas that poked through them. Hastings had helped to steer Wisconsin through the treacherous fiscal waters of the wartime years and would soon accept a seat on the hospital's board of trustees. By then he would be out of state service and active in a half dozen local enterprises.[43] He was also a trustee of the Northwestern Mutual Life Insurance Company in Milwaukee, where he had made the acquaintance of the firm's secretary, Amherst Kellogg. Their mutual interest in the hospital would have made it a lively topic of conversation. Did Kellogg open a window into the institution for Hastings that otherwise would have remained shut? Someone did, eventually prompting him to dig more deeply into hospital affairs than anyone had before.

Throughout his career Van Norstrand had prevailed in fierce encounters with all sorts of hard characters, but he had never run up against anyone like Samuel Dexter Hastings. Unlike the imperious Van Norstrand, Hastings was a diligent ferreter-out of facts and figures; unlike the impulsive Van Norstrand, he was a stickler for procedure. Above all, Hastings's polite, fastidious manner could give way suddenly to a scorched-earth fury. In a few years the fiercest encounter in the lives of both these tough-minded former Yankees would take place behind closed doors in the capitol building, within hailing distance of Hastings's old office.

ONE

The Fortune I Desired and Expected

By 1877, twelve years after the death of Romulus Kellogg, Abraham Van Norstrand was a banker in Green Bay, successful, comfortable, and well thought of in the business community.[1] He lived in a big house in a high-class neighborhood that echoed with grand Yankee names like John Jacob Astor and Washington Irving, who once owned land there, and he had set up his wayward son Fred in the lumber and coal business. Green Bay was far from the acid tongues of Madison. Settled by French missionaries and fur traders, it was the oldest town in the state, and it was prospering anew with lumber and paper mills.

On August 25 of that year, his birthday, he opened a leather-bound journal the size of a small gravestone, dipped his pen, and embarked upon a project that would continue to the end of his life. In his own way and at his own pace he was determined to set the record straight:

"Today at the age of 52 it may be of use to someone if I should modestly look over some of the events of my modest and uneventful life. To record some of my early thoughts, fancies, expectations and aspirations, together with my experiences as a child, youth, young man, student, teacher, physician, surgeon, speculator, superintendent of Wisconsin State Hospital for the Insane, merchant, lumberman, etc. etc."[2]

He simply cannot fake it. Time and again—in letters seeking

favors, in speeches to professional colleagues, and in these memoirs—Van Norstrand tries to elicit a scent of lilacs only to fill the air with swamp gas. In the first paragraph of his life story he is at his worst. He strains for humility but what flows from his pen is pure vanity.

But gradually the stage makeup is sweated away, and something real emerges. Forget the tin ear and false modesty, because underneath all that the reader detects lingering hurt. The man has been wronged, his reputation grievously wounded, and time is running out. Not that he admits to any such thing in the 154 densely lined pages that follow. Far from it. They are filled with a lifetime of bold risks and narrow escapes. Most of these tales are variations on the David and Goliath theme, the good doctor as the boy with the slingshot, while a succession of great names, roughneck thugs, and infuriating colleagues rotate through the Goliath role. His father had died young—at just fifty-eight—as Van Norstrand men had a history of doing. Abraham protests that in writing his life he intends only to provide a rainy-day pastime for his grandchildren, but the reader is not deceived. Clearly he has serious business to conduct while there is still time.

"In writing my opinions and thoughts, especially those of recent occurrences, I may allow my feelings to prejudice my judgment. I will endeavor to keep [this] thought continually in my mind while writing, thus assisting me to avoid recording feelings of hate or envy, still inherent in my nature of strong likes and dislikes, of never failing friendship and slowly ending hate."[3]

* * *

The Van Norstrands descended from a Jacob Jansen who landed in New York in 1638. Jansen came from an island off Holland called Noorstrandt, the source of the unwieldy and frequently butchered last name, which, ironically, was added in America to distinguish him from other Jacob Jansens. The family spread out along the Hudson River valley, intermarrying with French Huguenots.

Abraham Harris Van Norstrand was born August 25, 1825,

in a farmhouse among rocky fields on the east side of the Hudson River, near Poughkeepsie. His father, Frederick Frelinghuysen Van Norstrand, was solidly built, steady, and temperate. Raised a Quaker, Frederick had been forced to leave the church for "marrying out," his wife being a member of the Dutch Reform Church, but he lived the Quaker virtues of hard work, thrift, and patience, scratching enough profit out of a poor farm to eventually trade up to a bigger one, then a bigger one still. About the time of their son's tenth birthday, Frederick and his wife Elizabeth acquired over four hundred acres in Cayuga County, at the western edge of the state among exotic back-country folk who mistook the bulging parcels of clothes hanging from the family wagon for bags of money. Although sick with whooping cough, Abraham exercised his pride of place as oldest son to travel on horseback to this rich farming country, which he described as "better and more beautiful than we had been accustomed to." In time Frederick accumulated eight hundred acres.[4]

Abraham also aspired to prosperity, but unlike his father he was not, as he so often reminds his readers, a patient man, nor one to seek his fortune toiling on the land. The story of his boyhood and youth, played out through years of agrarian toil, was one of quiet struggle between a father who pressed his first-born to follow in his footsteps and a son determined to leave such drudgery behind.

Education became Abraham's bridge to the world, but into his mid-teens his attendance at so-called "district schools" was interrupted by chores. Hay needed cutting, hickory nuts did not gather themselves, nor could his father erect a house alone. Back in school he was frustrated by the repetitiveness of the lessons. When he was ready and eager for fractions, his teacher cycled back to "the rudiments of grammar and arithmetic."[5] He made up his mind to go off to boarding school. In a skirmish destined to be fought again and again, his father first adamantly rejected the plan, then conditionally objected, and then, sadly, and with a clumsy sort of grace, dug about in his pocketbook for the money Abraham would need. For three months Abraham lived at an academy near the shore of Lake Ontario, thrilled to make the acquaintance of algebra and other heretofore exotic subjects, before returning home and settling for an occasional tutoring session from a medical student apprenticed to the family doctor, a man he identifies as Dr. Palmer.* In the fall of 1843 he set off by foot for a teacher-training course offered at Auburn, fourteen miles from home.[6]

At eighteen he took a job at a country school and discovered that "boarding around" among his students' families opened up a whole new social life. He was flattered by the deference accorded him as teacher, scholar, and at times, family therapist. But grand as he may have felt in a family parlor, he was not happy with the petulant taskmaster he became in the classroom, where fear was evident in the eyes and bowed heads of his students. The demands upon him were complicated, the distractions many. He discovered that under pressure he became a bit of a tyrant—impatient, probably sarcastic, and quick to punish. He described himself as altogether too "ardent."[7]

Those hours spent with his former tutor, the medical student, remained on his mind and suggested an alternative. The next spring he explored the issue with Dr. Palmer, who agreed to take him on as a trainee. For $1.50 per week he would get meals, office space, and access to the doctor's books and equipment. The deal was struck when Palmer loaned him a copy of *Bell's Anatomy* to study over the summer.

Of course this was not to his father's liking, and for about a year Abraham tried to do it all—work the farm, study medicine, and also earn his fees by teaching and hiring out during harvest season. It was too much. Again, the solution was to go off to study full-time. Palmer was on the faculty of the medical college in Pittsfield, Massachusetts, where, at nineteen, Abraham Van Norstrand joined a starting class of twenty students.

He managed to scrape by for a while but finally gave in and asked for help from home. The letter resulted in a visit from his

---

* This may have been Dr. Benjamin Rush Palmer, whom he was to study under at the Vermont Medical College.

father, a trip he would not have undertaken lightly. It was a bitter-sweet encounter. Again Frederick yielded to his son, agreeing to pay tuition and board, but in a last attempt to get him away from school and back into the family he held out the promise of a new overcoat if Abraham would accompany him on a visit to relatives in Albany. Abraham was tempted—he dearly needed a coat, or the money it would fetch—but he sent his father off alone. There would be no overcoat, nor a first son to carry on at the farm.

Even with his father's help, day-to-day life was tight. He could not join other students dissecting a body because he lacked the fifteen-dollar fee. "I never indulged in a glass of soda water or an apple," he recalled.

Once he paid a visit to his father's side of the family. "I attended Quaker church and visited much among them and must say I like the Quakers and many times later in life I have regretted that I did not adopt at least outward Quakerism."[8] Perhaps in middle age he was tempted to idealize the road not taken. It is a revealing confession. He yearned for the simplicity and sense of community that he felt among the Quakers, but unlike his father, who broke a rule but remained a Quaker at heart, Abraham was alienated from the church by his own temperament.

The Berkshire Medical School in Pittsfield was associated with the Vermont Medical College across the state border in the small town of Woodstock. In effect, Woodstock was a satellite of the older, better-known school in Pittsfield. The Pittsfield school was in session in the fall, Woodstock in the spring. Most students and faculty migrated between the two. Itinerant medical teachers and students were common, some faculty teaching in three, even four schools a year, while students were able to cram what was supposed to be a three-year course of study into two.[9] So when Dr. Palmer packed up and moved to Woodstock, Van Norstrand and other students went along.

Woodstock and another private medical school at Castleton had put the medical school of the University of Vermont out of business. Nearly twenty years would pass before it enrolled another class. Considering the private schools little better than degree mills, the medical faculty at Burlington had raised admission standards and performance requirements so high that potential students had little incentive to apply, not with two seductively undemanding alternatives nearby. The attempt to improve the quality of medical education backfired, a reflection upon the state of medical education in mid-nineteenth-century America.[10] While medical research flourished in Europe, in America medicine was increasingly driven by short-term economic imperatives. Private schools succeeded in a marketplace that did not expect much from doctors. In the battle for public confidence, orthodox medicine—with its bleeders, purgers, and poisoners—was losing ground to alternative practitioners like the Thomsonians, who offered a do-it-yourself botanical cure for almost anything: simply clean out the system, raise the body temperature, and wait for better days.

That survival-of-the-fittest aspect of the doctor training business may have shaped Van Norstrand's expectations. Medicine for him became a means to an end, a way to accumulate capital, although he would remain a diligent practitioner. Nothing hurt a doctor's pocketbook more than a bad reputation.

At Woodstock he sat for another year of lectures, rooming first with a graying, dissipated scholar who could afford to romance one of the landlord's daughters while Van Norstrand, with his empty pockets, could not. Over time he detected—or imagined—a resulting chill from that side of the house, and so he moved in with another student, a carpenter and father of five who was making a mid-life career change and was as poor as himself. They all lived cheaply together and got along well.

The Woodstock faculty was receptive to new ideas. A staff member just back from France gave instruction in auscultation and percussion. Van Norstrand studied "Minute Anatomy and Physiology" through the compound microscope, a rarity in American schools. He witnessed a variety of surgeries and heard lectures from specialists in what were considered the seven parts of medicine—anatomy, physiology, chemistry, material medica, physic (including pathology and therapeutics), surgery, and midwifery.[11] Having met most requirements for graduation in twenty-eight months, young Abraham felt well-qualified to sit for the final exam, and in the spring of 1846, two months shy of his twenty-first birthday, he received his sheepskin.

His first choice was the army. War with Mexico had been declared. How exhilarating it would be to follow the flag as an assistant surgeon. Recommendations from his teachers were easy to come by, but money for uniforms and equipment was not. He couldn't even afford the trip to Washington to apply.

He settled for more prosaic work closer to home, first in nearby Dorchester, Vermont, filling in for a physician who was returning to school to upgrade his skills. He lasted seven unhappy months and was only 60 dollars ahead when he entered into another ill-fated arrangement. His senior partner sent a bottle of strychnine to a morphine addict who, expecting her usual delivery, promptly popped the cork and drank deeply. Fortunately it came shooting back up, thereby saving her life and the doctors' reputations as well.

This was not the future Van Norstrand had envisioned. "Charges were low," he wrote, "competition large and the amount of medical paying business . . . much too small to satisfy my youthful energy" or to start him along the path toward that fortune he longed for.[12]

It was time to break from the cold porridge of the east and chance feast or famine in the western territories. On May 1, 1847, he loaded a trunk of clothes and a box of books onto a stagecoach, climbed up beside the driver, and headed over the Green Mountains for a last visit home.

TWO

I Soon Found My Hands Full

A decade or so before Van Norstrand arrived, Wisconsin Territory was largely terra incognita. Law and order among far-flung pockets of soldiers, miners, missionaries, and fur traders was administered by a circuit-riding judge who periodically ventured across Lake Michigan to Green Bay, then set out over the so-called Military Road to Prairie du Chien on the shore of the Mississippi River, two hundred miles to the southwest. By mid-century not much had changed north of the Military Road, which was forested wilderness all the way to Lake Superior, but in the south federal surveyors were plotting and measuring, and new settlements were springing up everywhere, especially inland from Lake Michigan.

The young judge was James Duane Doty, and while plodding along on horseback he had plenty of time to ponder the land's potential to make a smart man rich. As late as 1835, for instance, the area known as Four Lakes remained a wilderness, "wild and desolate [where] the wild cat and wolf roamed at large." The Blackhawk War of the early 1830s had uprooted the Sauk and driven them west across the Mississippi. Crisscrossed by trails left by the Indians and the soldiers who had chased them to the river, the Four Lakes region was now home only to a Frenchman in a log cabin and a few Sauk and Winnebago tribesmen who had eluded the militia's dragnet to continue their old seasonal migrations. That year Doty and a partner bought over a thousand acres there and on paper turned them into a make-believe city. Doty then turned his prodigious energy and political savvy to bringing that city to life. That he succeeded is apparent to any visitor gazing down upon the city of Madison from the dome of the state capitol today. The layout is identical to Doty's original map; even street names are unchanged. In return for votes designating that stretch of wooded hills between two pristine lakes as the territorial capitol, legislators were given parcels of land in the fantasy city.[1]

"Pork eaters" is what the half-breed fur traders and wilderness men called easterners who arrived so ill-prepared for life on the frontier in the 1830s and '40s.[2] Lacking the stomach for wild game and the skill to bag it, they traveled for days in search of a bag of flour or a keg of pickled pork.[3] But by 1865 those "pork eaters" had become distinguished "old settlers." They were legislators, judges, bankers, teachers, and clergymen, and they looked back upon the early years of shared hardship with a misty sense of pride—the era of log huts and dirt floors, of communal geese and pigs roaming the muddy lanes, and a sense of all-for-one when crops failed or fevers broke out. For Yankees raised to believe that you had not earned your harvest unless you had uprooted a forest or hauled away yet another generation of rock, Wisconsin was sinful abundance. The black soil along the Rock River was so rich that each spring the Indians would burn off old prairie grass to make room for the new. New England had been survival; Wisconsin would be profit.

On through the forties they came. The southeastern corner of Wisconsin Territory was so thick with the rippling surf of prairie grass that a wagon drawn by a pair of oxen was lucky to make a dozen miles a day—considerably less when hills, marshes, and muddy river bottoms intervened. Even old Indian trails had a way of dwindling into little more than a notion through the wildflowers. All were struck by the beauty of the place, but its real beauty was in its potential to make a man rich. A New York couple making their accident-prone way to a farm near Fort Atkinson was so buoyed by the prospect of riches that when their wagon tilted dangerously in a bog, Mary Turner scrambled to dry land with a baby in each arm and gazed at the immobilized wagon, the helpless oxen, and her husband flailing his own way to safety, and still she was not discouraged. "I thought we should go back in a few years rolling in wealth," she recalled decades later.[4]

Eventually those Yankees were outnumbered by newcomers from Germany, Ireland, and Scandinavia. They liked to drink and have fun on Sundays, an outrage to puritans for whom Sunday remained a day of silent and earnest reflection. In Madison those immigrants called the old-timers "the codfish aristocracy."[5] But old New England still controlled the elective offices, edited the newspapers, owned the banks, and parceled out the land.

In early July, 1847, the steamship *Madison* docked at Milwaukee, and Dr. Abraham Van Norstrand promptly sought out two long-established physicians for advice. They told him to head for the Rock River, fifty miles inland, where he would find plenty of sick farmers to care for. The next day he and other new arrivals set out on a familiarization tour. They traveled in what he called a "hoosier wagon," sloshing across mud holes, creaking up hills, and racketing across stretches of "fearfully rough" corduroy before passing into a bright sea of prairie grass.[6] Occasionally a farmhouse drifted by in the distance, and now and then they tunneled through groves of towering oaks illuminated by cathedral-like shafts of sunlight.

The next day they arrived at a village called Aztalan, named for nearby burial mounds mistakenly attributed to a tribe of vanished Aztecs. Aztalan was a crossroads community with two hotels, a post office, and several hundred settlers expecting to profit from the rich black soil and a strategic location on a road linking Milwaukee, Madison, and the lead-mining district of Mineral Point. From muddy-booted townspeople Van Norstrand learned that there was no resident physician. That was all he needed to know. Aztalan it would be.

Back in Milwaukee he arranged to have his trunk shipped inland. He spent 21 dollars on medicines and 55 on a horse and saddle. As he neared town on the return journey he left his card at farmhouses and the occasional inn.

A Connecticut native named Timothy Johnson had been the

first to scout the area on horseback and canoe, camping in clearings left by the Indians and surveying the river for turbulent stretches where waterpower could turn trees into lumber and grain into flour. The town of Jefferson grew where he put up his first shanty in the woods. Later he wandered north to a rapids where a French trader had been murdered by Indians. There he built a house for his family, and the surrounding area became Watertown, before long the biggest and most productive town in the county, where German speakers tried to make sense of the Irish and vice-versa. Restlessly circling back east, Johnson built a sawmill, and that settlement became the creamery town of Johnson Creek—Danes and more Germans in uneasy shouting distance of one another. Johnson was the first to dig among those mounds where Aztalan later sprang up.[7] A few miles further west, dark and cool in the shade of giant oaks, was Lake Mills, and to the south, near Lake Koshkonong, stood Fort Atkinson, a soldier settlement turned Yankee village and now, increasingly, a market town for Norwegians and Swedes settling near the lake. In time Van Norstrand's practice expanded to embrace all these settlements, each destined to prosper, or fade into backcountry gentility, or disappear altogether in the great mid-century struggle to attract settlers, commerce, and above all, railroads.

"Filthy and slipshod" it may have been, but the Jefferson County Hotel was the lesser of two evils, and for two dollars a week Van Norstrand had a room, and his horse a stable and feed. A daily highlight was the arrival of the stagecoach, which brought the town to life at noon. While passengers lunched at the hotel, the street echoed with high-spirited obscenities from waiting drivers, stable hands, and hangers-on, much to the disgust of the young doctor standing at his office window. Even the Sabbath did not dampen their enthusiasm for all topics scatological. It was a melancholy reminder of how far he had traveled from dear old Vermont.

That former judge and conjurer of cities, James Duane Doty, was now known as Governor Doty, having served the territory in that capacity, and on a visit to Aztalan he and Mrs. Doty preempted Van Norstrand from his cramped room for a night or two, it being the nearest thing in town to a celebrity suite. Van Norstrand did not mind. Doty was garrulous and down-to-earth, his wife a kindly, nervous woman who busied herself teaching a hired girl how to knit. He liked the governor even more when he found him in the barroom later that night, "perfectly at ease in the midst of wagoneers, travelers, barn men, stage drivers, whiskey-fumes and tobacco smoke."[8]

Periods of homesickness were infrequent. He was too busy to brood. The area was infamous for a disabling malady known by many names—intermittent fever, ague, bilious fever. "All diseases strictly malarial" is how Van Norstrand described it,[9] and during the late summer and fall of 1847 whole communities were laid low. People believed it was carried by swamp vapors, decaying vegetation, even "noxious fumes" released by plows turning the sod of virgin prairie. It often struck at harvest time, as farmers struggled to bring in crops. Whole families were afflicted, the sick tending the sick.[10]

Woodstock had not prepared Van Norstrand for this. He knew about malaria but had never before encountered it, and he treated it by the book: "emetic, cathartic and attentive waiting until the tongue became clean to allow giving quinine and tonick." He was well aware that his own future depended upon the outcome. "I soon found my hands full. Many new cases every day and none getting well. Many of them were very sick and I needed 36 hours to the day." Norwegians and Germans did what they were told, but Yankees tended to be skeptical and unforgiving.[11] Reputation was everything. If your patients did not get well you would soon find yourself without any, and that meant a fresh start beyond the reach of local invective.

By luck, a Dr. Hoyt stopped at the hotel. Hoyt had passed through Aztalan the previous year, practicing just long enough to earn an enviable reputation. Van Norstrand asked him to consult regarding a certain Mrs. Wagner: "I was very much discouraged about her, in fact I expected her to die within 24 hours." Hoyt accompanied him to the farm. "We found her in the midst of her afternoon exacerbations, mentally wandering [and] rolling about. I really thought her about to expire." Hoyt did not bother with a physical exam. He advised four powders of five grams each of sulfite of quinine, to be given at two-hour intervals, a dosage so far beyond what Van Norstrand thought prudent that he shrank from taking responsibility for it. He asked Hoyt to make up the prescription. "He cheerfully complied and even exceeded the amount mentioned. I took a long look at my poor patient expecting never to see her alive again."[12]

Early the next morning he rode out to the farm. An empty bed tick hung from a line, and a pile of straw was burning in the back yard. "I said to myself—'There, I told you so—Well, my skirts are clear—I refused to deal out the medicine,' etc., etc."

He left his medicine bag hanging from the saddle. A woman laid out for burial had no need of medicine. But there was Mrs. Wagner in her chair, wide awake and cheerful. "Oh that medicine you gave me was just the thing," she told him.

When he got back to his office, Hoyt was waiting. "The old woman was up, wasn't she?" he said. He told Van Norstrand that he had practiced along the Wabash and other river valleys in the south, where heroic doses were the norm.

"I laid my books aside, so far as malarial diseases [were concerned]," Van Norstrand recalled, "and commenced the free use of quinine and at once my long list of patients [began] to convalesce, and I to get some needed rest. In three months my medical reputation was as good as at any time during the 25 years that I subsequently actively followed my profession."[13]

Quinine became his wonder drug. He prescribed it for "the first stages of typhoid fever, erysipelas [skin infections] . . . pneumonia, congestion of the liver and the first stages of the soldier-destroyer, chronic diarrhea."[14]

And that is all he had to say about his medical practice in the prewar years. He did not mention other diseases that doctors in the area encountered routinely, often with little or no success, from consumption and scarlet fever to, occasionally, scurvy and leprosy. "Prairie itch" was the scourge of the hardworking and unwashed. Pioneers had long memories of loved ones dropping a bucket or a hoe and crushing their backs against something abrasive—the bark of a tree or the corner of a cabin—and dancing in a gritty-faced reverie of pain and pleasure.[15] But Van Norstrand does not say a word about it. He may have spent hours each day going off on horseback to deliver babies, set bones, pull teeth, purge, and even amputate, but the reader would never know from his memoirs. Did he ever stay overnight with the sick, the dying? He doesn't say.

One year the area was swept by what he called "enteric fever"—probably typhoid. He and his colleagues employed their whole arsenal against the epidemic. One doctor blistered a three-year-old and then dosed her with mercury, turpentine, soap, and other poisons. Amazingly, she survived.[16] Van Norstrand does not mention the dread and sorrow at large in the community or the suffering of his patients. A quick box score—he lost only five percent of his patients while a competitor's practice was virtually wiped out—then on to other matters.

Dr. Thomas Steel, an Englishman who served a neighboring area, wrote to his father that the summer and fall of 1847 was "a very fatal season for youngsters because of dysentery."[17] Like Hoyt and Van Norstrand, Steel prescribed heroic doses of quinine and sometimes went on horseback to Milwaukee to renew his supply. He even asked his father to send it from England. Steel considered himself lucky to clear twenty dollars a month. Much was owed him but little was paid, especially after a poor harvest. He accepted bushels of oats. Several Irishmen split his firewood. Others plowed his land for planting.[18] Steel spent much of his life on horseback. He believed in bleeding and purging, and he remained with patients through the night as they suffered and died.

It was unforgiving work, and it wore men down. Steel knew of a nearby colleague who died of alcoholism, another from addiction to drugs, and another who went insane.[19] It didn't help that there were so many quacks, that patients fell prey to every passing fad, or that Yankee doctors in particular bad-mouthed the competition,[20] or that an angry widower or grieving father could turn neighbors against the doctor whose treatments failed. Bleeding and mercury-laced calomel weakened strong patients and killed the weak. Doctors lived daily with their own ineffectiveness in the face of so much suffering. In the words of one early settler in Fort Atkinson, "Of the pests we endured in the early days there were three—the 'shakes,' the Indians, and the doctors."[21]

Carl Schurz wrote that immigrant families crowded into shanties along low-lying riverbanks were struck down first by malaria and then by doctors who "poisoned [them] with all sorts of devil's rubbish."[22] But they also saved lives. Lucien Caswell testified to that. He was sick for months before his family sought out Dr. Billard in Janesville, ten miles away. From his bed in their lakeside shack Caswell watched the doctor approaching on foot, stooping from the weight of his heavy bags. He had walked the whole way. He slid a scalpel across Caswell's swollen neck, drained and dressed the wound, wrote up a bill for two dollars, and walked away. Caswell lived a long, eventful life.[23]

It is no wonder that many doctors sought out less arduous, more certain paths to prosperity. Some invested in land, others in factories and other local enterprises.[24] One of Van Norstrand's classmates at Woodstock got rich in the railroad business.

But it took money to make money, and like Steel, Van Norstrand collected barely enough to live on, much less invest. The cost of quinine may have been a factor for him as it was for Steel. Doctoring could be more expensive for the practitioner than the patient.

Yet in other ways, life improved. He had moved into a new hotel where he would not get kicked out of his room every time the stagecoach brought a famous name or single woman to town. His practice, as he proudly recorded, had spread far and wide, and doctors were coming to him for advice. Best of all, he could finally afford to conduct a proper courtship. The young lady was Miss Lucy Hebard, daughter of the hotel owner. He had been asked to treat Lucy for a minor complaint, was invited back socially, and thereafter he took the initiative.

His finances fluctuated wildly, but his father still came through when he needed help. The senior Van Norstrand left nothing to his sons in his will because he had already passed along their shares of his estate—amounting to $2,000 each—when they needed the money.[25] That may explain why Abraham was able to buy a house and several parcels of land in spite of his meager income.[26]

He and Lucy lived frugally, both being "possessed of common sense." Their wedding was attended only by a few members of her family. No white gloves, no honeymoon. For a year they lived on less than a dollar a day. "We were as happy as we have been in any year since," he wrote toward the end of his life, reflecting ruefully upon a lifestyle that eventually cost as much per month as they had spent during their first, and in retrospect, happiest year.[27]

From an outsider with a few dollars in his pocket and a saddle-bag full of medicine, he had become, in a year and a half, a pillar of the community with a successful practice. In place of a melancholy hotel room and meals shared with strangers he now dined with his wife in his very own house. Everything was falling into place, or so it seemed.

Then why, in October of 1849, did he walk away from this village that had been so good to him? What went wrong? He does not say, but once again Dr. Steel sheds light on one likely source of chronic irritation: "Amongst the Yankies, you are watched suspiciously, your mode of treatment criticized, and your advice probably altogether neglected in conformity with their ideas of independence . . . I have more than once taken my hat and walked off, advising them to get some other assistance."[28] How would Van Norstrand have reacted to a husband scowling over his shoulder and second-guessing his every move as he tried to examine a delirious woman, or to a mother's interventions as he fought to control a combative child? Run into him on the boardwalk on Main Street and he was a genial, hale fellow sort of guy. But he also had a hair trigger. If his "temperament was ardent" and his "patience fragile" in front of a classroom, what was he like with a challenging patient or an angry spouse? Imagine a duel of insults over a groaning child. He was less inclined to offer calming reassurances than to sniff out hostility, bully it to the surface and ridicule it, then wipe his hands of the matter. Anything short of undisputed triumph would have cast a chill over him long after he was back at the glowing hearth of his new home, with Lucy at his side.

On the other hand, he also demonstrated time and again that he was confident enough in his own judgment to dismiss the opinions of others without a backward glance. Maybe the practice of medicine was not a direct factor in his decision; maybe a business deal or a partnership scheme had gone sour. Whatever the reason, he confessed later that "severing connections with many friends and attachments" had been a mistake.[29]

It was not the last time he was to abandon a situation that had turned unrewarding personally and financially—nor the last time he did so without first lowering a lifeboat. What next? He had no idea. Lucy moved back to her family home in nearby Lake Mills while he went off on horseback to scout a new life for them both.

While touring villages to the northeast he overheard teamsters predict the imminent collapse of the Wisconsin Marine and Fire Insurance Company. Panic was spreading among owners of its bonds. Although banking was not yet legal in Wisconsin, Alexander Mitchell's insurance company operated like a bank (eventually it was chartered as one and became the state's biggest), loaning money to businessmen and exchanging currency, and Mitchell's influence was felt throughout the state. Van Norstrand could not believe that a shrewd operator like Mitchell would not come out on top. His gambler's blood was up: "I expended all the gold and silver I had with me in the purchase of those [bonds] at a large discount." It paid off, though he had to weather a few days of genuine poverty before the bonds appreciated.[30]

He chose Oshkosh, on the shore of Lake Winnebago, as their next home. It was twice the size of Aztalan and certain to prosper thanks to an endless river of logs from northern forests that kept its mills humming. He sank some of his windfall into a new building on the Fox River, at the foot of Ferry Street, and some into parcels of farm land near Aztalan. He was a landlord, a speculator, and was about to become a druggist, with the store below and living quarters overhead. But this venture too came to an early and abrupt end. Soon they were back in Jefferson County, this time in Lake Mills. Again he was broke, and again he set about building a medical practice.

Son Frederick was born in June, 1851, as anti-slavery agitation increasingly tested the patience of dyed-in-the-wool Democrats like Abraham. He was a law-and-order man, proud of his affiliation with the party of the common man north and south. Back home, he claimed, abolitionists had long been looked upon as troublemakers: "It was a very unpopular subject to advocate, even in central New York." His attitude toward "long-haired Humanity fanatick[s]" had not changed.[31] Those who challenged the status quo made him angry. "Many of us . . . felt that the Negroes were much better situated physically & perhaps mentally, as slaves, than they would be as Freemen. We felt . . . that the greatest good to the greatest number of Human beings would be to let the Institution pass on its quiet way."[32] The *Jeffersonian* voiced similar sentiments, though in a more discreet way, regretting that single-issue agitators like the Free Soilers and members of the new Republican party could threaten the general prosperity by whipping up a fury over "the most dreaded of all issues." All the more reason for Democrats to hang together: "We can see no good reason why any democrat, however unfavorable he may be to slavery, should desert his party and principles."[33]

It was about this time that Van Norstrand became politically active. He was well-known among that class of locals who considered themselves practical men—merchants, farmers, and others with a stake in sustaining a healthy business climate. First as chairman of the town's board of supervisors and then, in 1851, as the Democratic nominee for a seat in the state assembly, he played for keeps.

The nomination did not come easy. "I worked for it," he wrote. Actually, he bought it: "My opponent in [the county Democratic] convention was angry at his defeat and refused to support me. Without his aid I could not be elected. I visited him, being his family physician, and labored with him a long time. His obstinacy cost me a long effort, but he finally accepted some money and agreed to spend it for my advantage, which he possibly did." Bribery paid off. He beat the incumbent, a Whig, by twenty-nine votes.[34]

Of the 1852 legislative session in Madison he had little to say except that he supported a proposed banking law that later cost him a small fortune. Traditionally, Democrats had fought the legalization of banks, credit, and paper currency, all means by which the rich and powerful fueled their own wealth-generating machines at the expense of laborers and farmers, they believed. But Van Norstrand was an eager supporter of legalized credit because he had every hope of profiting from it. He was also appointed to the committee on prisons, which was arguing the death sentence. The legislature voted to abolish it, but Van Norstrand remained steadfastly in the minority. "I voted for it and never regretted it."[35]

The legislature met for only the first few months of the year, and by April he was back in Lake Mills, arranging to move his family a half-dozen miles to Jefferson, a town of eight or nine hundred on the Rock River. As the county seat, Jefferson was where land records were kept, an important consideration for anyone as involved in real estate as Van Norstrand, and of course it was the political heart of the county as well.

It was a smart move. Jefferson was growing. The population would soon reach 2,000. Land was a terrific investment. Two decades earlier, Enoch Darling had seen what was coming. He piled lumber onto a scow and moved his sawmill upriver from Koshkonong to Jefferson. As tavern, courthouse, and store, Darling's frame building became the heart of town.[36] Soon a flour mill was grinding wagon-loads of wheat hauled in by farmers who in turn spent their cash at stores on Main and Milwaukee and Racine Streets. Yellow brick factory buildings went up, and beer, blankets, and furniture were sent into the world. From nearby forests, German farmers hewed railroad ties by the thousands, and eager buyers sent them south to Beloit and Janesville, as the long awaited prize crept their way.[37]

The observations of Carl Schurz concerning nearby Watertown applied as well to Jefferson and Fort Atkinson: "All wealth here is self-made right on the spot ... The inhabitants have come here without means, and these same people you now see building mills, factories, railroads, gas-works, and great stores, organizing banks, etc. . . . Everything has been created out of nothing by mere industry, spirit of enterprise, and perseverance."[38]

Jefferson County's Germans were farmers and small shop owners. Most were Democrats. In 1854, during his second race for the assembly seat, Van Norstrand learned that his opponent had addressed an appeal to German voters that he considered "a little more demigogical [sic] than I expected or relished." Asa Snell was an old friend and "a rich man [who] stood well socially and morally." Even the *Jeffersonian*, the local voice of the Democratic party, acknowledged that Snell was a sincere man and a friend who "would aim to do all he promises." He just happened to belong to the wrong party.[39]

Van Norstrand obtained a copy of Snell's campaign statement before it was released to the public and was appalled. Snell welcomed the newly arrived Germans, said he was happy that more were on the way, and urged them to take a stand on the critical issue of the day: "I know that you hate slavery in your souls. I know that love of freedom is planted in your hearts."[40]

This was a low blow. As a Democrat and a physician Van Norstrand was close to the German community and considered it his constituency. He hitched up his team and sped north to the office of the *Watertown Anzeiger*, which Snell had paid to print the statement in German as a handbill. He asked the printer flat out to reject the job. But a contract had been signed; a deal was a deal. All right, Van Norstrand suggested, go ahead with the handbill, but let me write an unsigned editorial for your paper, and let me pay you for your trouble. A few days later the German community read in the *Anzeiger* that Mr. Snell, who had recently struck such a noble pose in his handbill, was in fact a liar and worse, a "Know-Nothing"—a member of a secret society of old-blood Americans opposed to immigration and the growing influence of non-English-speakers.[41]

The smear worked. Van Norstrand won by over 200 votes, but it hardly mattered. Democrats were overwhelmed by the missionary zeal of fiery Republicans who promptly sent a strong antislavery senator to Washington, replacing a conciliatory Democrat, and

cancelled contracts awarded by the previous administration for construction of a hospital for the insane, claiming the process had been
tainted by favoritism.

In 1856, he was talked into running for the state senate. It was
a lost cause from the beginning: "Even my personal friends seemed
to smell the approaching strife" and opposed him. He was soundly
beaten by a man named Samuel Bean, "called by those who disliked
him 'Windy Bean' because of his spread-eagle speeches on aboli-
tionism."[42] Lucien Caswell ran for a seat in the assembly in the same
election, carefully labeling himself "an independent democrat." He
lost and came to the same conclusion: "A [northern] Democrat at
that time was so under suspicion of being in sympathy with slavery
that his prospect of being elected . . . was not over bright. Sentiment
against slavery was so strong scarcely any other political question
was considered."[43]

Van Norstrand had no patience with those who presumed to
occupy a higher moral ground than enterprising live-and-let-live
types like him, but he was genuinely distressed by the slavery debate,
primarily because of the implications for his personal fortune. By
late in the decade he was betting heavily that the center would hold,
reason would prevail, and some sort of peaceable resolution would
restore both the local economy and the value of his investments.

He had not abandoned his medical practice, which he continued out of his office in downtown Jefferson. He also served as
superintendent of schools and was a trustee of the new Wisconsin
State Historical Society in Madison.[44] But throughout the decade
he devoted most of his time and energy to business ventures. The
first was a partnership with a pair of brothers just back from the gold
fields of California, "full of money and ready for a speculation." The
Frys were to put up most of the capital for a new general store; Van
Norstrand would do the brain-work.[45]

For a while business was good. He had detected a need and
filled it, but the brothers proved a liability. They helped themselves
to merchandise, refused to do bookwork, and generally got on his
nerves. "I kept the books & cash and could easily have retaliated

five to one, but of course I could not entertain such a thought." He tried to buy them out but they refused, and so he sold out to them and gladly wiped his hands of them. Two years later they were deep in debt. "They knew nothing of business, drank to excess, and employed dishonest clerks."[46] With this nest egg he added to his land holdings, which in turn he sold to the Chicago and Northwestern Railroad for shares of railroad stock.

For years he juggled several businesses, any one of which could have been a full-time job for a less ambitious man. In addition to overseeing the new store, he served as president of the newly chartered Jefferson County Home Mutual Insurance Company. He also ran an advertisement in the *Jeffersonian* offering his services as freelance banker and real estate agent, and listing Alexander Mitchell and other high-profile names as references: "I am prepared to buy, sell or exchange notes, mortgages, real estate. I have some choice personal selections of land in Portage and Jefferson counties that I will sell or exchange for good notes, cash, or other lands. I will act as agent for any person in buying, selling, or locating lands, lending or borrowing money, collecting debts."[47]

When the first chartered bank opened in Jefferson a few years later, A. H. Van Norstrand was the cashier.[48] There was one competitor in the area, the Koshkonong Bank in Fort Atkinson, owned by Attorney Lucien Caswell. The Caswells and Lucien's stepfather's family, the Churchills, had been the first settlers at Lake Koshkonong, arriving from Vermont in 1837 when Lucien Bonaparte was ten. He loved life on the lake, especially the springtime when great rafts of logs floated by on their way to a mill on the Bark River. These became the lumber with which Fort Atkinson, Jefferson, and other towns were built. In the fall the lake was "like a meadow," dense with wild rice. Later it was dammed and the lumber and rice disappeared, but Caswell commemorated that vanished era on his bank's currency, which featured an Indian couple gathering rice in a canoe.[49]

There had been no state-chartered banks until 1852, when the legislature passed the first banking law—with the enthusiastic support of Assemblyman Van Norstrand. At the time the federal government did not circulate currency. Each bank issued its own paper money, guaranteeing its value with state or federal bonds deposited with the state comptroller. Bankers quickly discovered that high-yield, low-priced bonds issued by southern states paid better than federal bonds or those of solvent northern states. Banks proliferated as more and more settlers bought land, more crops were hauled to market, and more implement makers, merchants, wheelwrights, draymen, machinists, cheese makers, brewers, tannery operators, and harness makers struggled to start up or expand. Money loaned brought returns on a clockwork schedule while at the same time those risky-on-paper but generous-in-fact southern bonds continued to pay off. How seductive this elegant system must have appeared to Van Norstrand as he watched it pump so dependably on, filling the coffers of the Bank of Jefferson and the pockets of its owners. No messy ambiguities here. No fault-finding, no second-guessing. Transactions were clear-cut and formulaic, the payoffs predictable on into the misty future.

Trouble was, by late in the decade the system was neither simple nor dependable. In 1857 railroad stocks collapsed. Farmers who had been induced to mortgage their land to finance railroad expansion found themselves deep in debt and as isolated as ever from their markets. Instead of stock profits and the sound of a daily local carrying their produce to the cities, they were left high and dry, with a handful of fancy paper. Soon the *Jeffersonian* was full of column after column of foreclosures and sheriff's sales.

Fort Atkinson and Jefferson had bought railroad bonds expecting in return that the line would come through their towns. When the railroads ran out of money for expansion the whole system imploded. Towns defaulted on their bonds, farmers on their bank loans. A good share of the capital that railroads had raised so aggressively had gone not for land and labor but into the pockets of legislators who would select the winners of the choicest routes. Most damaging to the bankers, however, was the growing fear of secession, which undermined southern bonds. As the bonds lost value, so did their currency.

Caswell and Van Norstrand saw the crisis differently. To Caswell it was time to get out. To Van Norstrand, the gambler, it was time to get in. It is tempting to conclude that Van Norstrand sensed the coming storm, feared it would foreclose any possibility of his longed-for fortune, and so drove himself to take greater and greater risks while there was still time. His railroad stocks had turned nearly worthless, his properties languished, and time was short. On the other hand, he may simply have been convinced that a grand opportunity had presented itself. He had played the contrarian before, tempting fate when he sank his money into Alexander Mitchell's bonds, only to come out a big winner. Not all of his ventures had paid off, but by the late 1850s he had reason to trust his instincts. Although barely into his thirties he was a big man in Jefferson County, a civic leader with a growing family (his daughter, Felona Belle, "the homeliest baby I ever saw," was born in 1858). He was a well-regarded politician, businessman, and physician. He was also a practical man with an ear to the ground. It also helped that he had learned the banking business from the inside, which may have steeled him to risks that scared off less adventurous types.

A trip in 1858 to St. Louis and up the Missouri to Leavenworth, Kansas, had only whetted his appetite. Day after day a horizon of unbroken grassland passed before his eyes. "The lawlessness of the border" was apparent in every raw settlement, but it was "the vastness of the country" that impressed him most of all—such abundance, such potential for wealth from all the teams and plows yet to materialize and all the roads and rails and towns yet to be built to service them. You had to strike fast and to hold your ground through the storm that was about to break, because to hesitate was to lose out.[50]

The gamble was consistent with his politics, just as selling was consistent with Caswell's. The Democrat was betting that he could turn bad times to his advantage by taking over the bank while the gathering crisis made it a bargain, hold it through hard times to come, and then count his profits when fuses lit by the extremists were snuffed out by practical men working together on a common-sense compromise. The new Republican had resigned himself to a bloody showdown as the only way to clear the political air and rid the nation of slavery.

Caswell warned him of the risks, but "Van Norstrand, a man of considerable means, took a different view of the situation and did not believe we would have war, and he clung to his faith in the bonds."[51] The ones Wall Street had sold to the Bank of Koshkonong were from North Carolina.[52] "Dr. Van Norstrand wanted our bank, and we wanted he should have it, so we sold it to him." That was in December of 1859.[53]

Van Norstrand promptly doubled his risk by buying $25,000 in Missouri bonds, raising the bank's capitalization to $50,000. Eventually he held bonds from Georgia, California, and Tennessee, as well as North Carolina and Missouri.[54] Business was lackluster in the red brick building Caswell had built on Fort Atkinson's Main Street, and so in February of 1861 Van Norstrand transferred the Koshkonong Bank to Jefferson.

The Bank of Jefferson, his old employer, had recently moved into a massive new structure of Waukesha stone, becoming "one of the most substantial and ornamental banks in the state," according to the local paper.[55] So while his competition prospered in what was already known as "the bank building," Van Norstrand had to run the Koshkonong Bank from his medical office a few blocks away, where his father-in-law, George Hebard, served as cashier. There the doctor maintained a sweaty-palmed vigil, waiting for the politicians to come to their senses before the nation—and his bonds—went up in smoke. By late 1860, Missouri's bonds had fallen to 68 cents on the dollar, North Carolina's to 79. The plunge continued into the next year.[56] The election of a polarizing figure like Abraham Lincoln made depositors and creditors more anxious than ever to exchange local banknotes for federal gold and silver. To make good on the face value of his sinking currency, Van Norstrand had to draw down his own savings. "I was full of courage. I determined to work through it, but it went from bad to worse. Ruin seemed to stare me in the face.

I looked the matter over, dayly and nightly, and made up my mind to find someone to buy me out."[57]

First he approached a banker in Watertown who knew too much to take the bait. Then he went hunting for a well-heeled bumpkin. He found Isaac Savage, "a regular frontier man, who knew nothing of the business but had some village property, and I sold it to him so far as papers could make it."[58]

Although he calls the transaction a sale, he had every hope of regaining sole possession if only he (and the bank) could survive the political crisis. The bank continued to do business out of his office, and the death watch went on. "I tried to engineer it into a safe port, knowing Savage would transfer it to me again when the apprehended ruin had passed. Things moved slowly on, I trembling at the approach of every stranger, lest he had more of the bills than I could redeem in gold." The last customer turned out to be former Governor Doty's son-in-law. Van Norstrand could not redeem his four hundred dollars worth of banknotes. He did not have the gold and could not raise it. The date was April 2, ten days before Confederate artillery fired on Fort Sumter. It was the end of the Koshkonong Bank. All he had left to show for the thousands he had lost was a ring made from a ten-dollar gold piece, which he wore on his little finger for the rest of his life.[59]

The pain lingered in the form of lawsuits. Van Norstrand was accustomed to being the plaintiff in foreclosure proceedings against farmers and others unable to pay their debts.[60] Now the tables were turned as he became the defendant in a case destined to drag on for years.

He had gone out on a limb, but the tree was full of men who had come to Wisconsin to get rich. The affliction was not full-blown gold fever of the sort that sent folks racing to California in the late 1840s, but it was a low-grade version of that virus. Even high-minded types like the German refugee, Carl Schurz, caught the fever. In 1854 he wrote his wife that in a few years they too would become "made people" in the west. Schurz went into debt speculating on land near Watertown, which he lost in the crash of

1857.[61]

Bribery, vote fraud, a disdain for the rules generally had become commonplace. Urged by a friend to enter politics and rescue the state from "unprincipled men who have made her name a byword and a reproach among the nations," the respected land-dealer Cyrus Woodman begged off: "To clean such an Augean stable Hercules is needed and I am but a pigmy."[62] In the late 1850s, two immigrants—one a German and a Republican, the other an Irishman and a Democrat—reflected upon the corruption of public life in the state. Carl Schurz warned that "the spirit of materialism" had become "the dark side" of life in Wisconsin. Wealth seekers who prided themselves on being "practical men become apt to regard even scruples of conscience as mere obstacles to be overcome. Successful in attaining their material ends, they often appear wise, when they are only sly, efficient when they are only trickish, smart when only base."[63] Edward Ryan, an attorney, declared that Wisconsin was becoming a "paradise of folly and knavery," and that "success had replaced honor" among people who, barely a generation ago, had been known for rectitude and public-spiritedness. Both men spoke from experience. Each had overreached in some way and had regretted it, Schurz with his land speculation and Ryan as a lawyer for the railroads. Something important had been lost from public life. Somehow the people and their leaders needed to find their way back to higher ground.[64]

That great purifying event was approaching fast.

THREE

My Blood Is Up

As chairman of a committee that welcomed Stephen Douglas to
Jefferson during the 1860 presidential campaign, Abraham Van
Norstrand got to see his party's nominee up close and was not encouraged: "He appeared as if he was just waking up from a prolonged
drunk."[1] The encounter was an omen of the long hangover in store
for the Democrats.

All but a few dozen pages of Van Norstrand's memoirs are
devoted to his two and a half years of wartime service in the army.
It was the most exhilarating time of his life. He was the surgeon of
the Fourth Wisconsin, which suffered the third highest death toll
of the state's 58 infantry regiments, but he expressed few sorrows
and no regrets. In page after densely scribbled page, he comes off as
a real-life Harry Flashman, crossing swords with towering figures
like Winfield Scott and Dorothea Dix and with villains like Thomas
Williams, a general despised by his own officers but revered by the
ladies of Baton Rouge. Van Norstrand cut them all down to size.
Like Flashman he had a gift for attaching himself to local gentry on
both sides of the conflict and basking in their flattery. He delighted
in recalling many a feast laid out for his pleasure and many a bottle of
aged brandy or claret urged upon him in one white-pillared mansion
or another. As head of the biggest hospital in the Department of the
Gulf, he saw Fourth Wisconsin comrades die lingering deaths and
was himself worn down by illness and exhaustion, to say nothing of
the frustration of being locked into middling rank. But again and

again those lavish encounters with the privileged—slave owners or not—and every favor and deference granted him as surgeon, officer, man of the world, energized him. And finally that old seductress, easy money, caught his eye.

Picture him in his mid-fifties—stout, brooding, no longer radiating the old heartiness—sitting at his great ledger book with pen in hand, the family heritage of early death constantly in his thoughts as through wartime letters and his album of military papers he recreated the part he had played in the great national crisis.

By the spring of 1861 he was angry at extremists on both sides—southern leaders who in their "eternal bombast and overweening pretension" demanded that "we must assert and proclaim that the institution was of divine origin, [and that when a slave escaped] every man must turn Negro-catcher*" and abolitionists "willing to sacrifice all their wife's relations but [taking] precious care to keep their own bodies out of harm's way."[2] Not that his opinion mattered anymore. Republicans held sway in Madison and Washington. In repudiating his politics they also undermined his livelihood. For the first time ever he found himself on the wrong side of history.

On Monday, April 15, he was at the depot when travelers arriving from Chicago brought word that Fort Sumter had surrendered. He asked a friend to tell Lucy that he was off to Madison, and he hopped aboard. "I sought out Governor Alexander Randall, an acquaintance of nearly 10 years, and offered to take any duty he wished to order me to."[3]

By the end of the month he was back home and had raised a company of volunteers so eager for action that he feared many would defect to units in Illinois unless called to duty immediately. "My blood is up in this matter," he warned the governor.[4] Webster P. Moore from the town of Beloit in nearby Rock County had brought a dozen young men with him and in return won a guarantee from Van Norstrand that he would be second in command.[5]

What a month it had been. At the beginning he had been

---

* This is in reference to the Fugitive Slave Law of 1850.

struggling to keep his bank solvent and praying that war would be avoided. By the end he was impatient to muster into the Union army as the captain of a spanking new rifle company proudly calling itself the Jefferson County Guards. It had not taken him long to get back on the right side of history.

Although he claimed to be "well-pleased" as a leader of fighting men, he also recorded in detail his efforts to exchange his captaincy for the green sash of regimental medical officer. He went back to Madison to negotiate with the governor and to urge supporters to "stiffen the governor's back" against other contenders for the position, eventually walking off with a promise that he would be appointed the ranking medical officer of the Fourth Wisconsin as soon as Congress authorized the upgraded position. Thus did Abraham Van Norstrand make his stand for posterity. He had been, if only briefly, a leader of fighters for the Union; now he would play the part he had been trained for.[6]

Ironically, the first time soldiers of the Fourth Wisconsin went face to face with an angry foe, it was to put down a bank riot. Milwaukee banks were refusing to take their own currency in exchange for federal gold and silver, or did so only at severely discounted rates. Laborers paid in banknotes could not even buy groceries. Pacing behind the ranks of troops Van Norstrand must have considered the plight of Alexander Mitchell—sent running for his life as a mob trashed and burned his offices—and thought, there but for the grace of God. Financial ruin was bad enough. At least he had not had to flee from a lynch mob. A soldier killed in a freak accident was put to rest with more ceremony, he darkly noted, than the hundreds who died later in Louisiana, where trips to the "death house" became routine.[7]

For the most part, the summer of 1861 was a high-spirited campout for the Fourth Wisconsin. Social barriers between farm boys, lumberjacks, store clerks, and boarding-school students melted away under the white canvas roofs that sheltered them and in dawn-to-dusk drill. Van Norstrand and his fellow officers eagerly set about acquiring the trappings of office—uniforms, saddles, holsters of a certain type. He was thrilled with his mount, which he described as "splendid, nearly white, young and beautiful, the most beautiful I ever saw in the field. It had a very fine ear for music [and] seemed as much pleased at a parade as a child."[8] In that, horse and rider had much in common. If this was military life, Van Norstrand was hooked. And it could not have come at a better time. Even soldiers refused pay in the form of "stump tail," as they called the paper money printed by Wisconsin banks, holding out instead for federal coins.[9]

At stop after stop their eastbound train was greeted with a blur of flags and tables spread with corned beef and baked goods tended by patriotic ladies, but the festive mood gave way to boredom as the regiment spent the following months in drill and guard duty at a variety of locations in Pennsylvania and Maryland. With time on his hands Van Norstrand practiced his gift for eliciting favors from people of distinction and influence, including Dr. James Hall, former president of the American Colonization Society.[10] He dined with Attorney and Mrs. Henry Stockbridge and was courted by Dr. and Mrs. Dorsey, he pro-union, she "a violent secessionist but a Virginia lady."[11] When he fell ill, Mrs. Dorsey sent him dinners, and the Stockbridges took him on a steamboat excursion down the Chesapeake Bay.

At one parade he caught the eye of a Mrs. LaSalle, a "very aristocratic . . . and intelligent secessionist" and, she claimed, a descendent of an early governor of Louisiana. "She was a great admirer of fine horses and I think, of good riders." She invited him to pay a visit. This was the sort of grand flirtation he relished. "I mounted, dressed in my best, well armed and spurred, and made my call. I found a black servant at the door of her magnificent house to take my horse, and herself just within, evidently much pleased at my effort at soldierly becoming and armament. She showed me the many fine paintings and other works of art," then sat him down to "the most elaborate lunch I ever saw, several kinds of fruit, cake, preserves, cold meat, coffee, etc., etc. She could not have treated me with more consideration if I had been President Lincoln or General Scott."[12]

Van Norstrand's most remarkable coup occurred during a trip to Washington in the aftermath of the disastrous battle of Bull Run. He passed through streets "full of dirty, begging, vagabond, defeated soldiers of disorganized regiments, everybody inquiring 'What can be done?' and the barrooms full of drinking officers." Hardly a good time for an obscure militia officer to seek an interview with the general commanding this stunned army, but that is what Van Norstrand did. Winfield Scott had been his boyhood idol, "my idea of the perfect soldier . . . the tall, fine-looking hero of Lundy's Lane,"[13] but the old man he was introduced to was "large, squatty and decrepit," too feeble to rise from his chair. Scott gazed at the pages of an enormous Bible, appearing as shell-shocked as some of his soldiers.[14] "He took my hand between both of his and blessed me," Van Norstrand recorded. "I said to myself, 'Great God, we need a leader.'"[15]

In October he was put in temporary charge of the U.S. General Hospital in Baltimore: "I was visited by Miss Dorothea Dix. She must have been near 60 years old and by fate forbidden woman's influence in the domestic circle. She chose to be a follower of Miss Nightingale but failed badly, through excess of desire for notoriety and lack of Christian humility and general good sense.[16] She subsequently did get a little credit for pushing the cause of the insane, but I think I am warranted in saying . . . that she was a terror to her friends, they always feeling that 'good-bye' was the best remark she had made during a long visit . . . She bade me to discharge some of my nurses, but I paid no attention."[17]

Another disappointment was William Hammond, soon to be appointed surgeon general of the army. Hammond commanded a nearby hospital and asked several surgeons including Van Norstrand to consult with him. An old soldier had taken a ball through the tibia, just below the knee. "The poor man had [taken on] that ethereal look that is a sure precursor of death," Van Norstrand wrote. He and others recommended immediate amputation, but Hammond refused, hoping to save the leg. The soldier died. "It was not the only foolish thing that Hammond did while he was surgeon general."[18]

His bitterness toward these and other figures is revealing. True, he was not alone in thinking Winfield Scott too old and weary for the challenge facing him in 1861. It was also true that Dorothea Dix's imperious manner brought bile to the mouths of many a legislator and hospital administrator, and that William Hammond, who was later credited with remarkably upgrading the medical services of the Union army under the most pressing circumstances, made some mistakes. What is striking about Van Norstrand's criticism is its intensity and apparent inevitability.

He also fumed over the presumptions of colleagues and underlings and delighted in their comeuppance. The regimental quartermaster rode beside him during a dress review for their commanding general, Van Norstrand "stiff as iron" while the know-it-all quartermaster cut loose with "an immense flourish" of a salute at the wrong time. Van Norstrand was delighted.[19] The incident merited a paragraph in his memoirs. So did his assistant's failure to connect with the ladies, and so did any number of mortifications suffered by enlisted men from time to time. He found "amusing" the terror of civilians who fled at the approach of Union soldiers, such as when a teacher ran out the back door of her schoolhouse and into the woods, followed by "twenty tow-heads in single file, casting back their frightened faces to see if we were pursuing them."[20] Impatience and contempt were ever close to the surface, just as he was readily seduced by praise and flattery.

The reason for the underlying anger is not to be found in the memoirs. It must be remembered that he was looking back two decades. By the late 1870s he saw his army life through a prism clouded by more recent events and in particular an obsession with an adversary who came into his life after the war and so shows up only indirectly in the memoirs. The wisecrack about abolitionists who wouldn't fight but eagerly sacrificed "all their wife's relations" was obviously a dig at Samuel Hastings, the hospital trustee and former state treasurer who was never far from his thoughts.

He started writing in 1877 and died six years later. Presumably he worked in fits and starts—when he had the time, felt the inclination, and his health permitted. The man who emerges from these wartime pages is restless and ambitious, ever-curious, quick to take offense but also quick to make friends. He is confident in his own skill and judgment. He has acquired the trappings of office, a surgeon's sword and sash, and loves to display them at parades and reviews, especially when there is a civilian audience to impress. He is fond of his stately and much-admired horse, and he is especially fond of "Nigger Jim," his personal servant.[21] Van Norstrand does not tell us where Jim came from, or how this relationship came about. Whether they met up in Maryland or later in Louisiana, Jim's job was to take care of him—to make sure he did not go hungry, to look after his uniforms and personal gear, and, when out of doors, to improvise shelter. That Jim was resourceful and reliable is obvious from the admiration Van Norstrand expressed repeatedly.[22]

In early November the Fourth Wisconsin was ordered on its first active campaign, the so-called Eastern Shore expedition into northern Virginia, which amounted to little more than an extended training exercise through Princess Ann and Snow Hill in Maryland, and Oak Hall and Eastville in Virginia. If rebels were nearby, they had melted away. For Van Norstrand this rambling campout was memorable mostly for the comradely feelings that deepened over suppers of fried pork, coon, and sweet potatoes purchased from a frightened farm wife, or while basking in the awe of country folk who watched the expedition's galloping cavalry and booming artillery on maneuvers, or during a tricky night march across a tidal plain, Van Norstrand in the lead, his white horse a beacon for the soldiers who followed.[23]

Colonel Halbert Paine, commander of the Fourth Wisconsin, had practiced law with Carl Schurz in Milwaukee. At 35, Paine was about the same age as Van Norstrand but looked younger in spite of his chin whiskers. Lanky and angular, with a face all sharp-edged jaw and cheekbone, Paine was blind without his spectacles. A passing acquaintance thought him the strangest man he'd ever seen.[24] Paine was a Republican and a true believer in the abolitionist cause. As a young college graduate he had taught briefly in Mississippi, an experience that would tend to either fire the idealism in a young northerner or extinguish it.[25]

Another dedicated abolitionist was the second in command, Lieutenant Colonel Sidney Bean, a former mathematics professor at Carroll College in Waukesha, and a student of oriental languages.[26] At 28, Bean was the youngest of the regiment's senior officers, and he comes to life in Van Norstrand's pages as a pink-cheeked, clean-shaven scholar and "a very fastidious bachelor." He was so short that his sword dragged on the ground. A few sips of wine turned him into a hopeless giggler. Paine described him as "more like a pretty girl than a boy," but also "gifted with a brilliant genius." Van Norstrand delighted in tweaking Bean's prissiness. Once they were served a meal by a woman who was nursing a child. "Her dairy appendages were a little in the way of our knives and forks," Van Norstrand wrote. "I finally whispered to Colonel Bean [asking] him what we were going to do about it. He replied in his solemn way, 'Oh, ain't it awful!'"[27] Three sons and a son-in-law went to war from the Bean family, officers all. Only one survived.[28]

But Van Norstrand's soulmate was Major Frederick Boardman. As a recent graduate of Annapolis assigned to the side-wheeler *Susquehanna*, Boardman had accompanied Matthew Perry on his historic expedition to Japan and China in the early 1850s, earning a reputation as a hell-raiser by climbing the walls of Canton one night after the gates were locked, among other pranks and adventures.[29] By 1861 he had been out of the navy long enough to become frustrated with the state job arranged by his uncle and hungry for adventure once again. The Boardmans were from Connecticut. Fred's father, a Yale man who had come to Milwaukee to practice medicine, died when Fred was 16. An only child, young Boardman was taken under wing by his uncle Josiah Noonan, an influential newspaper man and a Democratic party boss who opened many doors for his nephew. Depression and restlessness ate at Boardman when life was routine. His antidote was action. Even before the war he had put in for a commission in the regular army, and when he learned that the Revenue Service was looking for men to command its coastal cutters he applied for that position as well.

But with war came a proliferation of volunteer regiments desperate for experienced leaders, and he promptly enlisted as a private in the Wisconsin militia. Determined to stand out from the crowd, he beat the bushes for recommendations. Soon the governor received a letter signed by eight members of the state legislature and endorsed by General Rufus King, a West Pointer and publisher of the *Milwaukee Sentinel*, urging Boardman's appointment to the rank of major—evidence that Uncle Josiah was still using his influence on Fred's behalf.[30]

Frantic, insecure, convinced others were scheming against him, Boardman nonetheless comes across in Van Norstrand's account as a free spirit—brave, good-hearted, an altogether charming guy. It seems to have been both his curse and his gift that although chronically dissatisfied and fearful that less worthy men would outmaneuver him in the struggle for recognition, he maintained a high level of energy and good cheer. "I am well liked," he assured his uncle.[31]

He and Van Norstrand shared the same suspicions about certain fellow officers. Both were conservative by temperament. Neither could stomach boat rockers, be they secessionists or abolitionists. Boardman considered even Colonel Paine a shamelessly ambitious grandstander.[32] But of Van Norstrand he had only good things to say: "Dr. Van Norstrand is a first rate fellow and keeps the best regulated hospital I have ever seen."[33]

Van Norstrand may have been fortunate that he was out of the race for promotions that so preoccupied others. A regimental surgeon held the rank of major and could advance no farther. The creation of so many volunteer regiments had opened up positions of high rank that drew ambitious applicants like a land rush. "Unmanly jealousies are springing up all over," Governor Randall wrote to Noonan: "Every disappointed applicant thinks every appointee a d—d fool."[34] It was a mixed blessing to Van Norstrand that he was spared that turmoil and so could circulate comfortably among fellow officers whose relationships were often complicated by suspicion and rivalry.

Another friend was Captain Joseph Bailey, an enterprising land speculator and construction engineer, who sported a preposterously oversized handlebar mustache. Bailey once supervised the movement of a small town, which was loaded on flatbed wagons and drawn by teams of oxen to the anticipated site of a rail line. If the railroad would not come to Newport, then Newport would come to the railroad. Eventually the name was changed to Wisconsin Dells.[35]

Finally, Captain Webster Moore owed his position as commander of Company E (formerly Van Norstrand's Jefferson County Guards) to Van Norstrand. He would rally to the doctor's defense in hard times to come.

Slavery had been little more than a debating topic for these northerners until they marched onto Confederate territory. As Van Norstrand and Boardman savored a meal of fried chicken, cornbread, and peach brandy in Snow Hill, Maryland, their host boasted of the business he had created. He ran a sort of temp agency, buying "vagabond negroes" at bargain prices from the local jail, then hiring them out.[36] At such times the doctor was appalled. Other times he was amused, as when blacks who had gathered at a fence to watch drilling soldiers fled in terror from the roar of cannon fire. On still other occasions, especially when the guest of a flattering patrician, he was clearly seduced by the wealth and status that slavery had made possible.

Typically, his account of these weeks on the march is peppered with incidents of one-upmanship—the quartermaster officer too busy entertaining rebel women in his quarters to attend to business; the young doctor with too much rank and too little experience; a "tongue-brave" company commander whose bravado proved to be just for show.[37] All suffer from encounters with the regimental surgeon.

FOUR

The Best Specimen of a Tyrant

In early March, 1862, the soldiers of the Fourth Wisconsin finally embarked upon a real adventure. At Newport News, Virginia, they were ferried to a new steamship called the *Constitution*, reputedly one of the largest vessels afloat. "Imagine yourself [on] one of those floating palaces [on] the Mississippi," one of them wrote. "Increase its splendor, magnificence and size by about four times; imagine the sounds of bugles, drums, silver bands and military hubbubs on the decks above and below."[1]

There was no celebrating during the next day's storm off Cape Hatteras. One humorist observed shipmates "heaving up offerings to Neptune, in glorious profusion. It was a sublime spectacle to see nearly every man bow at the same altar . . . using the same form of worship."[2] In the midst of his retching Captain Joseph Bailey vowed that he would return home via the Mississippi River or not at all.[3]

Days later Lieutenant Colonel Sidney Bean sank his hand into a bucket of Gulf Stream water and found it "warm as blood." He watched beacons and lighthouses of the Florida Keys pass in the distance, and he stayed up one night to see the Southern Cross. But mostly he worried about the men below: "Picture 3000 men in one ship. It reminds me of all that I have read of the horrors of the slave trade. [The men are] packed away like cattle."[4] Paine tried to convince the captain to put ashore at Key West so that the living quarters below could be flushed out and more fresh water brought aboard, but he was outvoted by the colonels of the other two regiments.[5]

Fred Boardman felt sorry for the men but mostly for himself. The whole operation was a mere sideshow, he suspected, contrived to profit politicians and contractors. (Leasing the *Constitution* reportedly cost the army $2,500 a day.) He blamed Paine. It was Paine's outspoken abolitionism and his conniving for promotion that had jinxed the regiment. That was why it had been banished from the main event in the east and sent off on this backwater boondoggle.[6]

Doctor Abraham Van Norstrand brooded over the loss of his beautiful white charger, which had to be left behind. He was consoled somewhat by the status of the man who bought it, a New York colonel rumored to be the illegitimate son of the Emperor of Prussia, and by the price—well over double what the horse had cost him. Like other officers free to roam the deck, he was struck by the "magnificence and grandeur" of a gale off Cape Hatteras, the schools of porpoises accompanying them through the smooth green water of the Gulf, and especially by "flying fish by the hundreds . . . very beautiful, like little snowbirds." He did not mention the misery of the men below decks. Perhaps he found solace in being simply a tourist, if only for this week at sea.[7]

Officers were curious about the new brigade commander, Brigadier General Thomas Williams, a second-generation West Pointer. At 47 Williams had campaigned for most of his life, chasing Indians from Wisconsin to the Everglades to the far West. During the Mexican war, as an aide to General Winfield Scott, he was cited for bravery. Never in his army life had he lived as lavishly as he did aboard the *Constitution*, with its "table cloths and knives and forks clean and white; and my table for self and staff as good as any man could wish."[8]

Michigan-born, he was exhilarated to command a brigade of western soldiers. His three regiments were from Wisconsin, Michigan, and Indiana, and thus, he believed, certain to fight better than eastern regiments filled with city boys. These were "large, strong, active" men, accustomed to the rigors of outdoor life. He considered them natural soldiers, "the only [Union] men who have showed prowess and spirit,"[9] and he assumed that the fondness was mutual, though in fact his officers did not know what to make of him.[10] Sidney Bean wrote, "He is an old soldier—has been through the Florida and Mexican wars—is a fine looking soldier—and that is all I know about him."[11]

The destination was Ship Island, little more than a sandbar six miles long off the coast of Mississippi. The Union's master plan in the West was to cut the Confederacy in two by fighting up the Mississippi River, using Ship Island as the staging area, as well as downriver from the north. Details of the southern half of that plan were to be worked out by Major General Benjamin Butler, commander of the newly designated Department of the Gulf. Williams's brigade was one of three that had been shipped to Butler—a total of 15,000 troops.

By the end of the voyage fevers were percolating throughout the stifling compartments below.[12] Conditions on Ship Island were unlikely to be much of an improvement. In mid-March the *Constitution* dropped anchor beside what Boardman called "one of the most barren spots on the face of the globe."[13] The first of several horrific storms blew over them that night, prompting those at sea to pray for their sodden buddies already ashore and vice versa.

A green blur miles to the west marked the swampy southern tip of Louisiana. The coastal waters between Ship Island and the shores of Louisiana and Mississippi were patrolled by scores of Union men-of-war, frigates, and mortar boats. The soldiers were safe from rebels but soon discovered that on this strip of sand and muck nature was the enemy: dark squalls and a dazzling glare that inflicted a kind of snow blindness. Sharing the beach were slumbering gators and the occasional cottonmouth rattler, and everywhere and always, the mosquitoes. On one end of the island stood the walls of an unfinished fortress; on the other was an oasis of sorts where pines, scrub oaks, and palmettos grew among the marsh grasses, attracting most of the wildlife. In between stretched sand and pools of quicksand where in stormy weather, one soldier recorded, the south wind "takes off the tops of the waves, wisps them up, and flirts them clear across the island."[14]

While touring the beaches Boardman and Van Norstrand came upon a group of wild men lingering over a meal of wild boar. They turned out to be a fatigue party of home state boys. More storms blew up. Lightning killed four men. Tents were leveled—including Van Norstrand's hospital—and blankets and clothing tumbled into the sea. A New England soldier bathing too far from shore became food for the sharks.[15]

Weeks of unhealthy extremes at sea and on shore added to the sick lists.[16] Van Norstrand's hospital tents filled with fever cases, and there was much coming and going of nurses hauling pails. Within ten days of landing, he wrote, everyone had diarrhea from army food and bad water. He put suspected small-pox cases in a so-called "pest tent," and he treated cases of malaria and typhoid, but a debilitating strain of diarrhea was the biggest problem. Sanitary conditions were not helped by the scum line of human waste and putrefying aquatic life accumulating at the edge of the beach.[17]

General Williams was determined to shake his soldiers out of their lethargy and toughen them for duty in the tropics, and his method was drill—in wool uniforms, with rifles and full knapsacks. Williams believed that away from the civilizing influence of wives, sisters, and mothers, men turned brutal and coarse, and that the only antidote was discipline. "And I'll give them plenty," he assured his adjutant.[18] He ordered his officers to put them through three hours of tactical maneuvers every morning and afternoon in addition to simply marching them back and forth through the deep sand. In fairness to Williams, many senior officers and even some doctors believed that the best way to protect soldiers from the wasting effect of the tropics was to flush their bodies of noxious vapors inhaled from pestilential swamps and soil, even if that meant sweating them to the point of collapse.[19] Williams called the exercises he had devised "Order of Combat," but they were a departure from the army's standard battle drill, which the volunteers had only recently mastered through months of endless repetition. His variations at first bewildered them and then gave birth to a thrilling suspicion among the officers that they knew more about tactics than he did. It dawned on them that if you stripped away that aura of West Point invincibility you would find a man who didn't know what he was doing. An old-time campaigner he might be, but could he command a brigade? Increasingly, they concluded that he could not. Occasionally he conducted the drills himself, with disastrous consequences. One afternoon his anger mounted as junior officers and their riflemen, unprepared for his unorthodox commands, turned battle maneuvers into a circus. "He completely lost his head in this novel attempt to command troops," Paine wrote. "He cursed and swore fearfully, with nothing to swear at except his own idiotic tomfoolery."[20] The mounting contempt of the officers was picked up and amplified by soldiers, some of whom began to taunt Williams by calling out "Order of combat!" whenever he appeared.

Soldiers already shaky with fever keeled over during these ordeals. Each day the regimental surgeons excused more of the sick from drill. Williams fumed that they were deliberately undermining him. The doctors talked it over and decided that one of them had to make their case personally. Van Norstrand had been in uniform longest, and he was convinced that no one else was up to the task: "Most of them were timid, knew what they ought to do but lacked courage to do it." He wrote a letter explaining that in this climate these "hardening" drills had the opposite effect than Williams intended."[21]

He timed the letter to arrive after the general had finished dinner, imagining him in a more serene mood with a full stomach, but that happy vision vanished as soon as he approached the general's table. "I found him in a petty rage. There was more whiskey in his head than sound sense. . . . He accused me as head conspirator in rebellion against his authority."

Williams passed the insubordinate physician on to General Butler, commander of the Department of the Gulf. At the time, only two men in the nation ranked higher than Butler—Secretary of War Edwin Stanton and President Abraham Lincoln.[22] Butler got right to the point: "I am informed that you and other surgeons have conspired to break up our drill. Half of your division was excused from drill yesterday and today. And you sent a very disrespectful paper to General Williams. What have you to say?"

Van Norstrand insisted that he was doing his duty as army regulations defined it. But clearly he was shaken. He was the first officer in the regiment to cross swords with Williams and one of the first to develop an abiding hatred for him. There would be many more.

But ironically he became a life-long admirer of Benjamin Butler, who, although fierce, foul-mouthed, and funny-looking, was above all a "wonderful man"—rare praise indeed from Van Norstrand: "He is much crossed in his eyes, dresses a little loud, sits on his horse like a tree-toad on a chip, is fearfully profane when in a rage, [but] is the best specimen of a tyrant I ever saw, and what is very remarkable in a tyrant, he is personally brave."[23]

Spirits soared when the *Great Republic* appeared on the horizon, but the hopeful mood lasted only until the soldiers were aboard. For two weeks they languished, "stowed as closely as sardines," Van Norstrand wrote, eating "boiled sour ham and hard-tack."[24] "The water for the men stinks, and there is not enough of it," Sidney Bean wrote in his diary.[25] Too sick to make the journey, a hundred members of the regiment had been left on the island, many to be discharged and shipped north to recover or die.[26] Meanwhile their comrades on the *Great Republic* lived in their own waste. The ship "emitted a stench . . . that would knock a man down."[27] The greater the misery, the greater the rage directed at General Williams and his staff, who lived well above the squalor in the roomy saloon. Sidney Bean wrote, "There is nothing but hatred and contempt toward the General and his staff. . . . The man is so swamped by his vanity that [there is] no imbecility he may not be guilty of."[28]

One day an argument broke out between Williams and Butler. Paine overheard Williams shouting, "Before I consent to it, I'll fight, Sir! I'll fight!"[29] Poor Williams. He was a crusty old regular caught between an amateur general above and amateurs below, and like Butler, the Massachusetts politician, and Paine, the ambitious do-gooder, they all seemed to be lawyers.

With his "florid countenance and precisely cut grizzly hair and a mind pickled twenty years in alcohol, [Williams] appears determined to wage war by means of inspections," a Michigan officer wrote.[30] "Gen. Williams hates the 4th Wisconsin regiment," Paine unloaded in a letter home. "He hates me. His pretensions are disgusting. I am among heathen men, in an atmosphere of hell with an idiotic child of hell for a general, an imbecile puerile drunken malignant shallow cowardly traitorous incompetent blockhead, [who is] surrounded by a staff of empty-headed lickspittles."[31]

Van Norstrand recorded one burial at sea.[32] "I seriously think that if the *Great Republic* in its present condition could be moored for twenty-four hours anywhere within gunshot of New Orleans," a soldier wrote of the stench, "the city would of necessity surrender."[33]

They lingered in purgatory as Rear Admiral David Farragut's fleet headed up the Mississippi toward New Orleans, fighting its way through a flotilla of Confederate warships and the guns of rebel forts flanking the river. A cloud of songbirds, assumed to be refugees from the flames and fury upriver, descended upon the *Great Republic*, too weary or disoriented to resist the soldiers who took them in hand and petted them.*

The first of May came as a literal breath of fresh air. The Wisconsin soldiers had exchanged the toxic fumes of the *Great Republic* for a sunny deck on the captured steamship *Diana*. Patriotic music from their brass band drifted out to passing plantation houses, and the intoxicating sweetness of citrus groves and creamy-pink magnolia blossoms wafted over the soldiers. "The slaves, the women more particularly, would drop their hoes and run to the levee asking most earnestly to be taken on board," Van Norstrand recalled. "[They] danced most energetically to our tunes. Many of the plantation houses were shut up and several had hoisted the French flag."[34]

Near New Orleans the levee became a black moonscape of cotton bales that had been slashed open and burned. Warehouses

---

* This was Paine's impression (Paine, p. 14), but these were probably migratory birds exhausted by their flight from the Yucatan Peninsula.

full of tobacco and sugar had been torched, and the river was a slurry of dumped molasses and rice. Determined to deny the approaching enemy the fruits of their slave labor and cottage industries, rebels had chosen to destroy them.[35]

At the foot of Canal Street, wobble-kneed soldiers thundered down gangplanks and through a mob whose curses were drowned out by "Yankee Doodle" and "Star-Spangled Banner," courtesy of the Fourth Wisconsin band. For all their indignation and spite, locals grudgingly submitted to life under an occupying power after little more than one high-visibility hanging and some hard-hearted threats from the pen of General Butler. A surgeon with the 21st Indiana declared the citizens of New Orleans "the most easily sub-jugated people I have ever seen. They look and act like dogs which you catch stealing, and whip."[36]

Two incidents stand out. In his memoirs Van Norstrand boasted of an encounter with a cook on the *Great Republic*. A fellow officer had gone to the galley to fetch water for a sick soldier but came back empty-handed, "pushed out by the great black greasy Negro. I raised my Bowie from its sheath and marched into the [galley] and took the cup and took the water, in the meanwhile informing the nigger that if he interfered he would need a wash-tub in which to carry his stomach."[37] He also recalled following Halbert Paine down the gangplank into the mob and urging Paine to slap a few heads with his sword.[38] A young officer whose specialty is violence backs away from a fight, and the commander of a regiment of fighters deliberately keeps his sword sheathed in the face of provocation. Of all people, it is the physician who rushes into the breech on both oc-casions, threatening bloodshed in the first instance, urging it in the second. Here, years later, is the "ardent" young teacher whose temper chilled his classroom. No wonder Dr. Van Norstrand admired Ben-jamin Butler, "the best specimen of a tyrant." Such was the baggage he would later bring to the hospital in Madison.

FIVE

A Severe Punishment of a Deluded and Spiteful People

Shortly after the war a young officer traveling upriver from New Orleans described the view from his deck chair: "Eastward there is naught to span the horizon but one far-reaching level of swamp or trembling prairie. Westward, two miles back from the river-bank, bold barriers of forest, dense, dark, and impenetrable, shut off the view. In front lies the eddying, swirling, boiling bosom of the Mississippi—the winding highway to the North."[1]

General Williams's soldiers contemplated that view often during a spring and summer of constant movement up and down the river. Soon they were begrimed by soot from bonfires made of railroad ties, by swamp mud, mosquito splatter, and the silt of accumulated sweat. They scouted, foraged, tore up miles of railroad track, and once again sickened in the below-decks purgatory of ironclad river steamers poised for the long-anticipated move against Vicksburg.

A Wisconsin boy had vowed to "steal all I can lay my hands to" if he ever got to New Orleans.[2] Chances are he did pretty well, if not there then at Baton Rouge or any number of river hamlets and plantations the regiment was destined to strip clean over the years to come. Sometimes that was their mission. Sometimes they were desperate for fresh meat, or they needed farm animals to pull their wagons, and sometimes they could not bring themselves to leave behind books and candlesticks and things of beauty and wonder they had never seen before. Often, what they could not carry they trashed or burned.

The Fourth Wisconsin and Sixth Michigan in particular gained a reputation for pillage and plunder: "These regiments," Williams wrote, "appear to be wholly destitute of moral sense [believing] that pillaging [is] not only right in itself but a soldierly accomplishment."[3] The hostility between Williams and his volunteers—in particular their senior officers—only worsened. "Our volunteer system is radically bad," he believed, poisoned by the political ambitions of the officers and the brutishness of the men. As an old professional he held that "the only relation between the private and the officer [should be] a purely official relation, which exacts discipline and compels instruction without fear, favor or affection."[4] But to volunteer officers like Paine, Bean, and Van Norstrand, Williams epitomized the dark side of the professional army—the spiteful martinet who inflicted needless suffering on his soldiers. Only Boardman, still yearning for an appointment to the regular army and ever sensitive to any sign of slight or favor, had anything good to say about Williams. He speculated that Paine was jealous of him because "I have been favored by the General and Paine is too small minded to be generous."[5]

Over the following three years soldiers of the Fourth Wisconsin would be sent on expeditions as far north as Vicksburg, as far west as Texas. They took part in one decisive campaign, many lesser battles and running skirmishes, and periodic guerrilla roundups, but they would spend most of their days policing, scouting, foraging, plundering, sickening, and dying along the river between New Orleans and Baton Rouge.

General Williams communicated through his adjutant, a young captain named Wickham Hoffman. Hoffman was a busy man. He might show up a half dozen times before noon to revise an order, recruit men for details, or pass along still another petulant query or edict from his boss. These were not urgent tactical communications but irksome recalibrations of the brigade machinery by its peevish master mechanic. Prepare your regiment to disembark. The general wishes to know why your soldiers remain on board against his orders. Suspend disembarking until further orders. The general wishes to know why some of your soldiers remain on the levee and others on the boat. Paine and his officers referred to this unfortunate messenger as "Miss Nancy," and their blood boiled whenever "Miss Nancy Hoffman" came strutting their way.[6]

"It is a peculiarity of the General never to let us know *how* he wants a thing done until after we have done it," Paine wrote. "This secures to him a chance for a wider range of pretexts for cursing us for not doing the thing in the way he wished."[7]

Van Norstrand often accompanied the troops into the field, on one occasion "in water up to [our] arm pits." "Alligators and soldiers were mixed up in the general confusion," a soldier wrote, "and I am inclined to the opinion that those interesting creatures outnumbered the soldiers." This writer had seen General Williams plodding through the soup as well, "and not being a very tall man, he was not visible more than half the time."[8]

Rank had its privileges, and the next day Doctor Van Norstrand was offered a seat on a captured handcar. He turned it down, choosing to soldier on with the men: "This was the hardest march I ever made. Col. Paine, who always prided himself on his endurance, at last yielded his arms to me and I carried them with my own." Sure enough, General Williams "and some of his louty staff" came along, "occupying the place on the [hand] car declined by me."[9]

It was the conduct of the troops on this operation in the vicinity of Kenner's Landing that led Williams to condemn them with such fury. Van Norstrand and Paine saw the matter differently. Everyone was exhausted and famished. The soldiers had taken hostile fire. No wonder they returned to the steamboat "well laden with beef, pork, chickens, wine, etc., etc."[10] As young Norton DeHave explained: "We don't get anything fit to eat except what we steal."[11] Paine enjoyed watching his "nude giants" relaxing along the bank of the river, washing their clothes and "plung[ing] into the river in jolly style."[12]

* * *

On a lazy afternoon in late May the steamer *Laurel Hill*, with General Williams and most of the Fourth Wisconsin aboard, approached the shoreline near Grand Gulf, Mississippi, forty miles south of Vicksburg, to take on firewood. Suddenly the bluff overhead erupted with "a storm of grape and ball."[13] Van Norstrand had been watching a game of dominoes in the saloon. He lit out for the stern of the boat to distance himself from the boilers. Just then the captain swung the vessel sharply downriver, a maneuver that placed Van Norstrand in the rebels' line of sight: "I could look into the mouths of the guns [and] see the smoke well out of the cannon before the ball commenced singing. General Williams was standing at my left, his right hand on an upright stanchion, and with his left hand twirling his mustache. I was a little depressed by fear, but put my left hand on the same stanchion, and through my hate of him, resolved to be as unconcerned as he was." But to his eternal disgust he could not sustain the pose, ducking involuntarily when a round came near. "On coming to a perpendicular I discovered a sneaking smile on the General's face, which added much to my ill feelings towards him." One of the balls had gone through a soldier lying on deck nearby, reading *Harper's* magazine.[14]

A plan was hatched for a retaliatory raid. Gunboats fired into the bluff and the nearby village, and four companies of angry soldiers were landed on the levee, led by Major Boardman. They chased the fleeing artillery batteries through the village and beyond until a mile or so inland, deep in the woods, they came upon a scene that cooled their bloodlust. "There we met with fugitives—men, women and children, who had fled from the bombardment," one participant wrote. "Women and children were weeping piteously. Night was coming on and the woods was their only shelter, and strange soldiers, their enemies, were occupying their homes. We sympathized with their misfortune and gave them words of comfort, telling them to return to their homes and none of them should be harmed."[15]

Boats continued to come under fire from Grand Gulf. The area became a grand nuisance. In mid-June an expedition composed of Wisconsin and Connecticut rifle companies and some Massachusetts artillery landed deep in a bayou to the rear of the village. This time Colonel Paine commanded, and Van Norstrand went along: "It was a beautiful sight to see the movements of our skirmishers . . . creeping over the bluffs and among the bushes, with their long guns in the usual position of grouse hunters in a stubble field, looking out sharp for the enemy." Van Norstrand was sitting atop a nag Jim had scavenged for him, chatting with a country doctor, when a battery of Massachusetts artillery came thundering up the road, shocking him into action but not his dull horse, which was unmoved by his shouts and kicking heels. The soldiers and their lathered mounts and creaking gun carriages barely missed him. Later his spirits were rallied by slaves who abandoned their labor among the cotton fields and flocked to the men in blue, shouting, "God bless de Lincolnites." Still later he commandeered a team of oxen so that his men could gather up soldiers felled by sunstroke. A flag lettered "4 Wis Hospital" was always nearby, and his staff was equipped with stretchers, canteens, medicine, and whiskey. Mostly they were bandsmen, not the most reliable stretcher-bearers when balls were flying, but tolerably efficient otherwise. In spite of the withering heat and his own fatigue Van Norstrand carried on with his usual vigor, proud of his little organization and above all his own rugged, composed, take-charge self.[16]

Wisconsin troops ran off the rebel battery, and the next day they overran a recently abandoned infantry camp, killing a rebel officer and capturing a piano and steaming pots of corn and beans.[17] They continued into the town of Grand Gulf and, as ordered by General Williams, set it ablaze to the last chicken coop. Van Norstrand estimated the displaced population at five hundred women, children, and old men.[18]

In the opinion of young Newton Culver, destroying the town was "entirely uncalled for," but his disgust was not widely shared.[19] Van Norstrand did not shed any tears: "On arrival into the village the soldiers at once commenced firing the buildings and shooting pigs, calves, cows, etc. . . . I made an effort to save a little church, but it was soon consumed, with every other roof in the place, a severe punishment of a deluded and spiteful people."[20] In a letter home, Norton DeHave wrote simply, "We burned the village, that was nice and then left."[21] No mention this time of terrified civilians watching from the woods as their town was reduced to a forest of blackened chimneys. Mississippians had a term for what remained of a place after incendiary blue-coats had passed through—"Chimneyville."[*]

That night Van Norstrand turned his horse loose and went aboard the steamboat weary but at peace with himself. "We soon had a fine supper cooked and eaten," thanks to the plundered pantries and barns of Grand Gulf.[22]

Finally the western soldiers elicited grudging praise from General Williams: "[They] conducted themselves after a trying and oppressive day, like soldiers fighting in the cause of their country. [I] hope that in another place, and upon a larger scale, this regiment will soon have an opportunity to exhibit the same conduct, and the same courage."[23]

* * *

Such missions were secondary to the army's guiding obsession during 1862 and most of '63, which was to open the river to Union traffic. Rebel guns on Vicksburg's towering bluffs were rocks in the gears of the federal machine, paralyzing it. If the army could take Vicksburg the river would become a Union expressway, with cotton and sugar steaming north past Union reinforcements and supplies

---

[*] Others were Jackson, Friars Point, Prentiss, Holly Springs and Oxford. (John K. Bettersworth, *Confederate Mississippi*, (Baton Rouge, 1943), p. 279–80) As for the formerly prosperous Grand Gulf, which in the 1830s and '40s had been home to 1,200 people, a thriving cotton market, plus hotels and stores and a railroad link to inland communities, it had been triply cursed even before the war, first by typhus, which wasted the health of the community, then by a tornado that destroyed many of its structures, and finally by the angry river, which consumed its shoreline. Plunder and arson by the Fourth Wisconsin was the coup de grace, although the dead town's surrounding bluffs continued to be a thorn in the Union side. The following summer rebel artillery was back in greater strength than ever and repelled a Union flotilla of gunboats and troop transports sent by Grant and Porter as part of the Vicksburg offensive. (Vincent H. Cassidy and Amos E. Simpson, *Henry Watkins Allen of Louisiana*, Baton Rouge, 1964, pp. 12–13; *The War of Rebellion: A Compilation of the Official Records of the Union and Confederate Armies*, series 1, vol. 15, War Department, Washington DC pp. 26–35.)

flowing south. Also, the defeat of Vicksburg would split the western Confederacy in two, each half more vulnerable to collapse without the support of the other.

In late June Butler sent Williams upriver with about three thousand soldiers and spades and shovels by the wholesale lot. Williams was to capture the rebel stronghold "or have it burned at all hazards."[24] Failing that, he was to divert the river so that it bypassed Vicksburg. What made that option attractive to distant generals studying their maps was a finger-shaped peninsula of Louisiana clay that poked the state of Mississippi sharply in its rocky ribs and channeled the river around the finger's tip, directly under the Vicksburg bluffs. Sever the finger by digging a canal across its mile-and-a-half-wide base, and Vicksburg would no longer be a river city.[25] Thus would northern genius for engineering vast construction projects trump the citadel mentality of the south.

Before the war, when southerners embarked upon high-mortality projects like this—draining swamps, digging canals—they hired gangs of expendable Irish laborers rather than risk valuable slaves.[26] But the laborers Williams had brought along, the soldiers poaching in those incubators of fever and misery below decks, were ailing on a diet of salt-cured pork and river water even before they could be put to work.[27] He would need a healthier workforce, and one was readily at hand. He sent soldiers ashore to round up contrabands. Frederick Boardman was one of those pied-pipers, seducing blacks by the hundreds from plantation after plantation with promises of freedom and protection.[28] Unwilling slaves found themselves press-ganged. Williams estimated that his transports ferried nearly 1,500 blacks to the site of the dig,[29] where, under the supervision of Sidney Bean and Joseph Bailey, they were divided into teams and put to work felling and uprooting trees and hacking at the hard clay.[30] They had little to eat and they slept where they worked.[31] "They shout as they work, thinking they're working for their freedom, and if the canal is a success [they] shall have it," Williams wrote to his family."[32]

Van Norstrand flourished even as the health and morale of those around him was eroded by bad water, mosquitoes swarming out of the miasmal slop ringing the lowlands, the reek of rotting animal carcasses, and a torpid, foul-tempered shipboard routine. For soldiers, the days were an endless cycle of fever, chills, and despair. In the words of one of them, they were "spirit-broken men."[33] Van Norstrand lived in a manner the enlisted ranks below could hardly imagine. He had a servant to look out for him, a stock of canned meats and coffee, and a private room, presumably above deck. Soldiers would have settled for fresh drinking water, but Van Norstrand, Bean, and Paine "felt a necessity of claret wine," and so one night they improvised a bottle or two from water, vinegar and sugar.[34]

But as more and more home-state boys fell sick he inevitably became submerged in the misery around him. Some from his regiment were cared for on the hospital boat. Others filled an on-shore hospital that he had improvised in a derelict cotton gin.[35] Many were bound to die unless sent north for better care and climate, and so he braced himself for another confrontation with General Williams. The general sat in grudging silence while he made his case. The sickest patients could be shipped south, presumably to New Orleans, Williams told him, but no one had the power to send men north. "I asked if the men must die here. He said, 'Yes.'"[36]

By mid-July, dysentery had struck down most of the enlisted men and many officers. Funerals, he wrote, "were numerous and increasing." A Massachusetts man dropped dead on guard duty and was buried by his two sons, who soon followed him to the grave.[37] Meanwhile gunboats continued to bombard the Vicksburg heights and the town beyond. An assault remained a theoretical possibility, and sharp engagements flared whenever one side or the other probed for weaknesses. After one of these, Van Norstrand dealt with awful casualties as well as wasting fevers. Williams's aide, Lieutenant DeKay, was hit by buckshot while off on an adventure with Major Boardman.[38] Van Norstrand detected the smell of urine in one of the wounds and told DeKay's friends that this would prove fatal. DeKay rallied long enough to taunt Van Norstrand for his prediction, then died.[39] Another man peppered by buckshot at short range was carried in with a deep thigh wound, a shattered elbow, and a ball directly into the nose that lodged against his cheek. "His groans," Paine wrote, "while [Van Norstrand] was probing and dressing his wounds, were pitiful."[40] An exploding shell killed six Wisconsin sharpshooters when the steamboat *Tyler* ventured up the Yazoo to take on the much-dreaded rebel ram *Arkansas* in its lair. Sheathed in plates of railroad iron and fitted with a pointy beak to gut Union boats, the *Arkansas* looked like a prehistoric creature and lashed out with the ferocity of one. Three Wisconsin soldiers were decapitated, including David Bertram, an early enlistee in Van Norstrand's company. Survivors were splattered with the remains of the dead.[41]

Through all this Van Norstrand managed to remain an upbeat campaigner. His recollections of these hellish weeks are full of comradely affection for Paine, Boardman, Bailey, and others in the regiment. He praised the navy and its flag officers, Farragut and Davis. His sentiments toward blacks laboring on the canal were generous and compassionate.

The success of the canal project depended upon the river continuing to rise. Instead, it was falling. On July 17 Williams wrote to Butler, vowing to redouble the effort. He would round up more blacks, more "shovels, axes, carts, wheelbarrows, scrapers, etc . . . and make a real canal . . . to the depth of, say some 35 to 40 feet . . . which will take three months."[42] Should the canal fail, he would assault the heights and seize the enemy's guns or spike them.[43] His feelings toward those who would have to fulfill that promise wavered from pity to contempt. He chewed out Paine because the men were filthy, although that was like blaming them for the falling water level. "Filth and dirt," he wrote Butler, "with all the authority and supervision I could exert, abounded on vessels and men to a disgusting and of course most unwholesome degree."[44]

To the soldiers this expedition was already a lost cause. Disease had reduced their effective numbers by over half, and few of those still standing had the stamina—to say nothing of the spirit—for a foolhardy attack uphill against rebel guns. "As to the health of our regiment—got none!," a soldier wrote: "I am sick, and so is everybody around me."[45] All scorned Williams and his ditch, "where the insubordinate water would not run up hill."[46]

Ever since Ship Island, Van Norstrand had preached the gospel of quinine: when in doubt, give more. Determined not to run out, he went beyond government channels and local pharmacists, paying planters and other private citizens up to five dollars an ounce, often from his own pocket. That he continued to be profligate in its distribution is evident from a sketch written by a member of his regiment in which an unnamed doctor at sick call dispenses folded papers of white powder for every complaint from ankle sprain to bilious fever. "Our Surgeons and assistant Surgeons are totally incompetent, and I may say, inhuman," the soldier wrote,[47] sentiments not shared by Paine, Boardman, Bailey, and many others who, however sickly, emerged from fevers of one kind or another well and grateful. When Van Norstrand's supply of the precious remedy ran low, Boardman asked his uncle in Milwaukee to send more.[48]

Except for the western emphasis on heavy doses of quinine, Van Norstrand's methods reflected his conservative New England medical education, which encouraged doctors to assist nature with proven therapies and to recognize their own limitations. His top priority was to provide his patients with a rich, varied diet. He was always looking for fresh vegetables, meat, and dairy products for the hospital kitchen.

The surgeon of the Seventh Vermont invited him to dine aboard their vessel. The Vermont regiment was the sickest, most demoralized organization in the brigade. Their doctor toured him through sick bays filled with wretched souls laid low by malaria.[49] Van Norstrand urged his host to uncork the quinine bottle, but the doctor replied that he was saving it for an emergency![50] Van Norstrand was ahead of his time. In years to come quinine would be widely accepted as a stimulant and fever-fighter even in New England.[51]

He had come for a meal and was determined to enjoy it: "It seems to me that I [ate] more than all the Vermont officers." Meanwhile they mooned over their plates. The remains of a popular captain, one of the few to have started the previous day fit for duty, had been sealed in a barrel of whiskey for shipment back home. He had avoided fever only to catch a rebel cannonball. "I gently tried to assure them that they would soon be in better spirits. They said, 'Yes, like our friend in the barrel.'"[52]

It was Butler, down in New Orleans, who came to the rescue. In mid-July he sent a dispatch warning that enemy forces were gathering near Baton Rouge. An attack was possible there or against New Orleans. General Williams was to give up on the canal and hurry back to Baton Rouge.

For those not too fever-brained to comprehend it, this was welcome news indeed. For others it came too late. Van Norstrand had to cart his most feeble cases from the cotton gin "hospital" to the steamboat, a rough trip under a sweltering sun for desperately ill men. An old friend from Jefferson died on deck after being off-loaded from the wagon. Another delirious patient apparently sleep-walked off the side of the boat, never to be seen again.[53]

There was one group for whom the order to pack up and leave was not good news—all those black laborers and their wives and children who had sunk their hearts, their health, and their futures into Butler's Ditch, trusting the Lincolnites to keep their word. Their work had come to nothing, the ditch was dry, and now the people who had lured them there were about to leave them behind. Hundreds were returned by steamboat to points along the shore near where they had been found.[54] Many more were left crowding the levee, "poor beseeching creatures clamoring to accompany us," Van Norstrand wrote, "saying their masters would kill them." To Paine as well their anguish was "most pitiful." Soldiers with bayonets kept them away from the boats while others rolled barrels of flour and meat to the levee. It was cynical charity at best. Rebels and masters would decide who got the provisions. "Many were crying and some praying as we swung into the current and departed," Van Norstrand wrote, "leaving many new graves filled with our comrades."[55]

SIX

The Whole Camp Still as Death

"The faces of officers are changed, as if by ten years of care and trouble," wrote Edward Bacon, an officer of the Sixth Michigan who watched from the levee as soldiers trooped down the gangway. "The men appear like wretches escaped from the dungeons of the Inquisition. Confused processions of the sick, some in ambulances and wagons, some in litters, and some staggering along on foot, present scenes of horror in every street."[1]

Young Sarah Morgan saw men in blue sprawled "all the afternoon in the hot sun, uncovered on the ground, in every stage of sickness," one of them "too far gone to brush the flies out of his eyes and mouth."[2]

So far, Baton Rouge had survived the war relatively unscarred. As the seat of state government it boasted a grand and spacious home for the deaf and dumb, a prison, and its crowning glory, a Gothic revival statehouse with Arthurian turrets that towered over surrounding magnolia trees. Mark Twain called it "a little sham castle," evidence that the curse of Sir Walter Scott blighted even this "otherwise honorable" town.[3]

Idlers taking cover from the sun under verandas along the riverfront commercial district kept a squinty-eyed watch on the river and its traffic. Finicky rooftops and prosperous steeples poked through the rolling meadow of treetops behind them. The town was bordered by grassy fields in the east, woodlands and a cemetery in the north. Folks here tended to be better-off than most Louisianans. They were also better educated and more sensitive to public opinion outside the South. Unlike the hotheads of New Orleans they had mixed feelings about secession, although in April they too had stacked their cotton along the levee, soaked it with whiskey, and set it alight. "There lay the work of thousands of negroes for more than a year gone by," Sarah Morgan wrote in her diary.[4]

The first blue uniforms had appeared at the landing in early May. To everyone's relief these soldiers and naval officers were proof that the South was not alone in producing gentlemen. "Fine, noble looking men they were," Miss Morgan wrote. "One cannot help but admire such foes."[5] General Williams returned the compliment. "The good people of Baton Rouge," he wrote his wife, were "too humane to encourage civil war, and too much attached to the Union to aid its enemies."[6] His officers might despise him, but the ladies were smitten. One gushed that he was "a noble, upright, gallant man, who . . . always combined courage and skill with *courtesy* and *humanity*."[7] But it didn't take much to put both sides on edge. Buckshot from a gang of delinquents elicited broadsides from Union gunboats. People were killed; property damaged.[8]

Van Norstrand was glad to return to the airy, high-ceilinged hospital in the arsenal complex high on a bluff at river's edge, at the northwestern corner of town. Built after the British defeat at New Orleans, the federal arsenal consisted of eleven brick buildings plus shaded wooden barracks spaced around a parade ground. Soon the hospital building and others seized for the purpose echoed with the groans of the delirious and the dying. Van Norstrand had finally fallen victim to recurring bouts of diarrhea himself, but he had no choice but to soldier on. He estimated that two-thirds of the 7,000 soldiers in and around the arsenal complex were not fit for duty. The rest were only marginally healthier in that they could stay on their feet and control their bowels. Half of the Fourth Wisconsin was on the sick list: "Many times I was up [at night] ten times an hour to attend to my sick."[9]

Every man steady enough to lift a musket was immersed once

again in the tedium of drill under a tropical sun, often to the accompaniment of distant funeral calls, which drifted across the parade ground until nightfall.[10] By late July signs were thick that quiet times in Baton Rouge were about to end. Confederate regiments under a former vice president of the United States, Major General John C. Breckinridge, were being shuttled by train from Vicksburg to a camp fifty miles northeast of the city.

Afraid of what was to come, locals began to pack up. By early August buggies and wagons jammed Highland Road, heading south. A graveyard calm settled over Sarah Morgan's lively hometown.[11] Tipped off that Breckinridge was about to strike, Miss Morgan turned to her diary. "These poor men!" she wrote. "Are they not dying fast enough?"[12]

"Our little pale malarial stricken army were being moved hither and thither, cleaning up arms, filling their cartridge boxes and caissons," Van Norstrand wrote. "Artillery horses were harnessed and hitched on. Riders and gunners were standing in place. The officers' horses [were] saddled and bridled, the whole camp still as death except a little fretfulness of the horses."[13]

On the night of August 4, he put all in readiness—sponges, bandages, basins, chloroform, long-handled knives, a variety of saws, a series of beaked pliers for squaring jagged bones, bullet probes like tiny candle snuffers, forceps, tourniquets, even candles of clean-burning wax to light the operating room in place of the tallow kind that sputtered and flickered—all laid out in formation like the soldiers to the north and east. He tried to rest but his nerves and churning bowels kept driving him outside to the sinks. "I was so weak and dizzy. . . . My servant Jim, stalwart and strong, kept coming in uneasily, asking what he should do." In the wee hours he took some brandy and a dose of morphine, steadying himself for what was to come.[14]

* * *

For the past week Halbert Paine had been marking time in a

hotel room in New Orleans, awaiting a clash of a different sort. A showdown between himself and General Williams had been looming for months, lacking only a spark to set it off. It had been struck in early June, shortly after Williams's brigade had taken up residence at Baton Rouge. The *Laurel Hill* had been a home to the Fourth Wisconsin during expeditions up and down the river. Between expeditions it turned into a sanctuary for escaped slaves. Whole contraband families had sought protection under the Union umbrella, some hiding below decks, others gathering in the arsenal grounds and camps of nearby Union regiments. They earned their keep by relieving soldiers of the drudge-work—cutting and hauling firewood, cooking, digging latrines and entrenchments, drawing water, and so on. Some became officers' servants. "Many masters were just outside [the arsenal grounds] to seize them and carry them off," Van Norstrand wrote.[15]

At wit's end, General Williams wrote his wife, "My time is more cut up even than yours with our daughter on your lap . . . with constant interruptions, applications of all kinds . . . a court martial, rations, guards, pickets, distressed inhabitants wanting passes, others asking for redress of grievances. . . . Such a whirl of solicitation, re- monstrance and enquiry I never expected to be martyr to."[16] Among his tormentors were slave owners demanding the return of their fu- gitives, and so on June 2, Williams ordered all contrabands forcibly removed from the *Laurel Hill* and handed over to those who claimed them.[17] An engineer was told to flush them from their hiding places using steam from the boilers if necessary.[18]

Halbert Paine was convinced the order was illegal.[19] He went over Williams's head. "My situation has become so intoler- able," he wrote General Butler, "that I cannot, with any shadow of self-respect, longer occupy it, if escape, by change of brigade, leave of absence, resignation, or other lawful means, shall be possible." Almost as an afterthought he added that it was his "painful duty" to forward charges against General Williams "for a violation of the new Article of War . . . which prohibits military officers from employing the United States forces for return of slaves." He reminded Butler that many blacks returned to their owners from the *Laurel Hill* "by most cruel means" had actively assisted Union forces by providing valuable information.[20]

A few days later Williams raised the ante. Citing the "demoralizing and disorganizing" effects on the soldiers of harboring runaway slaves, he issued General Order Number 46, requiring his men to actively "turn out all fugitives" from their camps.[21] Some straggled back in peppered with birdshot and bloody from recent whippings.[22] Among Van Norstrand's wartime mementos was a handful of lead shot dug from the scalps of fugitives.[23]

Again Paine objected. He argued the moral repugnance of delivering to slave hunters the very fugitives who had worked for Union forces or provided them with information about the rebels: "What their fate will be . . . is easy to predict."[24]

On June 7, Paine disobeyed an order to allow a certain Mrs. McGumpsey to search the garrison for her slave. Williams put him under arrest and appointed Sidney Bean commander of the regiment. Angry soldiers gathered outside Paine's office, cheering him on as he read from the letters he and Williams had exchanged. They hooted at every mention of the general's name. It was a scene Williams would have been hard-pressed to ignore from his office nearby.[25]

Van Norstrand fully supported Paine. Some contrabands came from plantations looted and burned by the Fourth's own soldiers, including Black Kate, "a six foot wench, utterly black, straight as a pole." He had put her to work in his hospital cook-house where she soon replaced two soldiers "covered in grease from head to foot" who had produced little that was fit to eat. "Black Kate did all the work done by both soldiers, had fine messes for the sick. . . . When she had nothing to do, she did my washing and sewing."[26]

Wisconsin newspapers were filled with outrage over Paine's arrest. The regimental chaplain had gone off to war a Democrat but had recently returned home "a raving abolitionist."[27] He told of slaves locked in ankle cuffs that were chained to collars bolted at the neck, and if doubters still remained they could see for themselves the spiked collar that had been sent to the State Historical Society in

Madison.[28]

In Washington, Senator T'mothy Howe upbraided Williams on the floor of the Senate. Williams was turning Paine into a martyr to the abolitionist cause. To his soldiers and folks back home the former Milwaukee lawyer stood taller than ever, but to Fredrick Boardman, it all reeked of shameless self-promotion. He told his uncle that Paine had "brigadier on the brain," and he may have been right.[29] Carl Schurz, a major figure in the German-American community, was close to President Lincoln. Earlier that year he had written to his old law partner, "You can well imagine how much pleasure it gave me to talk to [Lincoln] about you. The answer I got was such that I am almost *sure* that you will have the appointment [to brigadier general]."[30] Such heady assurances from high places may have made it easier for Paine to challenge the moral authority of his immediate superior.

Paine had been allowed to remain with his regiment throughout the Vicksburg expedition, but upon return to Baton Rouge he was arrested and sent to New Orleans. Biding time with him in purgatory were four Michigan officers charged with mutiny.[31] During his first three months as brigade commander, Williams had placed at least ten officers under arrest, including four from Wisconsin. One of these was Joseph Bailey. "This is laughable," Paine wrote, "inasmuch as one captain like Bailey is worth one million generals like Williams."[32]

At two in the morning of August 6, a messenger banged on Paine's door. A carriage was waiting for him and the Michigan men. "We hurry along the moonlit streets," wrote Major Bacon, of the Sixth Michigan. "Lights are on in the hall, sentries are on duty, and orderlies and officers are coming and going. We are ushered into the presence of Benjamin F. Butler."[33]

Confederate forces had attacked Baton Rouge, Butler told them. "He looked at me with his right eye," Paine recalled, "then with his left eye and then with his right eye again."[34] General Williams was dead, his head taken off by a cannon ball.[35] The situation was in doubt; another attack appeared imminent. The officers were released from arrest with orders to proceed to Baton Rouge, where Paine was to take command of the fallen general's brigade.[36]

From the deck of the boat carrying them north they hailed a passing steamer for news, but there was no response. The other boat was bringing critically wounded soldiers to New Orleans, but it never got there. In the dark it rammed a gunboat and sank. Forty of the wounded went down with the boat, and so too did General Williams, or what was left of him. He turned up miles downriver drifting atop flotsam from the wreckage, still in his coffin.[37]

* * *

Sarah Morgan heard several rumors about the death of General Williams, none featuring decapitation, although in one he was held to the mouth of a cannon by his own men and "blown to pieces."[38] In another a civilian sniper shot him from a window as he passed Piper's furniture store.[39] Dr. Van Norstrand also heard the one about mutinous troops turning on him, but he knew better. He was pulling on his suspenders shortly after sunrise when a cart rattled up bearing wounded soldiers and the general's body. He counted four entry holes but did not specify whether they were in front and thus presumably from enemy fire, or in the back. However, Williams had been on horseback rallying the Twenty-First Indiana, and Van Norstrand was convinced that he had died a soldier's death from enemy fire. His loyal adjutant, Wickham Hoffman, wrote that Williams was shouting "Fix bayonets!" when a bullet pierced his heart.[40] Whatever the circumstance, Van Norstrand was unmoved. "This was," he wrote, "the first time in my life that I viewed the dead body of a human being with no pang of regret or sorrow."[41]

* * *

In normal times few of the men on either side would have been fit to drive a team, stoke a furnace, or work a hoe. Undernourished and clothed in rags, many attackers had fallen gut-sick from bad water and fever during a forced march of nearly fifty miles. Others collapsed from sunstroke or were hobbled by lack of shoes. Even the unsick suffered from hunger and thirst. The battle was a brawl between the delirious and the dehydrated, about 2,500 miserable souls to a side. Union strength was increased considerably, according to Van Norstrand and others, by fever patients who left their hospital beds and rejoined their regiments.[42]

The Fourteenth Maine and the Twenty-First Indiana had missed out on the recent Vicksburg fiasco and so were less debilitated than General Williams's other regiments. He had put them in blocking positions on the east side of town, his first line of resistance, and these were the soldiers who stood fast as volleys exploded out of the fog at dawn and scarecrow apparitions came howling through a semi-wilderness of trees, briars, and wild-growing rose bushes. Some rebels came over the split-rail fences, others loped through Magnolia Cemetery and adjacent corn fields, and still others crashed picket fences of outlying neighborhoods. Return fire from Union lines added dense rolls of blue smoke to the fog and confusion. An artillery officer told Van Norstrand that to locate targets for his guns he had to sprawl on the grass and peer through the narrow window between ground and smog. There, he said, "I could then see legs and feet fly at every discharge."[43]

Maine and Indiana fell back, exposing the demoralized Seventh Vermont. An incredible racket of gunfire and yelling thundered ever closer behind a rolling curtain of smoke. Shaky from the start, the sickly Vermonters were given a badly timed order, or misunderstood it, and fired volley after volley into the retreating Hoosiers. Then they too fled to the rear, only to run up against General Williams in all his mounted fury. Here, just east of the orphanage and the penitentiary, the battle reached its crescendo as Williams sent orderlies charging this way and that with instructions: the Thirtieth Massachusetts and part of Nims's Massachusetts battery were to shore up the Sixth Michigan on the right, the Ninth Connecticut and Fourth Wisconsin to stiffen the wobbling center. Above all he endeavored to inspire or, if necessary, terrorize his fleeing soldiers and turn them back against the enemy.

That is where he fell, and where Union resistance finally collapsed. By mid-morning, every man in blue who still had legs to carry him had fled to the arsenal grounds, where they were shielded by broadsides from Union gunboats. Grapeshot and shrapnel whipped through streets littered with splintered trees, dead horses, and shattered glass. Ranks of panting Confederates hung back just out of range, waiting for their mighty ram, *Arkansas*, to come thundering downriver and scatter the Union gunboats. But the *Arkansas* was already a beached whale. Mechanical problems had driven it ashore and out of the fight. Breckinridge's soldiers had won the field, but they could not win the battle without help from their navy. Exhausted, hungry, and desperately thirsty, they too were collapsing.[44]

Civilians who had held steady through the first wave of panic now battled for space in a terror-driven crush of carts, buggies, and spooked horses flooding the only road heading south. To Eliza McHatton-Ripley, watching from her plantation house, they looked like "stampeded sheep ... some in slippers, some with wrappers hastily thrown over nightgowns; now and then a coatless man on a bare-back horse, holding a helpless child in his arms, a terrified woman clinging on behind; men trundling children too young to run in dirty wheel-barrows." Pantries and kitchens along the route were stripped bare in what Ripley called the "battle for bread."[45]

As his own regiment was held in reserve through most of the battle, Van Norstrand found himself underemployed, although he boasted that some officers from other regiments sought him out because they trusted him more than their own surgeons.[46] The commander of the Twenty-First Indiana was brought in with a bullet in his shoulder. The Indiana boys were hard-fighters, Van Norstrand conceded, but they were thieves: "The officers stole my [hospital] whiskey, and the men stole my blankets."[47] A Michigan officer had taken a pistol ball to the forehead. He came in on foot, "his face covered with blood. I laid him on my operating couch and probed the wound carefully, expecting to follow the ball into his brain." Instead he found a "roughened place" under the skin which he enlarged, then probed with an instrument: "Much to my surprise I found a flattened ball." The officer pocketed his souvenir and walked away.[48]

When melodious profanity echoed from the hallway he discovered a gang of Irishmen from the Ninth Connecticut cowering there. Eventually they ran off to plunder the abandoned city. Their lack of discipline upset him. Were Union formations breaking under pressure?

He went out to visit his regiment, whose last sixty ambulant and delirium-free soldiers waited in reserve along a depression on the northern flank of the battle. A stretcher-bearer ran by, heading to the rear. Van Norstrand recognized him as a bandsman and thus, in his mind, a "coward and poltroon." He drew his pistol. The man protested that his hand had been stomped on, the fingers mangled; he was not fit for duty. Van Norstrand's big revolver convinced him to return to his assigned station.[49] But his heart was sinking. It looked like the day was lost. He imagined ragamuffin rebels digging through his personal trunk and decking themselves out in his dress uniforms.[50]

He went to the hospital of the Fourteenth Maine, and a ghastly scene it was. These soldiers had absorbed the first shock of the assault. Sarah Morgan was told by a relative on the other side that unlike other bluecoats, the men from Maine had stood fast and "fought like devils."[51] That they paid dearly for their stubbornness was apparent from the washtub full of arms and legs.[52] Van Norstrand counted forty blanketed figures strewn over the floor still awaiting the surgeon's blade. Their doctor did not make a good impression on Van Norstrand, who suspected he was drunk: "At any rate he was very free with his tongue and his knife. I was senior surgeon and therefore, outranking him, I soon made my influence felt, thus saving many limbs from amputation."[53]

The next morning he was asked to help out on the battlefield. He and Jim rode out together. "Many of the dead were still unburied. . . . [They] many times huddled together. Several had crowded to the corner of a fence, taken off their coats and placed them under their heads. Jim, who was a negro and Indian cross, examined the dead rebels and contemptuously remarked that they were 'niggers' and asked me to observe that, 'They were not starved. See how fat they are!'" Van Norstrand knew better: "What [Jim] saw, in face and body, were the effects of decomposition."[54]

Van Norstrand insisted that sick as they were, Union forces had triumphed in the battle of Baton Rouge. They had whipped the enemy on the field. "Not one of their horses tasted Mississippi water."[55] More to the point, the western regiments had won it. Van Norstrand was now a westerner through and through, with a westerner's sensitivities and chauvinism.[56] To him, Pop Howard, an old soldier from the wilds of Sheboygan County, exemplified the soldiers who had prevailed at Baton Rouge. So painfully ruptured he could barely stand, Howard had dragged a kitchen chair to his guard post where he sat out his tour of duty, rifle across his knees and pipe grimly clenched in his teeth, scowling into the rebel-held woods.[57]

SEVEN

The First Negro Hospital

At midnight on August 6, Halbert Paine walked ashore a liberated man. He spent the night inspecting the perimeter, a series of rifle pits spread in a semicircle through the eastern edge of town. Over the following days he raced to construct new and stronger positions around the arsenal grounds. He sent infantry companies into the countryside to recruit black field hands—and their wives, if they were willing to dig. No house servants need apply.[1]

For Paine this was a labor of love. The tyrant was dead. At last he was free to make a name for himself. "Oh what dreams of fame and glory danced before my eyes between the 7th and 20th days of this month!" he confessed to his wife. "I should surely have won a very high position amongst the generals of our army."[2] Apparently Fred Boardman was not so paranoid after all. The fantasies of the gaunt, bespectacled visionary Halbert Paine were much like his own.

He reorganized the barracks and hospital buildings, emptied the penitentiary, and sent the prisoners to New Orleans, where many were soon outfitted in Union blue. He also ordered the wounded and sick evacuated to New Orleans. When Van Norstrand learned that patients from his hospital had been left to the mercy of hard-hearted civilians, he stormed to the levee and kicked civilian passengers onto the sun-blasted deck, moved his patients into the shady interior, and posted a guard over the ice bucket. Even so, according to a doctor on the receiving end, many of the sick "were enveloped in their winding sheets before they reached New Orleans."[3]

Paine refused an order from General Butler to burn the city. Dozens of houses and several arsenal buildings (including Van Norstrand's "perfect" hospital) did need to be destroyed to create clear fields of fire.[4] But Paine held out against leveling public institutions like the statehouse and the asylum or damaging the commercial and residential districts beyond what was necessary for the defense of their position. Butler relented, and thus did Paine add another feather to his cap.[5] With his conscience as his guide he had once again prevailed against a formidable superior.

Paine was itching for a fight, but he had to settle for a duel of words with a former vice president. A letter arrived under a flag of truce. Major General John C. Breckinridge, C.S.A., was irate. He charged that Union forces were violating the rules of war by destroying private property, arming slaves, and forcing white citizens to load coal onto Union boats. Cease and desist, Breckinridge threatened, or he would "raise the black flag and neither give nor ask quarter."[6]

Paine worked up a response and read it to Van Norstrand. The destruction of property was military necessity, he told Breckinridge, and therefore not a violation of the rules.[7] Furthermore, forces under his command would not sink to the level of Breckinridge's troops regardless of atrocities already committed against Union soldiers by the other side. Then he plunged his own sword: "I shall never raise that black flag which all civilized nations abhor. But I shall try to maintain the flag which you have so often promised to defend."[8]

But the prize Paine craved for all his hard work—a showdown on the battlefield—was not to be. Late in the month Butler ordered him to bring his forces south to defend New Orleans. Meanwhile, Breckinridge marched north to Port Hudson and put his soldiers to work converting the surrounding bluffs into a hornet's nest of artillery and rifle pits, a little brother to Vicksburg upriver.

Paine was proud of his treatment of the blacks who worked for him. "At Vicksburg Genl Williams left 500 crying on the bank of the river," he wrote his wife later from Carrollton. "But when I left [Baton Rouge] I brought away every man, woman and child that wished to come and they are all now well taken care of, well fed, well covered in tents and happy. God only knows what sincere satisfaction it gives me to see the poor wretches so happy."[9]

He kept a young man named William Bird as a personal servant. The light-skinned Bird, Paine wrote, was the son "of a notorious Rebel, Capt. Bird." The boy's mother worked in Van Norstrand's hospital and may have been the "Black Kate" he raved about. "I think I shall take them home," Paine continued, "the mother for your kitchen and the son for my barn. But perhaps if you come down you will be able to 'have your pick' to suit yourself better." Abolitionist to the bone, Paine was also a bargain-hunting Yankee and a deferential spouse and therefore not above shopping around in this buyers' market of escaped slaves desperate for protection and livelihoods.

There was slippage too in his stance on plunder. In a letter to his wife in mid-August he acknowledged the temptation: "[Baton Rouge] is full of beautiful furniture. Many of the officers have collected much loot. I might. But you know I have not the face to do such things." Two weeks later he boasted to her of all the furnishings he had seized for himself, from sofas to a "marble top stand for water cooler."[10]

Nor did Van Norstrand go empty-handed: "I went about among the camp and buildings and secured a great number of nice books and sent them home by the first opportunity, thus adding many fine volumes to my library."[11]

Meanwhile, soldiers and blacks alike roamed the town trashing what they could not steal, smashing windows, china, and abandoned furniture, and smearing or shredding anything remotely artful or elegant. "We left the place a wreck," a soldier wrote. "Imagine the burning of Troy or any other city, and its frightened and crazed people fleeing, and you will have a slight idea of Baton Rouge before and at our departure."[12] Sarah Morgan's home was among the most "shockingly treated," according to one of her sisters. By one estimate, barely two-thirds of the original homes were still standing.[13] Paine attributed the mayhem to local "scoundrels" determined to make his soldiers look bad.[14]

* * *

It was the rainy season when his brigade settled into camp at Carrollton, north of New Orleans, among orange groves, banana thickets, and giant oaks draped with Spanish moss. The health of the soldiers soon improved, thanks in part to the abundance of citrus, which eliminated scurvy from the ranks. By autumn, Carrollton was dry, cool, and just about perfect, and Dr. Van Norstrand had time to collect his thoughts. "Valuable Advice from an Experienced Surgeon—Let it be Read and Heeded," proclaimed a headline in the *Milwaukee Sentinel*. Proud of his record, he passed along the lessons he had learned in the form of a letter to doctors of newly organized regiments still in training. Proper diet was everything, he asserted, and providing that diet was the first duty of the regimental surgeon. "A sick man fed standard army fare will die, and his case is put down in the register, 'Died of such or such fever,' when in fact it should be, 'Died of starvation!'" Salted meat with army beans was not a healthy diet for the well, much less the seriously ill. Put others in charge of paperwork and ward duties, and dedicate yourself to scouring town and countryside for fresh meat, vegetables, and milk: "Perseverance will procure both ... a good cook [and] something good to cook, and when they are acquired your battle with disease is half fought." One more thing: bring "plenty of quinine and opium." His own regiment had been on duty for fourteen months, traveling, by his estimate, nearly five thousand miles and encountering every sort of disease, but it had suffered a fourth as many deaths as companion regiments with less time in the service—thanks to the priorities of its medical staff.[15]

This was a theme he was to repeat in the annual reports he wrote later as superintendent of the Wisconsin Insane Hospital. A rich, healthy diet is half the battle. With rest, exercise, kind caregivers, and good food, the patient soon recovers his physical health, which in turn makes possible the restoration of psychic health.[16]

These were the views of a responsible, conservative practitioner, and they reflected his New England medical training.[17] Hardly the sort of man, you would think, to abandon such common sense medicine for personal gain. But a few years later some trustees of the hospital in Madison had reason to suspect that his priorities had changed.

At Carrollton he took up another cause. Perhaps the blacks Halbert Paine had brought from Baton Rouge were well cared for, but most in the area were not. "They lay on the ground without shelter," Van Norstrand wrote. "[They] were only half fed. Many were sick and very many died—anywhere, by the road side, beneath the shade of a fence or a bush, covered by the heavy dew at night and swarms of flies in the day time."[18]

Their suffering evoked scant concern from most northerners. Immersion into the world of the black underclass had hardened them. "Negrophobia," became a common affliction. To soldier thugs like some of Billy Wilson's New York Zouaves, blacks were easy targets, the equivalent of cheap crockery to throw against a wall. "They don't fight worth a cent," Van Norstrand wrote of Wilson's crew, "except among themselves, or better—some poor Negro whom they meet. Wo betide [that] poor Negro, especially if he was small, crippled, or sick."[19] To officers charged with their care they were a deeply resented distraction from more important tasks, an ever growing swarm of heads to be counted and mouths to be fed. "I can fight for this race more easily than I can eat with them," wrote a Massachusetts soldier. "I revolt at shaking hands with a darkey or sitting by him. Southerners don't feel it, Europeans don't feel it; strange that it should be confined to Northerners."[20]

An artillery officer took a utilitarian view. Why waste valuable Northerners in a sickly climate when the supply of potential black soldiers was inexhaustible? "If a nigger dies, all you have to do is to send out and get another."[21]

"The eternal nigger question . . . was a source of much annoyance and ill feeling," a soldier wrote home. "Every mess had its two or three cooks, every officer had his quota, varying from one to as many as he wanted. It was nigger!! nigger!! nigger!! They peered out of every window and door, brooded over every fire, lay stretched in every shade. The help became a nuisance and a bore."[22]

Van Norstrand resolved to do something about the problem. He showed up at the commanding general's tent to present his case. It turned out that General John Wolcott Phelps, a "grizzled, shambling" Vermonter, was also deeply concerned about the welfare of the contrabands flooding into camp.[23] He ordered Van Norstrand to look after the sick. "Take any house you want and send me a blank requisition. You can put anything in it you want."[24]

Van Norstrand had already set up a hospital for soldiers in Carrollton, but seizing the right building had not been easy. This time he ran into even more resistance. The first house he examined turned out to be a hornet's nest of scrawny women and kids who ganged up on this overfed Yankee, badgering and shaming until he fled. The next place to catch his eye was already providing services of a certain kind, judging from the steady soldier traffic in and out. This time he took a less direct course of action. A letter arrived, telling the ladies that the army was about to seize their basement for use as a pest house for small pox cases. No further persuasion was needed. They were soon packed and gone. Van Norstrand assigned an old Jefferson acquaintance to run the place. Assisting him would be a staff of "four stout wenches." Van Norstrand would provide general supervision. Bentley, the Jefferson man, was "a sort of herb doctor, a pretty good nurse and a great negro lover," who no doubt took advantage of his position to install "a wench or two in his bedroom."[25]

It is tempting to see Van Norstrand dashing off this salty item with a smile on his lips and no thought whatever to its implications. Suddenly he is struck by an exhilarating realization. By creating what he believed to be "the first Negro Hospital ever established by the United States government" he had done something historic. Here was proof of his own practical humanity: "Here I am, an old line democrat, the party charged [with] entertaining [no] love for [the] Negro, surrounded at home and in the service by an army of blatant abolitionists who practically did nothing for the suffering, dying Negro. It perhaps would be immodest of me to say—[my actions] exhibited the difference between a good heart and a good tongue." The "blatant abolitionist" he had in mind was almost certainly Samuel Dexter Hastings, who spent the war years at his desk in Madison and never came face to face with the human consequences of the crusade he had championed. When Van Norstrand warned the reader that he was a man of "slowly dying hate," in his mind's eye he saw Hastings.[26]

* * *

In September, Wisconsin veterans of the failed canal at Vicksburg and the near-defeat at Baton Rouge relished a one-sided triumph, running down a band of mounted Texans in a cypress swamp. If, as rumored, these were the legendary Texas Rangers, they didn't live up to their billing, Van Norstrand concluded. In their panicky flight they left behind an unranger-like trail of clothing, blankets, and weapons. Horses and guerillas alike were shot down and "left as food for the alligators." Van Norstrand likened the affair to a squirrel hunt. He came away with a Texas doctor's instruments and a good horse, which he later sold to the army. He was learning that even in uniform it was possible to turn a profit.[27]

A bloody encounter of a different sort left him equally satisfied. Colonel Billy Wilson's notorious regiment of New York Zouaves— "the terror of the country," he called them—had become their neighbors in Carrollton.[28] "Murderers, thieves, pickpockets, prize-fighters, and hard cases generally," is how he described them. One of these hard cases, a howling drunk, was brought to the hospital with a bayonet wound inflicted by his own sergeant. Two assistants were unable to control him, so Van Norstrand took over and threw him into the hospital lock-up, "his head coming roughly into contact with the stone work."

It was not the last time he rolled up his sleeves and stepped into a ring from which lesser men had been vanquished. His willingness to take on the belligerently unhinged and the criminally vicious became a source of pride, much like his stamina in the field and his skill as a horseman. In the bayous he had outmarched even the proud Halbert Paine, and no one outranked him in the saddle. When it came to a physical showdown, no man had yet triumphed over Surgeon Van Norstrand.[29]

By late December he was restless: "I had a few hundred sick on my hands, but no wounded. I began to crave something more exciting." What he craved even more was a visit home, and he jumped at the first opportunity. The Department of the Gulf had chartered a boat to take unfit soldiers to New York, including some who were insane. A doctor was needed to accompany them. Van Norstrand signed on.[30]

Named for a French theologian, the *Fenelon* was about to embark on a voyage of the damned. Van Norstrand gloried in this tale of high adventure, with its burials at sea, ship-killer waves, and threats of mutiny. For a month, with only his trusty Jim and a multi-talented private from Jefferson at his side (Alonzo Brown, later the sheriff), he cared for 155 virtually helpless soldiers and tried to shelter them from a crew of pickpockets and low-lifes who hovered like vultures. It was a preview of the challenges he would face as superintendent of an insane hospital—surly employees, belligerent patients, and the daily grind of meeting their basic needs. What did this experience reveal about him?

The type of insanity most frequently encountered in the army was a form of depression called "nostalgia." Homesickness. Nostalgia was a creeping malaise that could destroy a regiment as effectively as an epidemic, and when symptoms appeared in their ranks commanders tended to react harshly.[31]

Van Norstrand may have read Bucknill and Tuke's *A Manual of Psychological Medicine*, which was published in 1858 and remained the standard work on mental disorders for decades. Parts of the book had appeared in America's only journal devoted to the treatment of insanity, including a long discussion of nostalgia. The authors cited its prevalence among Swiss and Dutch soldiers with Napoleon on the retreat from Moscow. Especially vulnerable were country boys bewildered by hostile surroundings. They gave up, sank into despair, and died. Benjamin Rush described the condition in his 1812 book, *Medical Inquiries and Observations upon Diseases of the Mind*. Van Norstrand would have been familiar with the symptoms and with treatments advocated by the assistant surgeon general of the army, Dr. Dewitt C. Peters, who urged doctors to be gentle healers, using "kindness, free exercise, bathing and agreeable associations, while [improving] the tone of the stomach and bowels by generous diet and tonics."[32]

But most officers and many surgeons took a harder line. To them, nostalgia was a kind of rot, eating away the vitality of their command, and the way to deal with it was to keep young men too busy to brood by ratcheting up their sweat-level—more drill, more work details, more active campaigning. Above all, show no pity: "Sympathetic words" made matters worse. One regimental surgeon employed a kind of shock therapy consisting of heavy doses of shame: "A system was inaugurated to impress them that their disease was a moral turpitude. [It] was looked upon with contempt—that gonorrhea and syphilis were not more detestable. This course excited resentment,—passions were aroused, a new life was instilled and the patients rapidly recovered."[33]

Like most of his colleagues, Van Norstrand had no stomach for moody soldiers or for the recommendations of the experts. Yes, he had challenged General Williams on Ship Island, but that did not mean he protected crybabies. "Shirkers and cowards" were dead weight, using up hospital beds needed by the demonstrably sick and wounded.

The patients destined for the government hospital in Washington were certifiably insane, but he estimated that about fifty "hospital bummers" were also on board. Upon recovery from wounds or sickness, some soldiers remained too frail or troubled for combat but helped out as laborers, cooks, or ward attendants. But those he called "bummers" were beyond redemption. They too had recovered physically, but they did not perk up and pitch in. "Self-pollution" was believed to be a contributing factor, adding to their pariah status.[34] Some turned furtive and crafty. Others sank into a maddening state of inertia. Many wouldn't even leave their bunks. Unmoved by kindness, punishment, or public humiliation, Van Norstrand's "bummers" had fallen so far that the army was washing its hands of them. Some may have been shirkers, skulkers, and cowards. Some from New England states in particular may have joined for the bounty, intending to cut out at the earliest opportunity. But for others, official cruelty exacerbated an already severe depression. Dietary deficiencies or undetected neurological damage may have been contributing factors as well.

Van Norstrand could not stand them. He used a shovel to lever a 200-pounder from his bunk, then slapped his head with the blade. Later he taunted the man into eating salted herring until he vomited.[35]

He had courage; he did not back down from a fight. He had stamina; if there was a problem that lesser men could not handle, he would see it through to a conclusion. But woe to the patient who did not fall into line. Then the gloves came off.

In New York he turned most of the soldiers over to women from a nearby government hospital. "The ladies came like Angels, with Spirits and Wine and Kind Words for the poor feeble remnant of the army of the Gulf. [They] cheerfully took them off my Weary Hands."[36]

On occasion Van Norstrand seems to have stepped back from what he had just written to see if it had the desired effect. That is when doubt surfaced, and he felt compelled to cover his tracks with an added sentence or two of overripe sentiment like those about the "Angels" and "Weary Hands." It is as though he discovered that he had been lured from his original objective, which in part had been to depict the life of a man of principle, modesty, and compassion. In hastily touching up this self-portrait—Abraham Van Norstrand as he wanted to be seen—he did battle not only with enemies who told a different story but with revelations about himself that had slipped onto the page almost against his will.

In Washington he delivered his remaining charges to the government insane hospital and then enlisted Senator James Doolittle to help him lobby army brass for a furlough. As surgeon and hospital administrator he had routinely turned down applications for furlough submitted by his patients, yet he was soon homeward bound on his second "medical leave" in two years.[37]

Probably he was reunited with his family. Perhaps young Fred, now approaching twelve, had shed his childish ways, and Felona Belle, five, was eager to show him how she made her letters. The strain of his long absence may have affected his wife's appearance or manner. He may have commiserated with local families who had lost sons in the South. But he says nothing about all this. His family is mentioned only as he is about to leave them again: "I bade my wife & children a sorrowful good-by and turned my face toward New York."[38] Other things were on his mind when he sat at his desk to record his recollections.

Rebels inflicted some casualties, but heat, exhaustion, and feet bloodied by constant marching inflicted more. One way to rest screaming feet was to mount up. Load-bearing animals began to disappear from farms and plantations and were lassoed from prairies. Slaves led some soldiers to herds hidden in the woods or along streams.[8] To men of the Fourth Wisconsin and two other regiments traveling bareback on mules and plow horses, this was an upgrade not only in mobility but self-perception, the first step in an undreamed of transformation from infantry frogs to cavalry princes.[9]

As a grand offensive the expedition was a washout. The enemy kept melting away. But as economic warfare it was a triumph. Soldiers picked the countryside clean of everything from cotton to contrabands, molasses to mules, and sugar to sweet potatoes.[10] It was also valuable on-the-job training for Banks's new brigade commanders, Halbert Paine and young Geoffrey Weitzel, who months ago had been a mere lieutenant in the regulars.

Washington was not happy with Banks's meandering. "Eccentric" is how General Halleck, the frustrated general-in-chief, described this excursion.[11] Coordinate with Grant, he urged. In late May Banks crossed back to the east side of the river and concentrated his forces under the heights of Port Hudson. As Grant had besieged Vicksburg, so Banks would endeavor first to besiege Port Hudson, then overpower it.

Thus there was an urgency to Van Norstrand's efforts through the hot weeks of April and into May. Fresh produce returned to markets. Live oaks were dense and green, and magnolias flowered, but the most impressive sights were at the landing: "Soldiers are arriving and departing constantly. Transport after transport [and] steamer after steamer are headed towards Port Hudson." Signal flags flashed between gathering warships. "Camps for the wounded are being established all over the city and outside among the groves," a solder observed. "Churches are taken, also a number of the large private residences converted into hospitals."[12]

Van Norstrand's hands were full. The steamy, mosquito-breeding heat of early summer combined with collective melancholy to swell the ranks of the dangerously ill. He needed beds and mattresses by the hundreds, but lumber and straw were hard to come by. "Till quite recently there were no beds," a soldier from Massachusetts wrote. "The sick lay on their one blanket till putrid, running sores were the result. No one stood near to brush away the flies and insects."[13] His own regiment sweltered under canvas and wasted away of nostalgia: "Going home is the great topic with us. We see only the wilting of our sick and the burial of our dead. The soul-eating monotony has often been broken by the funeral procession with its mournful music. 'Died of home-sickness' should be written on many a grave."[14]

By mid-April Van Norstrand had only five assistant physicians to help with the care of over seven hundred patients.[15] Still bothered by diarrhea, he was at his office by 7:00 each morning and worked until 7:00 in the evening. To his assistant physicians he distributed medicines, condensed milk, beef broth, a punch made of milk and whiskey, and other "delicacies." He toured wards and kitchens, chaired meetings of a board charged with evaluating soldiers for discharge, supervised his clerks, and pored through the paperwork they generated.[16]

"Flies and mosquitoes are in swarms & our men are already suffering from Bilious and Typho-Malarial fevers & Dysentery," he wrote Lucy, "many dying daily." So many, in fact, that he had assigned four men the task of hauling the dead to the cemetery with a wagon and mule team. One morning he watched their supervisor, a German soldier he called "Dutch John," walk among the coarse wooden coffins and kick each one to distinguish the empty from the occupied.[17] "Last night we buried the assistant surgeon of the 50th Regiment of Massachusetts Volunteers," he wrote in mid-April. "I bury from two to four or more every day."[18]

The army no longer shipped dead officers home for burial. It "took too much time," he explained. "[Furthermore] the hot climate made the bodies very unsightly in a short time." The cemetery was divided into separate sections for enlisted soldiers, officers, and blacks.[19]

He put soldiers to work tearing up the floor of the abandoned penitentiary. "I organized a corps of cot builders and they furnished one cot every ten minutes, and in a few days we were supplied."[20] The demoralized Massachusetts soldier took comfort knowing that hospitalized friends were finally off the ground in beds and protected by mosquito netting. The tents of the infantry regiments were still ovens, but the hospitals, he wrote, had become "airy, sweet, and clean."[21]

By mid-May the U.S. Army Convalescent Hospital, Baton Rouge, occupied the town's most substantial public buildings and some private homes, each location with its own physician and staff. "No sooner was one [building] ready," Van Norstrand wrote, "and I went [on] to another." Yet with a flood of battle casualties expected any day, he still had barely enough staff and space to accommodate the sick. On May 19, forty wounded arrived from Port Hudson, half of them rebels. Eight days later, the night after Banks's first major assault on the heights, casualties arrived by the boatload. When smoke hazed the northern sky he knew that after nightfall another shipment of groaning litter cases would show up at the landing. Four blasts of the steam whistle alerted him and his corps of fifty black stretcher bearers that the hospital boat *Sallie Robinson* or some other bloody-decked steamer was approaching. "I kept my horse saddled and tied at my door, ready to go to the landing and superintend the handling, some of the wounded swearing and praying to be left alone [to] die. All my seventeen [surgeons] were active and busy, [and] I was compelled to fill in on them."[22]

The streets and shaded porticos of Baton Rouge were corrupted by odors wafting from open windows and under tent flaps, including at times the eye-watering stink of chloride of lime used to wash waste buckets, floors, beds, and stretchers.[23] After a few weeks, a new population appeared around town, "pale, emaciated," idle men lacking an arm, a leg, or an eye.[24] "The hospitals are in excellent order," a New England man wrote, "and many of their stricken inmates are really jolly."[25] Profoundly relieved, more likely. A disabling wound was a ticket home. For them the war was over.

Nature and the triage process practiced in field hospitals separated those with survivable wounds from the hopeless. Arkansas and Mississippi infantry on the heights of Port Hudson, peering from behind a woven thicket of spikes, branches, and tree trunks, fired smoothbore muskets loaded with a one-ounce lead ball and often with buckshot as well. Such old-fashioned weapons were deadly at close quarters, the spray of buckshot lacerating soft tissue, the round ball capable of crushing joints and tearing organs. Union soldiers and rebel sharpshooters fired conical balls from rifled barrels. These were effective at much longer ranges. The spinning ball cut a funnel-shaped path, a clean entry hole giving way to a widening shock tunnel through soft tissue, and a large, ragged exit. Intervening long bones tended to be split lengthwise.[26] Most gut-shot soldiers typically coughed up blood and died of shock on the battlefield. Some survived a jarring trip to the field hospital, where doctors could do little but numb their suffering with morphine and await early death from peritonitis or hemorrhage. Penetrating chest wounds were also unlikely to survive transport to Baton Rouge, though some did. A few soldiers even survived for days with a lead ball in the brain—comatose or convulsing or, in at least one case, up and about until he fell into a coma and died. Field doctors designated likely survivors for transfer to Baton Rouge. Stretchers were mounted in ambulances and driven to Springfield Landing. Some died waiting for the hospital boats, others on the trip south to Baton Rouge. Still others, the lucky ones, eventually showed up on crutches on the sidewalks of Baton Rouge, soaking up the sun and counting days until their trip north.

"On June 8, I wrote my wife that I had buried ten men that day and I was of the opinion that it would not be less each day for the next ten days, that I had 2,085 sick and wounded in my immense hospitals, and the stench from the wards was awful. On the 14th I wrote that I can hear the wails of the wounded in my wards many rods away and some dying every minute. On June 21, I wrote that I was in good health but poorer in flesh than she ever saw me—202 pounds, which is 65 less than when I went in the service. My hospital consisted of 2,848 sick and wounded for whom I had to provide food, water, provisions, medicines, lint, bandages, cookery, bedding, nurses and medical and surgical attention. [My assistants were] good men, but some became sick and one crazy."[27]

Like his recent adventure at sea, this job was a test of his leadership under great stress. It was this experience, in fact, that later qualified him for consideration for the hospital vacancy in Madison. Like the superintendent of a public insane hospital he had to closely monitor his patients' diets. When the commissary issued "sour" meat, or short rations, or did not supply food that officers were billed for, or fresh beef and rice for sick contrabands, Van Norstrand shot off sharply worded memos demanding prompt action. He set aside time to respond to messages up and down his chain of command and for other paperwork, including requests and complaints from patients and their families. An Italian took offense when his wound was described as "a humbug." As an officer in Garibaldi's army, he said, "I was always a soldier of honor I never was able for humbug. The leg is weak, the grease of knee-limb is dry and I am by my age [54 years] not able for duty. I pray you, Medical Director, to please to give me furlough for any weeks to New York."[28] A German with chronic diarrhea requested discharge from the army citing failing vision, rheumatic pains, and teeth so rotten they could no longer tear open a rifle cartridge. "Besides," he wrote, "I am very old."[29]

Soldiers wasting away in a ward set aside for diarrhea cases pleaded that going home was their only salvation; to remain in the south was to die. Van Norstrand urged them not to give up hope, while privately acknowledging that they were as good as dead. Until the river was open to Union traffic, hundreds upon hundreds of the very sick were destined to take their chances in Baton Rouge. Doctors tried purgatives, sedatives, strengthening tonics, and a concoction that included camphor, turpentine, opium, laudanum, cinnamon, ginger, and black pepper. Nothing worked for long. Van Norstrand was encouraged by the effects of a strychnine solution. He saw enough improvement in forty patients to briefly become a believer. But all soon relapsed: "When well established, [the diarrhea] never gave up its victim. All [standard treatments] proved of no avail. One at a time [they] went to the cemetery."[30] A few lucky sufferers, men of rank and influence like his friend Frederick Boardman, got sent home because Van Norstrand fought for them up the chain of command.

* * *

The following note arrived from Officers' Hospital:

> Sir,
> Capt. Mabbit requests that his arm may be amputated as soon as possible.
>
> Respectfully,
> L. M. Rice,
> Act. Steward.[31]

Van Norstrand obliged. He had hoped to save what remained of Mabbit's right hand—two fingers and the thumb—but infection set in and it ballooned into "a rotten mass."

"I put him under the influence of chloroform and made my circular cutaneous incision, which crossed an artery, which had been so enlarged . . . that it deluged me with blood." He had to pause and wipe it from his only good eye before getting back to work.[32]

In time he received a written thank you from Mabbitt's family in Rochester, New York: "Without your kindness he knows he would not have lived."[33]

He checked daily on another New Yorker, a scrawny, tubercular Irishman, "[expecting] to find his place vacant and he gone to the dead house." His arm was "the size of a large man's leg, and [appeared to be] filled with water." Van Norstrand resisted his pleas to amputate, fearing an operation would kill him. Finally he agreed to do it the next day, expecting to find the bed empty by then anyway. "When I entered the room the next morning he looked up brightly and at once said, 'You will cut it off?'" Eventually the one-armed veteran went home to Cayuga County.[34]

A soldier from his old regiment was shot through the bones of his neck: "I supposed he must die for several days, but he did not, and so it became me to consider the best position for his head, as the neck was very likely to be stiff and remain just as I placed it. Hence I concluded to place it at 'Attention'—head erect and eyes front. So I placed him and so the wound healed. When he recovered he was the finest specimen of a soldier at attention that I ever saw. I suppose he is just so yet if he is alive."[35]

Captain Nelson Craigue, also of the Fourth Wisconsin, took a ball through both buttocks—four immense holes. Sprawled belly-down in a cotton furrow, he had started to laugh when a nearby soldier joked about their predicament. His rear end shook just enough to draw the attention of a rebel marksman.[36]

On June 26, twelve days after Banks lost much of his army in a second futile assault on Port Hudson, Van Norstrand took up his pen and escorted his wife on an imaginary tour of the U.S. Convalescent Hospital, Baton Rouge. In the next room a half-dozen clerks scratched out discharges, death reports, transfers, and orders. Lined up outside his window were ambulances, supply wagons, and the dead house cart. It was not yet noon, and Dutch John had already made five trips to the cemetery. Eight hundred more patients had arrived with the dog days of summer, raising the population to over 2,800.

He asked Lucy to join him in a carriage and they set off to Buel Hospital, where the men were in bad shape, but "all clean and orderly. The doctor is an opium-eater but a good disciplinarian." Buel was the first of many stops, to include a converted theater, a factory, a court house, and other confiscated buildings public and private, plus an encampment of 150 tents in tree-shaded rows where those well on the way to recovery awaited discharge. "Many of the old veterans less a leg or an arm rise and salute me as we pass."

Next came a cavernous room filled with chronic diarrhea cases, "each row about 100 feet long. As we pass slowly along the aisles, a faint voice here and there calls out, 'Doctor, how long before I can go *home?*' My answer is, 'As soon as able.' Poor fellow. He will be at the home of the flesh in a few days or even hours."

Church Hospital, filled with amputees, "is clean but poorly led. Too many Negroes and women putting on airs. Some cases need amputation, others need bone taken out. We will come back tomorrow and give it a general overhauling."

Factory Hospital stood vacant, poised to receive the next wave of wounded, "everything in fine order, medicines, bandages, rags, adhesive plaster, bathing tubs, beds, pans, sheets, blankets, instruments, cook stove and large soup kettle, pails—all that I think may be needed [by the] doctor and steward who are sitting by the door waiting for [the] steamboat to blow the wounded signal."

Many at Court House Hospital were near death. "This is none too clean. The doctor drinks a little, and I have reprimanded him severely. Perhaps he is a little offended, for he comes slowly and salutes me coldly."

The doctor at Academy Hall Hospital was "slow and inefficient," and the place had required extra attention from Van Norstrand. "Many must die in a few days. But we must hurry."

Patients at Harvey House Hospital "had bones cut out of their arms and legs on the battlefield. Some I have been compelled to re-amputate because the bones stuck out when they got here. The bunks and floors look clean, and all is quiet and sweet. Lt. Maxon, of the 4th Wisconsin, [was] shot through the left lung. [He] has a small chance to recover."[37]

At Officers' Hospital, patients had every conceivable sort of wound—"some in the mouth or arms, eyes, hands, feet, legs, breast, back, head and bowels, but all pretty contented and happy."

He was proud of his fifteen "cook houses," as he called the kitchens, "some with white cooks, some with black, some women and some men, but all busy [and] mostly clean." Equipment varied from open fireplaces to cast iron stoves to "ranges built by myself."

Last stop was the dead house, which doubled as a lock-up. Disciplinary cases had a choice; they could sleep on the brick floor or on a coffin. A day or two there on bread and water was a potent remedy for pigheadedness.

"All this establishment I have to provide with food, clothing, wood, water—which we haul from the river, medicines, etc. Do you wonder that when I rise from bed in the morning I feel as if I could not attack my day's work?"[38]

He failed to mention the many nurses and other staff at each setting, but one patient described an extensive chain of command, including assistant physicians, a nurse for every eight patients, wardmasters, and stewards, all under a resident surgeon who made rounds at 10:00 every morning, "and woe to the unfortunate nurse whose ward is not in the most perfect order, or whose patients complain of the least neglect or remissness of duty on their part."[39]

S. K. Towle, a future editor of the *Boston Medical and Surgical Journal* (now the *New England Journal of Medicine*), ran the hospital that the army had installed in the Louisiana Asylum for the Deaf and Blind, a grand structure in the gothic style of the nearby state capitol. In late 1863 he wrote in a letter to the *Journal* that echoed the sentiments of his colleague across town, Dr. Van Norstrand: "I . . . believe more and more in the importance of nutritious food in any protracted disease, and feel much less anxiety when my stock of drugs gets low, than when my supply of fresh beef, mutton, chicken, oysters and eggs fails me." Like Van Norstrand he touted the effects of quinine in large doses for fevers, and he prescribed strychnine, opiates, and quinine for chronic diarrhea, although he considered these his "least hopeful" patients.[40] Towle and Van Norstrand worked under the army's medical director in Baton Rouge, but like Van Norstrand in his memoirs, Towle did not mention this fact in his letter. Each seemed reluctant to acknowledge that within the chain of command he was a link or two shy of the top, and more importantly, that he was not a free agent practicing his "art," but one practitioner among many who were struggling to find effective treatments for conditions they seldom encountered up north.

But Van Norstrand did acknowledge the work of hundreds of blacks who hauled refuse, dug latrines, carried stretchers, and buried the dead. He praised the courage of black soldiers at Port Hudson whose senior officers, both white, had gotten cold feet and stayed behind while their men, he had been told, "moved on almost double-quick notwithstanding the missiles [coming] awfully and sweeping them down." The two colonels showed up later at his hospital pleading illness. He told them that he had no cure for cowardice and sent them on their way.[41]

* * *

By this point in his story Abraham Van Norstrand had filled nearly 140 pages in his ledger book since his first entry on August 25, 1877. He was writing in haste, often copying long passages from the letters his wife had saved. He had been at work on the memoirs for nearly four years and was fifty-six when he compiled the section dealing with the summer of '63. His father had died at fifty-eight. In a few months he would suffer his first apparent stroke.

These pages written mostly in the present tense recall his proudest hours as doctor and soldier. Here, finally, is a detailed record of his conduct as surgeon, counselor to the mortally ill (and sometimes their wives and parents), and supervisor of temperamental subordinates laboring and sometimes breaking under grinding pressure day after sweltering day. Letters in his army scrapbook from patients, families (including relatives of wounded Confederates), and colleagues testify to his effectiveness. They brim with expressions of admiration, thanks, and even affection. Collectively they describe a very different figure from the weary, peevish, and sometimes boastful figure that emerges from his narrative. But then it was not a sense of a job well done that sent his hand slashing across page after page of his ledger book in old age. When his account of that summer at Baton Rouge was complete, his writing tapered off. By the time of his death a year and a half later he had added only a dozen pages. Illness may have been a factor, and also a deep aversion for the task ahead. Maybe he simply could not bring himself to relive those years at the Wisconsin hospital.

NINE

Friends and Enemies

When Union forces moved unopposed into Baton Rouge in the spring of 1862, Port Hudson would have fallen into their hands just as easily had they sensed its strategic value. Just twenty-five miles upriver, Port Hudson was an undefended trading center where rail ;and river commerce converged, a town of warehouses, saloons, and hotels for commercial travelers. But a year later, guns installed on its heights overlooking the river effectively confined Farragut's fleet to the lower Mississippi, and Port Hudson had become a thorn in the Union's side. As they climbed the wooded base of those bluffs, Nathaniel Banks's thirty thousand soldiers gazed up at a veritable citadel bristling with cannon and rifle barrels and protected by a manmade thicket of uprooted trees and other debris upon which crawling attackers could easily be picked off—those who had made it across the killing zone of wasteland between the edge of the woods and the heights.

Under fire from the Union fleet and batteries of field artillery, Banks's divisions emerged from the tree line and advanced on the entrenchments in ambitious but poorly coordinated attacks that foreshadowed the western front of a later war: storms of artillery fire that dim the sun but fail to destroy a dug-in enemy; elaborately planned assaults that spasm into ruin almost immediately, some ragged lines of soldiers climbing into smoky oblivion, others cowering in the dirt. The first grand attack was launched in late May. Many of those soldiers ended up on bloody tables before Dr. Van

Norstrand and his fellow surgeons to be picked clean of worms and maggots, chloroformed, probed, sawed, ligatured, elixired, and all too often boxed up, hoisted onto Dutch John's wagon, and carted to the dead house.

Especially hard-hit were those leaders—regimental commanders, company commanders, and others—who dared take their chances up front with their men. In the early hours of May 28, Sidney Bean started a letter home from the battlefield: "[As] we were crawling over and under the felled trees and through the branches, some of my best men fell. Captain Herron had his leg knocked off. Lieutenant Pierce was shot in the arm. Lieutenant Crittenden was hit in the breast. Our whole loss was about seventy killed and wounded, and three hundred was all I took on the field." Sheltering under the crest of a hill, his men took advantage of a clear field of fire to pick off rebels who had crawled atop a parapet to cheer their own artillery. "The number of their killed and wounded must have been great before they abandoned their guns," Bean wrote. The carnage was, in the words of Halbert Paine, "a dreadful spectacle, so ludicrous that our boys could not restrain their laughter. So does war petrify our hearts."[1]

Bean's letter was found in a satchel beside his body. Private Knute Nelson wrote that his "much beloved colonel" was shot dead crawling from company to company giving orders. Van Norstrand heard that he had been shot out of a tree while spotting enemy fire. One thing was beyond dispute. Sidney Bean was up front with his soldiers when a sharpshooter's bullet tore a hole through his right lung. Two years earlier he had been a silly kid who could not hold his wine. Now Van Norstrand referred to him as "Little Napoleon."[2]

The second major assault, on June 14, was even more costly to the Fourth Wisconsin—47 dead, 74 wounded, and 25 taken prisoner when they fought their way over the rebel parapet only to discover that the eastern outfits that were to accompany them had refused to go forward—"a wholly unexpected defection," Banks wrote Halleck, by "nine-months' men, who do not consider themselves bound to any perilous service."*

Halbert Paine was charging uphill with his division when a minie ball shattered his knee.[3] A storming party of riflemen and grenadiers were to keep the rebels hunkering under cover while following ranks dumped hard-packed bags of cotton into ditches, creating walkways over which massed infantry would cross into rebel lines. The initial phase apparently went according to plan, but the nine-month regiments—the bulk of the force—balked when Paine went down. "It is impossible to overrate the courage and endurance which Gen. Paine showed," wrote a correspondent from the *New York Times*: "[He] would not consent to leave the field, but remained there during the long sultry day to cheer on his men."[4]

In fact Paine had no choice. He was awkwardly folded upon his useless leg. He could not crawl if he wanted to and would have been shot if he tried. He managed to straighten his leg and pull his hat over his face as protection from the sun, but his every movement drew rebel fire. Marksmen "amused themselves all day" using him and other fallen soldiers as bait to lure would-be rescuers into their sights.[5] Two men from New England regiments were shot dead trying to reach Paine with a stretcher. Worms were already busy at his neck when he was dragged from the field after nightfall.[6]

The novelist John William DeForest, an officer with the Twelfth Connecticut, claimed that not a single officer from the regular army participated in the assault. All were safely in the rear: "The entire storming business was left to the management of volunteer colonels and lieutenant colonels. The ablest of these, [General] Paine, fell at the foot of the parapet; and with him fell what little military genius we had anywhere near the parapet."[7] Edward Bacon, a senior officer with the Sixth Michigan who was arrested twice for having a bad attitude, ventilated mightily about drunken generals, diabolical surgeons, and craven bullies (Joseph Bailey of the Fourth Wisconsin

---

* Too late to influence events at Port Hudson, Halleck wrote back: "When a column of attack is formed of doubtful troops, the proper mode of curing their defection is to place artillery in their rear, loaded with grape and canister, in the hands of reliable men, with orders to fire at the first moment of disaffection." Halleck to Banks, June 27, 1863. Official Records, series 1, vol. 26, part 1, p. 603.

was one of his favorite targets), consigning to hell just about every officer in the Department of the Gulf *except* Halbert Paine. To be excluded from Bacon's methodical character assassination was tantamount to high praise.

The wounding of Halbert Paine merited only passing mention in Van Norstrand's memoirs, probably because he did not show up at the Baton Rouge hospital. Van Norstrand was consumed by the needs of those who did. But he still managed to keep up with developments in his old regiment. After Sidney Bean was killed the next in line to take command would have been Frederick Boardman, but eleven months of recurrent diarrhea had virtually crippled him. He nursed his stricken gut under Van Norstrand's care in Baton Rouge, a pasty, skeletal ghost of his former self. It is not hard to imagine him writhing in anguish at having to pass up the position he had coveted for so long. Van Norstrand had added his name to a list of maimed officers ("musket ball through shoulder joint, . . . minie ball through shoulder blade and chest, . . . grape-shot through forearm, . . . ball through right lung, . . . canister through the arm and rifle ball through shoulder. . . . ") for whom he urgently requested early transport north. Even if Boardman survived, Van Norstrand doubted he would ever be well enough to rejoin the regiment.[8]

Next would have been Joseph Bailey, but he had been assigned to the staff of General Banks and was engineering gun emplacements and entrenchments at Port Hudson. So for the time being Captain Webster P. Moore took over the regiment. The irony was not lost on Van Norstrand. He had enlisted Moore into the Jefferson company, had orchestrated his appointment as his own successor as company commander. Had Van Norstrand retained his infantry commission, he—and not Moore—would now command the Fourth Wisconsin. Youngsters who only yesterday had struggled to become passable lieutenants now sported silver eagles on their shoulders, yet here he was, master of what he believed to be the second largest hospital in the army, stuck permanently at the rank of major.[9] Once again he had done everything right, only to come up short.

Half-starved on a diet of wharf rats, mule meat, and sugar—

there was always plenty of sugar—the besieged rebels surrendered on July 8.[10] The fall of Port Hudson was the third Union victory in a matter of days, a footnote to the strategic triumphs at Vicksburg and Gettysburg. In Van Norstrand's hospital the crisis atmosphere gave way to deep relief, then weeks of tedium. Beds emptied and were not filled. In August his census fell to about 700, down 75 percent from mid-July. Amputees and invalids on the mend crowded his office while clerks churned out discharge papers and authorizations for furlough. Grown darkly restless himself, he predicted that many would quickly sour on life at home. Isolated on farms and behind store counters they would grow homesick for the army and the intoxicating sense of being part of something grand and historic.[11]

As his workload declined, long-held grievances ate at him. If the army would not give him what he deserved, then he would find ways to compensate himself. The story of his last months in Baton Rouge lacks the clear chronology of his memoirs to that point. His family had joined him in November, and so he had no letters from this period to draw from.* He wrote the last few pages during the last year of his life, following at least one stroke and with only memory and his military album to guide him.[12] He managed to get down several more tales—and a strange assortment they are—but suppressed others. In 1860 he had estimated the value of his real estate and personal property combined at $1,200.[13] In late '62 his wife had warned that if he hoped "to save anything" he must come home to deal with creditors and pending litigation. Yet by early 1864 he was carrying over $10,000 in large bills. Where did this sudden wealth come from?[14]

Unmentioned in the memoirs are his dealings with a man named Goldsmith who wrote to him under the letterhead of a New Orleans liquor dealer named "Karsten, Diek & Company." Letters and receipts indicate that Van Norstrand bought at least 36 barrels of whiskey from Goldsmith, or 900 gallons. (Prices varied, but at $1.60

---

* Lucy had chanced a voyage down the liberated Mississippi, the journey made memorable by guerrillas on shore who peppered the boat with musket fire and artillery rounds, killing some cattle. Memoirs, p. 144.

a gallon Van Norstrand paid 40 dollars per barrel, which comes out to 25 gallons per barrel.)[15] Saloon owners commonly doubled the volume by adding an equal amount of water, a practice an operator eager to siphon money from the pockets of idle soldiers would be unlikely to shrink from, thus possibly increasing Van Norstrand's stock to a retail equivalent of nearly 2,000 gallons—enough to quench the thirst of an army. In his hospitals, whiskey, brandy, and wine were used as sedatives and stimulants, and they were mixed with otherwise unpalatable medications (i.e. "quinized whiskey"). Thus they retained an aura of medicinal legitimacy. Some regiments actually distributed a whiskey ration in the belief that it protected soldiers from malaria. It is not clear how medicinal alcohol was supplied to the hospital, but doctors had discretionary funds for procuring medications, fresh foods, and various "delicacies"—presumably including whiskey.

But the numbers suggest that he had other consumers in mind. He does not record how many patients remained in his hospital that fall, but given the downward trend well underway in August there would have been fewer and fewer—at most several hundred. In other words, the volume of whiskey he purchased went up as his patient population declined, leaving him awash in three to four gallons per patient.

He was in a powerful position. The army had forbidden liquor sales in Baton Rouge without authorization from the provost marshal.[16] The application of a civilian from New Orleans was unlikely to be treated with the deference accorded one submitted by the acting medical director, the position to which Van Norstrand had again been appointed. On November 5 Goldsmith wrote, "If you succeed in obtaining a license, please take it out in the name of my son-in-law, Henry Abraham. Now is the time to *act!* There is plenty in your same profession who undertakes all such work and without any exception they all making a *little fortune!*" In reference to an earlier shipment he wrote, "In case you have *sold out* (emphasis added) the same please advise me whether to ship you more."[17]

It appears that Van Norstrand had become the middle-man in an enterprise that paid off handsomely, even as other army doctors were discovering that the alleged medicinal properties of whiskey were more than offset by its pernicious effects. For one thing, a whiskey-soaked soldier proved to be as vulnerable to fevers—including malaria—as his "unprotected" counterpart. Regiments that distributed a whiskey ration tended to have more sick soldiers, not fewer. Finally, as a stimulant it was a bust, knocking out more soldiers than it spurred to action. A Connecticut officer wrote, "One-fifth part of the regiment keeps drunk all the time."[18] Seeing the effects on his own soldiers, one doctor went so far as to destroy his regiment's supply.[19] Van Norstrand had ample opportunity to observe soldiers, officers, and even doctors who, day in and day out, were too drunk to function. But it appears that he could not resist the lure of easy money.

He also profited as middleman in another enterprise. One day that fall a gregarious plantation owner named Pierce showed up in his office, spied a demijohn of brandy Van Norstrand had set aside for holiday partying, and offered a very good price for it. A deal was struck. Pierce invited the Van Norstrands to his plantation where he wined and dined them and even urged little Flora to take home a "pickaninny" as a sort of pet.[20] Van Norstrand seemed to interpret all this as a sign of his own prestige: see how this aristocrat doted on me? Days later, a cotton wagon loaded with sweet potatoes appeared at the hospital, a gift from Pierce for Van Norstrand's patients.[21]

It is as though he had been selected for an elaborate softening-up process. On his next visit Pierce brought a shopping list and told Van Norstrand that his family and the eighty slaves on his plantation would suffer unless he could lay in a supply of these items, which Van Norstrand did not identify. On his recommendation, Brigadier General Philip St. George Cooke, the army's ranking officer in Baton Rouge, authorized Pierce to buy the goods from the army and to transport them home through army lines.[22]

Van Norstrand depicts himself as a well-intended participant in a humanitarian transfer of goods. Yet ten days later Pierce showed up again. He insisted on privacy and handed over $2,275: "Your half of that venture in which you assisted me, and some more to come." Van Norstrand was stunned! "I had expected nothing and told him so and that I never on any occasion had received a cent for my influence while in the army." But he kept the money. Later Pierce came by and thrust a folded paper into his hand. Van Norstrand would have the reader believe that he stuffed it into a pocket and forgot about it. Only days later did he discover that it was a thousand dollar bill, "the first and last I ever saw." He kept that too.[23]

Something is missing from this portrait of a naive, good-hearted fellow caught off guard. Why Pierce's secrecy, and why doesn't Van Norstrand identify the goods? The planter's deep pockets are also a puzzle. The few sugar planters who had not already abandoned their estates were left with no markets, a rebelling work force, deteriorating fields and equipment, sugar houses full of unsold hogsheads of sugar and barrels of molasses, and empty pockets. Even in good times they depended on credit to feed their slaves, buy equipment, and survive the year until their sugar was sold. But here was Pierce flaunting wads of cash and playing the big shot. He may have taken an oath of loyalty to the Union, in which case Van Norstrand could not have been accused of dealing with the enemy, but even so something fishy was going on. One historian wrote that an "air of intrigue" hung over the sugar land during the war.[24] It appears that Van Norstrand was in the thick of it.

Why didn't he turn the money over to his commanding general? It is as though his object in telling this story is not disclosure but concealment. He boasts of his profitable connections while insisting that his hands are clean.

His windfall would have been greater had not another project fallen through. A rich Baton Rouge banker and planter named Pipes had made him a partner in a scheme to transport and sell cotton held by the Confederates. Van Norstrand believed that Banks and a Confederate colonel were also parties to the scheme. Pipes was to be paid one-third of the profits for orchestrating the affair, and Van Norstrand would get a portion of that for unspecified services should the scheme come off. Alas, he was out of the army before the transaction took place, if it ever did.[25]

Banks's hands were probably clean, unlike those of his predecessor, Butler, whose removal was prompted in part by allegations of blatant corruption. Banks had been ordered to harvest Louisiana wealth, cotton in particular, as a means of undercutting the Confederate economy.[26] But it is not surprising that Van Norstrand suspected him of illegally enriching himself. Greed at high levels was common in the topsy-turvy moral climate of the Mississippi valley. Many plantation owners along the river despised the Confederacy for its ruinous effect on their fortunes, while a good many Union officers embraced that same plantation aristocracy and bemoaned the demise of the slave system that sustained it. When it came to profiteering, planters and New England bluecoats proved to be equally cunning and opportunistic. At the other end of the spectrum, Irish laborers who had been brought south to work on high-mortality drainage and canal projects were press-ganged into rebel gray, while southern slaves were press-ganged by Union "negro drivers" like Joseph Bailey to labor at high-risk construction projects for the Union. Van Norstrand was not the only one to lose his bearings in such turbulent ethical waters.[27]

But there was a price to pay, and increasingly toward the end of the year he wanted out—out of the South and out of the Fourth Wisconsin, which had been reinvigorated with fresh faces from home and was fit for hard duty once again. It is as though that old impulse to flee had been triggered. Why else would he pull strings to avoid going back to his beloved regiment?

Joseph Bailey wrote to him from New Orleans. "I find that you like all men have your friends and enemies. There is a few here who make serious assertions as to alleged trouble that you should have. . . ." Van Norstrand or a protective family member obliterated the rest of the sentence. It is a pitch-black stain. What were they hiding?[28] Had old comrades grumbled to Bailey about his shady dealings? "It would be well to watch certain parties who are still connected with our regiment," Bailey warned.[29]

Van Norstrand had written to Halbert Paine, now deskbound

in Washington awaiting a wooden leg, for help getting reclassified as a "surgeon of volunteers," a title that would have brought him both a promotion and a new assignment. Paine urged him to come to Washington and sit for an examination, after which he would surely get the promotion. A month later Van Norstrand sent another letter, this time asking his support for a position of a different sort. He had heard a rumor that back home Governor James Lewis was about to organize a new cavalry regiment. Van Norstrand wanted to command it. He would seek recruits from among discharged soldiers eager to return to the colors including, he expected, a good many who had served in the Fourth Wisconsin. He would call the regiment "The First Veteran Wisconsin Cavalry." What did Paine think of this plan? More to the point, would he recommend Van Norstrand to the governor?[30]

Paine was not encouraging. He would gladly recommend any comrade from his old regiment for promotion, but the war had created many officers qualified to lead regiments, and Van Norstrand's years of medical service put him at a disadvantage in the competition for a combat command.[31]

Van Norstrand tried the governor. "No man can fail to dash his way to distinction with a cavalry regiment of Wisconsin men, if he has any ability in him," he wrote Lewis. "My heart has been in this war from the first as you very well know. Should I go out with a regiment of yours I would conduct it with honor and credit to you and myself, or I would not return." He provided a star-studded list of references, including Benjamin Butler, John Phelps, Halbert Paine, Fred Boardman, and Joseph Bailey.[32]

But he had other irons in the fire as well, and in December he sent a letter of resignation to the new medical director. His wife was in "very feeble health," he explained, and he needed to take her north to be cared for by relatives.

Yet he kept his family in Baton Rouge for a month after receiving his discharge.[33] He had signed over what was left of his hospital; he was out of the army. Why did he stick around? Was he still collecting whiskey profits? Were the Pierce transactions continuing to pay off? Was he waiting for the expedition Pipes had talked about to get underway?

The memoirs will soon end abruptly. At this point the reader might expect a summing up: the return home, readjustment to small town life, and so on. Nothing prepares us for the dark adventure that follows. But that story must wait.

Abraham Van Norstrand in 1863, a year of supreme accomplishment and great stress.
Courtesy Neville Public Museum of Brown County.

Halbert Paine. WHi-2366,
courtesy Wisconsin Historical Society.

Joseph Bailey. WHi-31815,
courtesy Wisconsin Historical Society.

Sidney Bean. WHi-28273,
courtesy Wisconsin Historical Society.

Recapturing the glory years. Van Norstrand in dress uniform, complete with surgeon's sash
and sword, outside his home in Green Bay.
Courtesy Neville Public Museum of Brown County.

The hospital a few years after Van Norstrand resigned. He oversaw the construction of the wings on the far left and right as well other major upgrades to the building and its elaborate grounds. Later he regretted carrying over "my energetic administration of out of doors affairs into inside discipline with patients and attendants." WHi-40020, courtesy Wisconsin Historical Society.

Group photo of hospital staff, undated photo.
WHi-11289, courtesy Wisconsin Historical Society.

Samuel Dexter Hastings in old age.
Courtesy Neville Public Museum of Brown County.

Abraham Van Norstrand, undated photo.
Courtesy Neville Public Museum of Brown County.

Fred Van Norstrand, the problem son.
Courtesy Neville Public Museum of Brown County.

TEN

A Second Class Man

In the fall of 1863 at the hospital for the insane in Madison, Dr. John Clement was consumed by resentments of his own. Unlike Dr. Van Norstrand, whose declining workload left him time to find ways to compensate himself for his good work, Clement contended with mounting disaffection within the hospital and poisonous rumors without.[1]

His predecessor, J. Edward Lee, had been sacked after only nine months on the job. Lee had been an assistant to Thomas Kirkbride at the Pennsylvania Hospital in Philadelphia, probably the most highly regarded superintendent in America and one of the founders of the Association of Medical Superintendents of American Institutions for the Insane (AMSAII). In effect, Lee had come to Wisconsin as a gift of the Association. For years he worked without pay as an adviser to the hospital's building commissioners, but once on the payroll as superintendent he became an easy target. Construction lagged behind schedule. Contractors had defaulted. A skeletal roof stood over expensive, space-hogging extras such as an unauthorized chapel. "The Institution was designed for practical utility," legislators scolded, "and not for mere gaudy show and empty splendor." Out went the commissioners and their designated man; in came a hastily assembled board of trustees to grapple with lingering financial chaos, equipment shortages, construction delays, and staffing dilemmas, to say nothing of mounting pressure from across the state to open the hospital's doors. Even so, it took the trustees a full day and seventeen ballots to settle upon Clement as Lee's successor.[2]

He barely had time to learn his way around and hire an assistant before the first patient was escorted up the front steps. By mid-December of 1860, a structure designed to house 32 patients in comfort and safety held 78. A few months later there were over a hundred. Clement struggled through those chaotic early years when pressure to make room—state-of-the-art care and treatment be damned—undermined the original plan to increase admissions only as the physical plant expanded wing by wing. He had to control men and women hauled in raging, terrified, or full of mischief, and to revive others dredged from jails, barns, and backrooms who arrived sprawled on wagon beds, pucker-mouthed, evil-smelling, barely alive. Books had to be balanced and supplies ordered for the teamster's daily trip to Madison. The grounds were still wild. There were trees to fell, stumps to grub, fields to clear, fences to erect. In time the hospital would be expected to raise much of its own food, and so livestock had to be acquired, sheltered, and cared for, vegetable gardens and fruit trees planted. And of course beneficial activities had to be organized for patients who grew restless with time on their hands.

Clement had symptoms of his own. He was a drinker, a shouter, a tightly wound man. Constant pressure to improvise, to bend without breaking, put an awful strain on a man who was by nature unbending. Relations with his subordinate, Harvard-trained Dr. John Favill, were bad from the start. Favill protested the dearth of meaningful activities and the overuse of belts, cuffs, straitjackets, and seclusion rooms. Clement was furious. His own assistant was undermining his authority, damaging him in the eyes of employees and trustees alike.

Although pressed to accommodate ever more patients, to shepherd the facility through its growing pains and to favorably impress legislators and taxpayers who came to marvel or gawk, he was primarily responsible for curing the sick. That is what the hospital movement was all about. It was why dozens of nearly identical facilities had gone up throughout the nation over the past thirty years.[3]

Specialized hospitals providing humane treatment could drive away madness for good. Like new-age asylum doctors of France, England, and Germany before them, superintendents back east had demonstrated this time and again. Some boasted cure rates of 70 to 90 percent.[4] Faith in the effectiveness of hospital treatment became so pervasive that one historian labeled it, "The Cult of Curability."[5] Thirteen of those eastern doctors came together in 1844 to form the Association of Medical Superintendents of American Institutions for the Insane. The association met annually, launched *The American Journal of Insanity*, and, as it grew, so did its influence with medical organizations, newspaper editors, and state legislatures. Members mostly took the high road, confining their public statements to conclusions gleaned from their own statistics—always an abundant crop, though of dubious value—while crusaders like Dorothea Dix staked out Main Street, noisily popularizing the same cause.

The superintendents' argument was as follows: small, private institutions had proven that insanity was curable if caught early and if the sufferer was promptly admitted for what they called "moral treatment." (The term meant, essentially, "mind treatment," but in fact "moral treatment" was a vague concept, more suggestive of an enlightened, nonpunitive attitude than of specific activities or medical remedies.) Now that there was a proven cure, it was the duty of state governments to establish much larger, publicly funded institutions for the many thousands of insane beyond the reach of the private hospitals. The association even prescribed how those new facilities should look (a series of wings extending from each side of a massive central building) and how far they should be built from the nearest town (no closer than two miles). The master plan speci-fied the proper building materials, the acreage of the surrounding grounds, the types of decorative trees and other plantings to set out, the maximum number of patients (250, reluctantly increased to more than 600 in the mid-1860s), the required number of wards (eight for each sex to provide for what they called the "proper classification" of patients), and the amenities required in each ("a parlor, a bath room, a water-closet, a dumb waiter, a speaking tube"). It prescribed the organization of the central building (offices, receiving rooms, private apartments for the superintendent and his family), the type of lighting (gas), and the heating and ventilation requirements (steam heat, forced ventilation). Mostly the work of Dr. Kirkbride, this model required an enormous investment of public money up front but would prove the most economical and effective in the long run, the association argued. In the words of Dr. Luther Bell, for many years superintendent of the McLean Asylum Hospital in Boston, "As the communities called to provide for the insane advance in familiarity with this duty and in means to meet it, the fatal error of cheap institutions will cease to exist."[6]

Bell could have been describing the process Wisconsin struggled through in the 1850s. Early in the decade, as counties pleaded for help with growing numbers of the insane, the legislature authorized a paltry $22,000 for construction of a facility modeled after the already outdated hospital in Worcester, Massachusetts. Dr. George R. McClane, hired from the east by the newly appointed Commissioners of the Wisconsin State Lunatic Asylum, set about raising the consciousness of those with power over the purse-strings, shepherding the three commissioners on a tour of eastern hospitals where they got a crash course in modern hospital design and treatment methods. Back home, they ditched the Worcester plan and contracted instead with a Philadelphia architect for drawings based on the more expensive Kirkbride model. But they could not convert the legislature, which was alarmed to discover in the commissioners' first annual report that contracts had been let for a leviathan of a hospital that no one had authorized and that there was no money to pay for. McClane was fired, the commission dissolved, the excavation and adjacent rock pile abandoned. The newly elected Republican majority made hay of the issue, and a taint of scandal lingered for years. But proponents kept the issue alive. In 1857 they brought a doctor from the Indiana hospital before the Legislature to preach the gospel of "moral treatment," a lavish outlay for special facilities in which to implement it, and the resulting certainty of high cure rates. "The age of experiment has passed," he assured his listeners.

"You have before you two generations of successful result."[7]

By late in the decade, a hospital had been authorized and funded once again. This time, the guidelines of the association of superintendents would prevail, even though the state was struggling through a financial crisis. As construction got underway, some doctors back east were making a painful discovery. The cure rates they had boasted of for so long were bogus.[8] Early statistics from the small private operations may have been accurate as far as they went. But doctors who ruled over the new public hospitals had been seduced by high expectations and naive assumptions. In those early New England hospitals, superintendents and patients shared a Protestant, Anglo-Saxon heritage. But big public asylums housed an explosive mix of bewildered immigrants, chronic drunks, worry-worn and bone-tired farm wives, epileptics and other neurologically impaired types, all manner of jailbird snakes and bullies, in addition to the classically demented and the desperately melancholy. Keeping order had of necessity become the first priority, treatment a distant second. Looking good in order to sustain public support was more important than accurately recording outcomes. The superintendents had hitched their wagons to the cult of curability, and there was no turning back even though many were losing confidence in the viability of moral treatment for such a hodgepodge of patients. Subtle shifts began to appear in their annual reports. Restoring physical health and personal cleanliness were realistic, attainable goals, and so some down played cure rates and instead emphasized improved quality of life. A hectoring, defensive note was struck. If only family members were a little more insightful into changes in a loved one's habits. If only they didn't wait so long to take action. Family and friends might claim the old man a "recent case," but upon admission he all too often proved to be beyond help, his dementia too deeply rooted to be touched by modern methods of treatment.

From his years as assistant physician at the Brattleboro asylum in Vermont, Clement may have been wise to the dilemma of deceptive statistics. In his annual reports he avoided the word "cure," with its suggestion of finality, instead claiming a "recovery" rate of

50 to 60 percent. But he did not dwell on statistics. Like other superintendents he was convinced that many so-called recent cases were "simply the outbreak of fires that have long been smouldering unsuspected within," thus already well-advanced.[9] He stressed improvements in patients' physical health and comfort, not their mental status. "A considerable number, once filthy to a disgusting extreme, have become habitually neat," he wrote in late 1861. "Several who were considered so dangerous at their former places of confinement as to cause them to be subjected to the most rigid and unremitting restraint, mingle here freely and harmlessly with the others. The uncouth and profane have, in some instances, become so far refined and correct in manner and language as seldom to offend the most delicate."[10]

Death rates were high. In the first two years nearly one of every seven patients died. Tuberculosis and old age were factors, as were epilepsy and suicide. But the most common cause of death, Clement wrote, was the negligence and abuse patients had suffered before they were brought to the hospital. The trustees echoed this claim: "It should be no wonder," they wrote, that such "frail material" perished, having barely survived "long and cruel suffering in ill provided places of confinement, where restraint by chains and brute force had been substituted for kindness and sympathy."[11]

It was not that patients lacked things to do, Clement insisted, but that most were too inert to do anything anyway. "A large portion of our patients are proof against the most enticing modes of diversion. Marching to drum and fife, in distant imitation of military drill, has been resorted to as a means of arousing and exercising the most stupid, and it has succeeded better than any other we have tried."[12]

During the summer, ladies were escorted on carriage rides and gathered flowers for the wards. There were picnics and "chowders," with music and dancing. A few males ventured into the lake to swim or fish. Mrs. Mary Halliday, the matron, hosted weekly parties, but it is not clear how well attended they were.

Farm and field work was the staple activity for healthy men, and a valuable resource they proved to be. In the first three years 30 acres were cleared for plowing, 150 fruit trees and 100 grape vines planted, as well as vegetable and flower gardens. The hospital grounds were graded and seeded, the drive from the road lengthened and improved. There was pasture land to tend and acres of undergrowth and dead trees to clear away. Finally, that old eyesore by the lake—the abandoned excavation for the original, scandal-tainted hospital, with its heap of stones—took work parties with teams of oxen a month to fill and clear.[13]

In 1862, a wing for females was completed on the west side of the central building. It corresponded to the male wing on the east side, but already it was obvious that more wards were needed. The trustees would have to appeal to the legislature for tens of thousands to add additional wings on each side of an already huge and hugely expensive structure that had proven to be surprisingly frail. With its faltering systems and random vulnerabilities it was like a sinking patient, subject to local infections like the reeking sinks in its water closets, and to systemic breakdowns like air shafts and heating ducts clogged with building materials. It had an insatiable appetite for labor and money—for cisterns to collect rain water, for new and stronger boilers to replace those that had failed within a year or two, for marble tiles to replace urine-soaked pine flooring in bathrooms, for a more extensive sewage disposal system to purge the place of the constant stink—and for fuel, a thousand plus cords of firewood each winter before coal-burning boilers were installed. The price of wood soared as nearby forests gave way to cultivated fields. The operating budget literally went up in smoke.[14] Even so, during periods of bitter cold, temperatures seldom reached fifty degrees in some parts of each wing. Mop water froze on the floors.[15] Pine flooring had been installed in the wings. Mopping urine-soaked pine guaranteed a floor that never dried.

It did not help matters that Clement and his assistant despised each other. Eventually he fired Favill, citing his "deliberate and incorrigible insubordination [and his] visionary and impracticable notions." Favill went back to his private practice across the lake, but he was not done with Clement. He complained to the trustees that under Clement, "Fear is the tangible basis of controlling power, abject, degrading fear." Clement had allowed attendants to throw a woman to the floor and kneel on her chest until she nearly choked to death. He was so vindictive toward another that she ran away. He ignored a dying man and hid his negligence from the trustees. He overused sedatives, solitary confinement, "the strength jacket," and other physical restraints. Patients languished in isolation for months, one naked, another without sheets. Cold baths were used as punishment, not therapy. Clement was "exceedingly excitable. . . . Not amiable in disposition [but] generally irascible." Furthermore, he was a drunk: "Within a year he [will] be a common sot," Favill predicted.[16]

Others chimed in. A physician on the Visiting Committee complained that medical treatment fell far short of "the plan of modern Psychiatrists" in Europe. The hospital lacked facilities "for the application of different sorts of cold and warm baths," hydrotherapy being the rage overseas.[17] Charles Ecklow, a former night watchman fired by Clement, accused the superintendent of forcing a "noisy" patient into a cold bath and nearly drowning him. He said he watched Clement share a bottle or two in the kitchen with colored musicians who had come to play for a dance. The inference was, here is a man so degraded that he will drink with anyone.

Employees discredited Ecklow as a bitter, devious man who had impregnated Miss Bunker, the second female hired at the hospital, and then abandoned her. The much admired matron, Mary Halliday, said she had never seen Clement drunk and that he treated everyone with kindness and used restraints only when necessary. After all, these patients were "filthy and violent . . . very destructive . . . throwing things out the window . . . tearing things in pieces." Former Governor Farwell picked up his mail at the hospital and had never seen Clement under the influence: "He has somewhat of a nervous temperament, but he controls it. He's affable and kind." Clement's new assistant physician, Dr. John Sawyer, thought the institution "was as well conducted" as Isaac Ray's highly regarded hospital in

Providence, Rhode Island, Sawyer's previous workplace.[18]

The trustees rallied around their man. The charges against him were "false and slanderous." Most felt that Clement had been humiliated without cause. They regretted having been duped into launching an investigation. Clement was "a faithful and efficient superintendent," they concluded. But it was too late. Seeds of doubt had been planted. Hostile patients and dissenting staff had been heard, and their back channel accounts of hospital affairs continued to infiltrate saloons and boarding houses where legislators gathered.

Clement hung on for another year, but in his report for 1863 he explained why he felt compelled to leave the hospital. It was a preemptive strike. Annual reports were read by state legislators, newspaper editors, and the medical profession, and were excerpted or summarized in the *American Journal of Insanity*. Clement wanted influential people to know what was going on at the Wisconsin State Hospital for the Insane.

"All is not smooth and pleasant in an institution. The tendency of modern reform is to go to the extreme and surpass what is practicable. A large portion of the inmates of all institutions for the insane still retain some of their mental faculties. [Some] are apt to cherish revengeful feelings for the restraint and authority necessarily exercised over them. When such a one can hold the ear of a Trustee, or Legislator, or a 'Visiting Committee,' for any length of time, the occurrence is boasted of among a sympathizing clique as a triumph over the tyrannical superintendent, and his authority and efficiency are proportionately impaired. Our motives are impugned, and our actions misrepresented, while the thousand little acts of kindness fall modestly into the background."

He reminded readers that he been on the job from the beginning, a one-man construction supervisor, personnel and training officer, admissions committee, and autocrat: "Between the legitimate obstacles and labors in arriving at our present condition, and the wearing trials arising from personal hostilities known to so many of you, my health has so far failed" that he felt compelled to resign. The position was too much for him. Too much, he implied, for anyone subjected to endless criticism and abandoned by his board of trust-ees.[19] The board decided not to wait the three months he had given them to find a replacement. They asked for his keys.

Apparently his message was heard back east. Trustees sent there to recruit a successor came home empty-handed. The editor of *The American Journal of Insanity* observed that in Madison, "The [trustees] seemed to be afflicted with perpetual unrest in relation to the medical superintendency."[20] The hospital had endured plenty of bad press at home. Now it was getting a national reputation. Dr. Sawyer took over as interim superintendent and soon came under fire himself. A patient "eloped" on ice skates and showed up in the governor's chambers to plead his case. He made a convert of Gover-nor Lewis, who set him free. Of course his spectacular escape made the newspapers. Under Dr. Sawyer, he contended, belts and bullying were as common as hash for breakfast. It was not what legislators liked to read about their new hospital.[21]

* * *

By March of 1864 Abraham Van Norstrand was back home in Jefferson, but he was hunting for bigger game than the same old small-town medical practice. His work in Baton Rouge was proof of his qualifications for a more challenging position and the rewards to match. He still hoped for a cavalry regiment of his own, but by then Governor Lewis had learned that the army only wanted more infantry regiments. It had enough cavalry.[22] It may have been Lewis who pointed Van Norstrand in another direction. Any number of men could lead a regiment, but precious few could run a hospital. Why not consider the vacancy across the lake, where skills like his were desperately needed?

Five weeks after writing to Lewis invoking visions of battlefield glory, Van Norstrand wrote another letter, this one to the board of trustees of the insane hospital. It is an amazing document. He sounds more like a consultant than a job applicant. As superinten-dent you want a man "of much experience in this special disease," he wrote, someone whose powers of "psychical influence will enable him to control these unfortunates without resorting to violence as is too frequently the case." In addition, you expect him to be a first-rate executive and a sharp money-manager. But you cannot afford someone with those qualifications, and so "you must accept a second class man, so far as experience is concerned," an adaptable man who can grow into the job. That man, he contended, was himself.

He claimed that in some unspecified way he had been responsible for the insane of Jefferson County years ago. Generals Banks and Butler would vouch for the care he provided thousands of sick, wounded, and insane soldiers in New Orleans and Baton Rouge. As for his executive skills and other qualifications, he reminded the trustees that most had known him for many years. Enough said.[23]

Recommendations from two Jefferson friends vouched for his skills as doctor and businessman and for his strong character. They called him "a great vigorous man" with "quick perception, sound judgment, an even temper, and a cheerful disposition, a man of acknowledged executive ability."[24] For all that, he was no shoo-in. Although he was the only candidate for the job, he got only six of eleven votes cast by the gathered trustees. But six was enough.

He was thirty-eight when he moved his family into stately quarters in the hospital's central building, he but he looked older, his heavy face lined and careworn. Lucy was thirty-six. Young Fred was thirteen, Flora seven. After years of financial ups and downs, he enjoyed a comfortable bank account thanks to his Baton Rouge windfalls, but the fortune that he had come west to find still eluded him. He was finally living in the kind of grandeur he aspired to, but it was not his. He was just passing through.

In labeling himself a second-class candidate he revealed ambivalence about the job. He had demonstrated time and again that he did not shrink from the decisive exercise of power in the manner of his hero, General Benjamin Butler. But for years he had tried to work his way out of the practice of medicine—as merchant, landlord, banker, and even, briefly, infantry officer. The hospital job would plunge him back into all the vagaries and conflicts of his profession, subject him to constant scrutiny from many quarters, and burden him with endless administrative responsibilities. It was medicine at its most controversial. He would be in the public eye as never before, and he would be responsible for a class of people that had consistently tried his patience in the past. The payoff was a prestigious title, a modest salary, and almost certain controversy down the road.

Still he must have marveled at the splendor of his empire in the woods. Even in mid-April, tramping among skeletal oaks and wincing from icy breezes off the lake, he could imagine what the grounds would be like with a deep green canopy overhead and wild greenery all around. Bordered by Lake Mendota on the south and west and by woods and fields falling away to the north and east, this was the sort of idyllic wilderness that could turn youngsters into happy barbarians, bring sighs of wonder from their mother, and inspire in a man like Van Norstrand a deep sense of possessiveness. Evidence that the area had been favored by the Indians survived in scattered effigy mounds in the shape of birds in flight, deer, even a panther or two.[25] The great stone hospital towered over a clearing midway down a gentle slope that shouldered into Lake Mendota, facing south toward its masters in the capitol.

Exploring its halls, a visitor deaf to the voices and immune to strong odors might mistake the place for a high class hotel. A half mile or more of corridors intersected at intervals where light through the windows brightened little oases of gentility—sitting rooms with rocking chairs and potted plants. Corridors of the central building were floored with alternating strips of dark and light hardwood. The walls bore floral wainscoting, and elaborate classical moldings merged wall and ceiling. The steps of the iron stairwells were emblazoned with stylized vines.[26] But in the patient wings, halls were mostly bare of decorative touches and the floors were of cheaper wood.

Van Norstrand had never before lived in anything like this, not by a long shot. Utilitarian it may have been, as the legislators had insisted, but grandly so, in the manner of public buildings born of high ideals and great expectations.

The press was enthusiastic about the new superintendent. "As a physician he has few superiors; as a business man he is accomplished and successful . . . In character he is upright, honorable. In address he is commanding, affable and popular. Indeed, in all positions in life, [Dr. Van Norstrand] has been successful and popular. We shall be very much mistaken if the friends of the Asylum ever have just cause to regret his appointment."[27]

After just five months on the job he submitted his first annual report, which began with a bow to the trustees and their long experience in the field. He humbly vowed to learn from them. Then he promptly went on the offensive. Some people complained that the hospital "was hardly accomplishing what they expected of it" and that it did not measure up to its big brothers back east. Those people did not know what the experts knew—"that the maximum per cent of cures is not reached for some twenty or twenty-five years from the organization of a hospital." Upon opening its doors a new hospital was mobbed by the neediest patients, "some epileptic, some idiotic, and some who have already passed through a thorough treatment in some other institution and been discharged incurable. With this unpromising class of patients all new State institutions commence their onward and toilsome career; they do not get freed from this incubus upon their prosperity in less than twenty years."

Having shown that if critics knew what they were talking about they would expect less, he then trumped them a second time by demonstrating that the cure rate at the Wisconsin hospital had already exceeded that of more established institutions. He tallied the rates given by 20 superintendents in their most recent annual reports and came up with an average of 43 percent, well below the 50 percent he claimed for his hospital in 1864. "With this success in the fifth year of our efforts," he concluded, "I feel that Wisconsin can reasonably claim consideration for our [hospital] among the prominent institutions of like character in the country."[28]

This passage, in which he listed hospitals by name alongside cure rates of from 15 to 68 percent, is at best misleading. He must have known how deceptive such figures were, how simplistic was this concept of "cure." Even in his general practice he would have encountered cycles of remittance and manifest craziness, the all's-well calm between bouts of drunkenness, the lingering obsessions, and the melancholy that bled body and soul of vitality. Evangelists within their own profession had painted superintendents into this corner, compelling them to somehow reconcile the gap between expectation and outcome. In their own annual report, the trustees reaffirmed that expectation: "Our institution was designed for a Hospital and not an Asylum. It is of the first importance to *cure* insanity." Unlike his predecessor, Van Norstrand did not shy away from the dicey issue of cure rates.

The trustees wanted a separate and cheaper facility for the chronically insane, but Van Norstrand disagreed. He did agree that violent patients and recent cases were the highest priority, but he called for enlarging the hospital to make room for all the insane in the state, pleading the awful conditions in which many currently lived: "three insane females chained to the floor or bedstead in the poor-house of one of the wealthiest counties, never taken out to walk, ride, or exercise. In another wealthy county, the [inmates'] quarters are less ventilated and more filthy than an ordinary stable, one woman being chained up in the barn because she was noisy."

In sum, the hospital was already more effective than many of its well-established brethren in the East. It was more economically run than ever, and the cost per patient would continue to decline if additional wings were built to make room for those desperate souls still confined to poorhouses and family barns throughout the state.

He considered one group of chronic cases an asset to the hospital. The acutely ill were no good on the work crew. They were too inert or too frenzied to be worth the trouble. But long-demented old farm hands and manual workers could grub out stumps, lay drainage tiles, level the clay surface of the carriage drive, spread crushed rock, plant trees, cultivate a garden, and shovel manure better than most hired men. That some might now and then drop their tools and break into a jig, or engage an attendant in a bizarre, stylized attack and retreat, or send quavering ululations to the sky hardly mattered. They were reliable, and they *needed* to fill their days with physical labor as much as the hospital needed workers. Through the years Clement and then Van Norstrand remarked upon the inexhaustible Henry Augustus, who labored literally under delusions of persecution, chopping underbrush, cutting wood, and tending cows and pigs. "He does as well as anyone that we could hire at $20 per month," Van Norstrand wrote. "We could hardly get along without him."[29] An old woman obsessed with "piles of money . . . is very fond of work and is never so easily managed as when allowed to scrub to her heart's content."[30] The pros and cons of separate asylums for the chronically insane were debated at the annual meeting of superintendents in Washington in 1866, and Van Norstrand made the case for the status quo: "I should most strenuously oppose a separation of the two classes. Most of the labor [at my] institution is performed by the chronic insane. During the winter our patients mostly remain within doors, and in the spring they are much poorer in health than they were in the fall. I think the labor, in season, which they perform is not only a source of economy to the institution, but of benefit to the patient. Four-fifths of all our farm labor is performed by the chronic insane."[31]

He was not alone in this opinion, although it ran counter to the Association's tenet that hospital beds should be reserved for those most likely to benefit. Thus did the superintendent's role as hard-nosed, pinch-penny executive of both a demanding physical plant and a vast agricultural enterprise conflict with and sometimes undermine his role as practitioner.

Van Norstrand concluded with the traditional inventory of projects undertaken and those still on his list. The hospital's well water was so hard that lime plugged pipes and flues, and so another cistern had been installed to collect rainwater for use in the boilers. Problems with the kitchen, laundry, and heating systems had been resolved. Stronger bars had been installed over the windows of one of the men's sitting rooms. Furniture was breaking down under hard use. Floors, door frames, and window sashes needed repair. Buildings were needed to house the hogs, poultry, and farm tools; the grim work of digging up and moving the dead remained to be done.

He signed off by praising his assistant, Dr. Sawyer, who "has no superior in his every day, faithful efforts." Employees who fell short of expectations, he noted archly, "have been permitted to seek employment elsewhere."[32]

He sounded like a man comfortably in charge.

ELEVEN

The Usual Little Jarrings in the Ward

The superintendent and his assistant charted in enormous casebooks, a fresh page for each newcomer. If he proved to be an attention-getter and stuck around long enough, that page eventually filled, and he reappeared deeper in the book and perhaps even in a subsequent casebook, like a magazine serial that went on forever. But few patients took up more than a page or two. Given the many demands on the two physicians, patient records simply were not a high priority. A new arrival came to life in the casebook only after a period of observation. The first note included background information from the application form, a physical assessment, a summary of his initial adjustment to hospital life, and any medications, special diet, or other treatments prescribed. Months, even years, might pass before the next entry. Serious illness, dramatic upsets, sustained periods of improvement or decline met the casebook threshold, but lives of quiet desperation tended to go unrecorded if not unobserved.

The application usually arrived before the patient. It provided basic information—age, marital status, occupation, and so on—and posed questions intended to elicit a profile: Describe the symptoms. When did they first appear? Were there "permanent delusions," or an inclination to attack others "from premeditation or sudden passion"? Had homicide or suicide been attempted? Was he "cleanly" in his personal habits? Were his parents blood relations, and were any relatives insane? Was he addicted to "intoxicating drinks, opium or tobacco, or any improper habits?" Doctors, jailers, and others with scant knowledge of the person dashed off little that was useful, but applications labored over by family members were often richly detailed and moving, even if the writer was clearly ill at ease with the task at hand.

"This is one of the outcroppings of the hellish Rebellion," Van Norstrand wrote of a man whose son had died in a rebel prison.[1] "Came in with very marked hallucinations, hearing spirits talk to him, etc. Was put on whiskey and quinine with nourishing diet." At least Gilbert Wilson steadily improved, although after sending him home Van Norstrand worried that he would show up again. Wilson was among dozens whose madness had been triggered at least in part by the war. They included widows, wives tormented by returned veterans, mothers convinced that the draft was a death machine stalking their sons, fathers and mothers whose grief had driven them berserk or sucked all the vitality from them. And there were the soldiers themselves. One arrived shackled, "irritable, morose, disposed to violence," and showing signs of secondary syphilis.[2] Another, the former fife player from Van Norstrand's old regiment, had been released from the Government Hospital in Washington where he had wasted away from the effects of nostalgia, obsessed with "liberating the Negro." His wife had refused to take him in, and so he showed up at the hospital.[3] Some had suffered head injuries—a fall from a horse, a blow of some kind, a glancing minie ball. A young German who had taken a bullet in the face went crazy in the Harvey House hospital across the lake and jumped through a third-story window "in fear of some approaching ev l."[4] Nathaniel Foster was paralyzed with guilt, confessing to the murders of his cousin and a woman while in the army.[5] When neighbors learned that James Dawson, a middle-aged veteran with four children, was in the county jail covered with filth and ranting about his many afflictions, they took up a collection and cared for him in a barn until the hospital could admit him.[6] A statement from another veteran's application might have been rubber-stamped on many: "Came home crazy."[7]

At least most of the war-related insane got better. Probably they were assigned rooms on the upper two wards, where the most hopeful cases were housed. Those on the first floor were not so promising, among them many with progressive, organic conditions. The German wife of a tailor had spent time at the hospital during Clement's reign, only to be readmitted and still in the house when Van Norstrand took over. Although run-down physically she carried on like royalty, ordering her servants about and expecting special treatment. "Her mouth had become gangrenous," Clement wrote. "The offensive smell infects the whole ward." Van Norstrand noted that carbuncles had appeared on her back. He ordered iodide of potassium (iodine). "The cartilage of the nose is absent," he wrote, suspecting syphilis. "Her husband has been requested to remove her but he refuses. The disagreeable smell from her body is unbearable."[8] Chauncy Leonard grew despondent when county officials rejected his plan for a road. Despair escalated into suicidal self-loathing, and he cut his throat with a razor. At the hospital he had to be force-fed through a stomach tube. "His delusions are most entirely melancholic," Van Norstrand wrote. "Is a nocturate masturbator and there is hardly much hope for him." Within months this driven, articulate farmer was eating vomit and feces and masturbating whenever he had the energy. Desperate inquiries from Chauncy's wife and parents continued to show up on Van Norstrand's desk until the very end, when he wrote in the casebook, "Is wretchedly profane, often asking with the most pitiable oaths to be killed."[9] A poor butcher, the father of five, came in feverishly boasting of superhuman powers. Nine months later Van Norstrand described a different man: "The expressionless eyes, puffy unsolid appearing flesh and incapability of speech all combine to form a picture most truly to be sympathized with, especially when we compare this wreck [to] the young man who stepped within the hospital doors commanding heaven and earth." Paralysis had wrenched his wasted torso and joints at frightful angles. "General destructive decay," Van Norstrand wrote at the end. "For the last few days [unable] to swallow."[10]

Twelve-year-old Elena Straus wrote for news of her mother, whom she had not seen for five years. "I have to keep house myself and go to school every day besides. And when you receive this letter do not answer back that you want money to buy clothing for her, because my Father is too poor and can not earn enough to clothe us and buy us food."[11]

Van Norstrand could not offer much hope. Elena's mother had assaulted men in the street, and her "strong venereal propensities" did not fade at the hospital. She had elicited only a few brief observations from him: she was still violent, noisy, and homesick. "Has been most of the time restrained by muff," his successor wrote, "being dangerous and at times quite violent." A year or so later, "Is now a confirmed dement," and still later, "Is very vain in spite of intense homeliness. Sometimes rubs the skin off her face in order to render herself fairer." She died after many years at the hospital and was buried there.[12]

Many epileptics were hospitalized in the belief that seizures were a manifestation of insanity. Effective medication was a long way off, but Van Norstrand tried old herbal remedies such as belladonna, stramonium, and valerian, which were considered "antispasmodics," or central nervous system depressants. He had better luck with the new bromides, in particular bromide of potassium; also with chloral hydrate: "Hydrate of chloral cuts short his spells considerably," he wrote of a man who may have been so overmedicated that his seizures simply became less pronounced. A note he wrote about another—"Died in a fit"—no doubt could have been said of many in spite of all the tinctures, powders, and pills with which they had been dosed.

Tuberculosis, or phthisis as it was called, was another frequent visitor. Long considered a disease of the restless and moody, the alcoholic, the poorhouse dement, it carried off a handful of patients every year. A tonic prescribed for those suffering extreme restlessness and so-called "night sweats" was whiskey with quinine, the latter to cut their fever and the former as a sedative.

Another class whose disease often proved irreversible was the severely depressed. A young student from a comfortable home in Janesville attempted to drown himself and was brought to the hospital expecting to be poisoned, suffocated in a sewer, dissected, and experimented upon. Frail and anorexic, he argued that treatment was useless, he was hopeless. "His countenance and conduct always display a great amount of mental suffering," Dr. Sawyer wrote. He ate only on threat of being force-fed. Eventually he gained weight and pepped up only to turn "mischievous," escaping his attendants to attempt suicide, first by throwing himself over a banister and then by jumping into a cistern. Eventually he came up with a plan that succeeded, more or less. In a vacant sitting room he poured kerosene from an unlit lamp over himself and rubbed it into his face and clothes. Back in the hall, he lifted the glass chimney of a working lamp and flared into a ball of fire. "His breast, neck, chin, part of his face and about the ears, were deeply burned," Dr. Sawyer wrote. "Most of his hair was burned off and his hands were badly blistered. . . . Frequently asks those around him to kill him."

His wounds were sprinkled with flour. He lingered for a week. Internal swelling slowly choked off his airway. Swallowing became nearly impossible. Breathing was a ghastly, foamy struggle. "He did not ever regret his suicidal act but to the last begged to have his head cut off, or his life ended in any way."[13]

Rope, poison, water, a blade across the throat—these were the preferred methods of self-destruction. One woman tried all but the knife and had jumped from a train as well. "Feels she is a burden to her friends and of use to no one."[14] Jumpers were drawn to cisterns and wells. Others arrived with razor scars or rope burns on their throats. The record of a female patient who died before Van Norstrand's time aroused his suspicion. She was alleged to have driven a knife through her throat with such force that it nicked her spine: "The mooted question [being] the ability of a suicide to put the knife down to the vertebrae."[15]

Guilt, self-loathing, dread of the next human encounter. An old hemiplegic farmer continued to drag himself through his dawn-to-dusk chores on crutches, convinced that he was falling behind and that "his stock was starving or dying of thirst, his children were coming to want, that he himself was covered with vermin." Somehow he managed to get his head in a noose and string himself up. He was cut down and taken to the hospital ("Lies in bed, constantly moaning over his sins"), where he died.[16]

Another old man blamed himself for the war, and still another—shades of Edgar Allen Poe—was "afraid he had done wrong. Thought his brother was under the floor, burning up."[17] A widow went crazy after her husband squandered his fortune, joined the army, and drowned. "Brooding, disconsolate, anxious about her children," she refused medicine and turned violent. Transferred to the lower ward among the most disturbed patients, she withdrew altogether, "her face concealed in her shawl. . . . Is quite emaciated. Exists like a plant, showing not energy or will, or perception, notices nothing in her vicinity." She did not last long.[18]

Quite a few women sought peace and security in the same manner, curled on the floor, heads buried in the skirts of their long dresses or under a blanket or a shawl. They got on Van Norstrand's nerves. He took their withdrawal as a kind of provocation, as though they had literally turned their backs on him. He was particularly irked by a middle-aged spinster who indulged in half-hearted suicidal gestures and ate only with constant prodding. He theorized that she and her sisters "early imbibed the false notion that it was improper for a lady to work. They therefore allowed the mother to do the household duties, and they were parlor ornaments, and received company, waiting for matrimony to relieve them from their poverty and dread of honest work. Matrimony came not. Poverty increased. Bright hope fled. Sexual systems became deranged. Hysteria and melancholy alternated. Insanity came on. The history of one is nearly the history of all three. They are reaping the fruit of false education and a misspent youth."[19]

A former clerk in the War Department was admitted in "a deep melancholic apathy, insensible to all voice or commotion." His painful stoop was the result of childhood rickets, Van Norstrand suspected. Force-fed a mixture of milk, eggs, and beef tea, he spent his nights "coughing and groaning." He was found dead one morning with foul-smelling pus all over his chest. Van Norstrand suspected that an abscess in the lungs had ruptured. Death from aspiration pneumonia brought on by overzealous application of the feeding tube was a possibility he either did not consider or refused to acknowledge.[20] A lumberman who guided log rafts down the Chippewa River lapsed into a suicidal funk after suffering a head injury on the job. He was also force-fed milk and eggs, although mixed with whiskey rather than beef tea. It was an ordeal he could avoid only by feeding himself, which he finally agreed to do, though only in small amounts. In less than a year he, too, declined and died.[21]

After going broke in his home state of Vermont, Earl Boswell decided to start over in Colorado. He got as far as Madison, where he was paralyzed by second thoughts. Boswell was a farmer, "industrious and temperate, but easily depressed by disappointment." He fretted over every conceivable hardship and contingency before finally setting out for Colorado. By the time he reached Leavenworth, Kansas, he was a nervous wreck. He gave up, turned back, and was taken into custody at the Madison post office, "shouting, singing, dancing, talking incoherently, etc." Van Norstrand prescribed morphine, whiskey, and an herbal concoction three times a day. Boswell was clean and docile, a model patient, and was soon deemed well enough to rejoin his family back east.[22]

If the prospect of fresh start in the unsettled West could bring an uptight Yankee to his knees, it was even harder on many immigrants. Nearly half the people in the hospital had come from Ireland, Germany, and Norway, and virtually every nation from Cuba to Russia was listed as country of origin at least once. Language and cultural barriers complicated life for patients and staff alike. Of an angry young German, Van Norstrand wrote: "His exact mental condition we can hardly ascertain as he does not speak English and our conversation must be carried on through an interpreter." Another German was brought from jail battered, starving, and "in low physical condition." He recovered enough to run off and steal a horse but was soon back on the ward. Nine months later he disappeared again. Eventually his body washed up on the shore of nearby Lake Monona.[23]

While her farmer husband was away in the army, an Irish girl concluded that her brain was on fire. She came in nearly bald, having cut off her hair to cool her head. She may have been suffering from pellagra, a nutritional deficiency that brought on painful dermatitis in addition to mental symptoms. No medicines were given but she got better anyway, probably because she was finally eating well. After six months she was sent home, "recovered."[24]

Negative reinforcement in spades was the approach taken with chronic masturbators. In ages past such "addicts" were considered beyond redemption, doomed to burn in hell, but in this enlightened era it was understood that they merely risked dissipation and madness. Little Elena Strauss's mother sexually assaulted men in the street, but her behavior was considered a symptom of her disease, not a cause. Not so masturbation, which was thought to lead directly to insanity. "Spermatorrhea" was the official label, but the records are full of colorful synonyms: self-pollution, secret vice, solitary habits, nocturate masturbator, onanism, etc. A young man from rural Princeton wrote to Van Norstrand desperate for help. He was convinced that he was being shunned: "I am so ashamed that I keep myself from society." A patient was seen urinating out the window but his real crime, his roommate reported, was masturbation.

These and others were prescribed a so-called "antaphrodisiac," typically an herbal tonic thought to have passion-suppressing qualities, plus whiskey and sometimes a sedating, opium-based narcotic. But the real shocker was a solution applied directly to the penis. "Prepuce kept sore with cantharidal collodian" was a common notation. Cantharides were dried, toxic remains of an insect commonly known as "Spanish fly." There was an immediate burning sensation. Blisters appeared, and sometimes open wounds. After one such application a fellow boldly walked off to his work assignment on the farm only to be stopped in his tracks by the friction of fabric against traumatized penis. He had to be helped back to the hospital.[25]

The typical drug addict was a well-off housewife. "Has taken enormous doses of opium, chloroform and other narcotics," Van Norstrand wrote of the wife of a lumber dealer: "Begging all the time for chloroform that she may have just a little ease, but morphine and chloroform are denied her altogether." He tried to ease her craving with a tonic of whiskey and valerian, a plant long used as a sedative. At night, she was strapped in bed. He did allow a deeply depressed woman to self-medicate with cannabis in pill form, but when even twelve grains a night failed to control her "nervous irritability," she was taken off cold turkey and within weeks seemed completely well. Back home she had a baby and went on with life, liberated from enslavement to "the use of Hash Heesh."[26]

Some patients simply lived in a different world. A woman named Jansen insisted on being called Mrs. Fremont, after the famed pathfinder, general, and presidential candidate, John C. Fremont, who in fact was married to the daughter of Missouri Senator Thomas Hart Benton. She also referred to herself as "Queen of the Earth." Melville Crumley was related to Queen Victoria, lived in a palace given him by Prince Albert, and owned gold mines in California. Several poor farmers had become big-shot cattle dealers, buying high, selling low, and driving their families deep into debt. Another patient was "a driving businessman, excitable [and] quick-tempered, [who] pretends to be the wisest, strongest and handsomest man in the world. At one time he is Abraham Lincoln, then Washington, Napoleon, etc. . . . " For some, the dark side of this manic euphoria was suicidal despair. For others it was an eruption of rage that often had to be contained within a tight cocoon of canvas and leather. In either case, the long-term outcome was often progressive dementia.[27]

There were mischief makers aplenty, psychopaths and thieves who hid weapons, beat up roommates, flooded bathroom floors, broke windows, set patients against one another, and taunted slumbering giants. On their wards assaults on attendants escalated—more head-butting, face-gouging, hair-yanking, and blindsided body blows. Llewellyn Thomas was the reigning tyrant at a prosperous farm nearby. A cantankerous veteran of eastern hospitals, he showed up several times a year, drunk, belligerent and ever eager to regale staff with that hallmark of the chronic repeater, rants about how much better he had been treated elsewhere. The anxieties and overwork of harvest time were almost certain to trigger attacks on family members, in particular his wife. Medicating himself with whiskey did not help. Sometimes the sheriff brought him in. Sometimes his sons or neighbors overpowered him, flung him onto a wagon, and dumped him at the door. "Readmitted, abusive, vile and profane," one doctor wrote. "Never for a moment loses his gift for fault-finding and abuse. He is the worst affliction that ever befell a madhouse." Allowed outside to give attendants a break from his harangues, "he was found visiting the neighbors and troubling the workmen and help about the house, attempting to instruct the cooks, the doctors, the farmers, the engineer, attendants and all hands. Talking in a vulgar manner to the girls, etc…" No wonder that when the trustees launched their first extensive investigation of the hospital in the spring of 1868, Van Norstrand sent him home. Within weeks he was back with broken ribs and a punctured lung following an encounter with a neighbor.[28]

Bernard LaRochelle, an epileptic half-breed from Prairie du Chien, was a wilderness man, a sawyer by trade, a self-taught Shakespeare scholar, and an early member of the Wisconsin legislature. He had killed a man, was declared insane, and spent over thirty years at the hospital, where he urged doctors to learn Italian to broaden their medical background. Gradually he came to live on his own terms— "comfortable & incurable," according to one doctor. He had a private room, roamed the grounds at will, and spent the passing years waiting for his imaginary Negro bride to show up. From time to time he eloped but usually came back on his own, happy to reclaim his room. That is, until the early spring of 1868, when he was spotted back home in Prairie du Chien, much to the concern of the town fathers. Unlike Van Norstrand they had seen him at his worst—murder, arson, and no end to threats of further mayhem. "The citizens are much alarmed as he has threatened the lives of several," one wrote to Van Norstrand. Van Norstrand insisted that LaRochelle was harmless, and letters and telegrams went back and forth, growing ever more petulant. The citizens of Prairie du Chien eventually prevailed, and LaRochelle lived out his life at the hospital.[29]

A laborer digging the foundation for a new wing witnessed an encounter between the superintendent and another of these hard cases. Van Norstrand was outside near a barred window where the patient stood watching. He asked the man to fetch a certain attendant. "The patient told the doctor to go be damned and call the [the attendant] himself," the laborer recalled. "The doctor asked again kindly, and the patient gave the same answer. [He] abused the doctor ugly. [He] said [the doctor] had more shit in his purse than he was able to carry. The doctor stooped down and took a piece of brick and threw it [at the window] guard." The patient was not hit. "I do not think the doctor was angry. He went socially away."[30]

Crazy people from politically influential families caused special headaches for Van Norstrand. He refused admission to a hopelessly mad former colonel in spite of the governor's intervention, but in the case of the abrasive Mrs. Hazel Roach he did succumb to pressure from the governor and lived to regret it. He did not like her and did not think the hospital could help her.[31] The president of the State Medical Society was a friend and loyal supporter of Van Norstrand whose son had died at the hospital. When he sought admission for a second son Van Norstrand readily obliged, although the young man was already, in his words, "a hopeless case."[32]

Of the hundreds of sufferers who came before him, none was more common, or admitted more regularly, than the woman carried in so care-worn and malnourished that she no longer experienced her "monthly turns." The last straw had been the death of a child, or just as often, the cry of yet another demanding mouth. Or she might show up barefoot, bruised, and bullied out of her wits, wild-eyed and weather-scoured from roaming night and day. "Grief and trouble and poverty," was the explanation given for poisoning her child, shredding her clothes, cutting her throat; "hard times, war, taxes, etc.," for her furtive, dirt-eating withdrawal. No wonder so many took refuge under cover of their skirts, their last sanctuary. Often relegated to strong rooms, or "dark rooms" as the female attendants called them, these ghostly figures comprised a sort of pagan chorus that repudiated Dr. Van Norstrand and all he stood for—iron tonics and rich diets, gumption, self-pride, and respect for authority. For them, the hospital was the end of the line, the final refuge. Just leave me alone.

Several discharged women came back to the hospital on foot, having been sent out against their will. One was sent out three times and came back three times, pleading homesickness for her old room. Another was dragged from the hospital by a dull brute of a husband. She fought all the way, beating him with her fists and sending him tumbling down the front steps. Still he managed to drag her aboard the small side-wheeler *City of Madison* just before its scheduled return to town. Van Norstrand argued that she should stay, but the fellow wanted her back, and that was that.[33]

* * *

By regulation, "the *law of Kindness* must be the governing one. All employed will find that to ensure success, great self denial and a wakeful control of the temper and disposition will be required. Attendants must treat patients with respect, kindness and attention. They must not use greater force towards the patients than is necessary to secure themselves or others from violence."[34]

Kindness versus control. The ideal versus the essential. It was every attendant's dilemma: the theoretical world of warm paternalism that shelters and nourishes versus the actual world of schedules, conflict, dominance, and submission. Attendants were expected to get up at the ringing of the 4:30 bell. They woke their patients and made sure they washed up and combed their hair. Breakfast time varied with the seasons, 6:00 or 6:30. Afterwards there were halls and rooms to mop, mattress ticks to hang out and refill with fresh straw. Because there were no nurses, attendants had to care for the sick. They cut hair and shaved the men once a week. Some accompanied the laboring patients to the farm. Others helped patients set tables for meals and, weather permitting, spent an hour or two outside with them. Dances were scheduled every other Friday night, though sometimes the fiddler didn't show or other problems intervened. Mrs. Halliday, the matron, organized occasional parties, and Mrs. Van Norstrand invited a select few to tea in the family quarters. Donated newspapers came from around the state. There were pool tables, some books, and nightly card games. Even so, for most patients the hours ticked by like days, and days turned as slowly as seasons.

The woman who smeared feces on the walls and the fellow who turned his into a weapon could corrupt a ward, to say nothing of the stink from those who routinely soiled their beds. Members of the Visiting Committee showed up one day when the wings were especially ripe. At the annual meeting that fall they urged acquisition of hand-cranked fans of the type used in Kirkbride's hospital—a bright idea but a hopelessly inadequate solution.[35]

Sometimes it seemed that everything stank—patients, wards, even the surrounding grounds. The reek from water closets snaked along hallways and into patient rooms. Breezes brought the smell of the nearby cesspool through open windows. Air hanging over the dirt floor in the cellar, which was fouled by overflow sewage and rainwater, was drawn up ventilation flues. The kitchen generated a miasma of its own from vats of morning hash and ovens filled with meat, the vapors seeping up stairwells and down hallways of the central building. Living quarters were especially foul in winter. "In almost every ward will be found some who are the subjects of offensive physical disease, and the natural propensity of the insane to habits of unseemliness, even under the most watchful supervision, manifests itself in ways innumerable. To this may be added the physiological fact that persons of many of the insane, when in a state of high excitement, exhale an effluvium at once pungent, penetrating and almost ineradicable. It is also a well established fact that the more depraved and noxious the air becomes, the less moveable it is." No wonder patients were sickly after being shut up behind sealed windows through the long winter.[36]

There was a chronic shortage of fresh water. Stored in an enormous iron tank atop the central building—150 tons of dead weight balanced over the living quarters of hospital officers and their families as well as sixty patients—the supply was depleted at a rate of 25,000 gallons a day. "Filthy" patients and filthy rooms used up a disproportionate share. For the others, a bath and a change of underwear were weekly highlights. It is not hard to imagine the dynamics of the Saturday bath. Tubs were drained and refilled after every second or third bather. W'll some lout elbow his way into the fresh water, or will the attendants choose a hulk reeking from days spent grubbing roots or tending hogs? Imagine the tension among the frail, the depressed, the ever anxious, dreading immersion into murky brine just vacated by someone who in other circumstances they would have crossed the street to stay upwind of.[37]

The well had been unsatisfactory from the beginning. Its hard water clogged pipes with mineral deposits and then dried up altogether. In the mid-1870s engine-house pumps activated a pipeline from the lake, and the problem was apparently solved. Sewer pipes were also extended into the lake, and for the next decade superintendents and trustees alike convinced themselves that the lake was the solution to both the water shortage and the sewage disposal problem. But there was no ignoring the great plumes of evil vegetation that blossomed around the sewer drain, just as "fresh" water from the intake pipe a third of a mile distant became ever more cloudy and pungent. Ice was harvested from the lake, and eventually even the ice house smelled like a sewer. A decade after both problems had been "solved," a colossal summer die-off deposited tons of fish virtually at the hospital's doorstep. Years later a typhoid epidemic left seven dead and sickened dozens more, patients and attendants alike. For the third time work crews descended into the troublesome well, finally drilling through layers of quicksand and rock and tapping into an artesian well vast enough to provide all the water the hospital needed.[38]

An attendant's work day ended when his last patient was bedded down and quiet. As his own room was just down the hall, this depended on when the last screamer shut up and the last excited newcomer quit pacing and got to bed. Like the superintendent, the assistant physician, and the matron, attendants had virtually no life outside the institution aside from an occasional evening or day off, granted by special permission. That did not stop some of the males from showing up at a notorious tavern nearby. Smith and Mooney came back drunk time and again. Once the night watchman found them throwing up on the kitchen floor. Much as these and others may have angered Van Norstrand, including a few who were quick with their fists, he was too short-handed to fire every attendant who broke the rules.[39]

It was no wonder that good workers were hard to come by, especially males. Superintendents across the country bemoaned the scarcity of the "right kind" of applicants. "They are in fact plain every-day men and women, with the common infirmities of the race, losing their temper under extraordinary irritations, and sometimes guilty of downright abuse of their trust," wrote Dr. Isaac Ray, a prominent eastern superintendent.[40] The annual turnover during Van Norstrand's tenure averaged over 100 percent.[41] The hospital employed from five to seven male attendants at any one time. Typically, one or two new names showed up on the payroll each month, while others dropped off. Men were paid 25 dollars a month, women only 14, yet women tended to stay on indefinitely, perhaps finding in the job a sense of community in addition to room, board, and a small income. Cooks, laundresses, seamstresses, the teamster, the carpenter, and others might help out in a pinch, but the routine good order, cleanliness, and tranquility of the wards depended almost exclusively upon the attendants. Thus year after year, about a dozen attendants, male and female, ruled over a patient population of from 170 to 180, or 15 per attendant. Pity those who waded into the lower wards each morning, urging the incoherent and the filthy from their straw-filled mattresses, or who threw open the doors of the fourth-floor strong rooms—here a wild-eyed stalker, there a lump in the corner, and down the hall, a ranting wall-pounder. But even on the second and third floors there were enough shifty characters to keep an experienced attendant on his toes, much less a new kid yet to be tested. In the words of Dr. John Wilson, who became assistant physician after Sawyer moved on, "Patients are more inclined to attack new than old attendants. Patients are cunning about that. They can look at a man and seem to know whether they can manage him or not, and whether the attendant has any stamina or not." The inmates did not run the asylum, but many tried.[42]

You would never know from the reports of the Visiting Committee that such strains existed. With a revolving membership of two trustees and a physician from the community, the committee was one of those checks and balances built into the system to detect problems. In theory, a member of the committee could show up at any time to observe hospital life as it really was and not as someone in authority wanted to depict it. Did patients seem fearful? Was there an overdependence on bed straps, straitjackets, or narcotics? Did patients complain of mistreatment? Were they kept active? Did the superintendent and his assistant appear at ease with their charges and in control? Was the food healthy and nutritious? Were the wards as tidy and clean smelling as circumstances permitted? Above all, did the superintendent generate a sense of confidence and optimism among patients and staff?

A year and a half after Van Norstrand took over, the Visiting Committee found room for improvement. Hallways were still dark and airless, sitting rooms as yet unadorned with artwork, the library hardly worth the name. But they had nothing but praise for the new superintendent. "We have seen perceptibly growing from month to month a confidence and trust on the part of the inmates in the officers of the institution, which has been well pleasing to your committee."[43]

A different view emerges from the letters of some patients and families. Chester Malloy eloped from the hospital early one March, arriving at his home in Oshkosh on frostbitten feet a week later. His wife wrote Van Norstrand that after an earlier escape attempt, an attendant "caught [Chester] and threw him on the cellar floor choking him until the blood ran from his nose. I never saw a person so thankful for anything as he was to get home, and he is so opposed to going back, I think I shall let him remain at home for the present." A delusional bachelor farmer composed a letter to his "beloved

Mary, My dearest love and devoted friend and eternal help for Eternity, in whose loving Arms [I] will soon be resting [my breaking?] heart & head on thy loving Bosom, nestling [my] face between as it were two clusters of Grapes as noted in one of Solomon's Songs of love." Woven among biblical allusions and evocations of an earthy soulmate are accounts of beatings inflicted by room-mates and attendants: "In said 2 General fights I had my head so pounded that Even to this day the left lobe of Brain is painful and causes the blood & slime matter to run out of my norstrill. I had also my left breast bone struck & my 5 left ribs dislocated from my back bone which causes me sharp pains."[44]

Letters alleging mistreatment were sent to Governor Lewis a few months after Van Norstrand took over. One former patient insisted that she and many other perfectly sane women were held against their will, anguishing over their families and "the injustice of [being] under lock and key. O that I could betell all I know concerning that house to some influential man who would interest himself for the sufferers who are imprisoned there." She was not impressed by Dr. Van Norstrand. "I do not think they have bettered [the hospital] much in changing superintendents."[45]

Herbert Bird knew hospital life. His father ran the laundry. His mother worked in the dining room, a sister in the sewing room. Herbert had started on the wards at eighteen: "It is not pleasant for new attendants. Patients will not recognize them as such or obey them. A new one has to speak authoritatively and make it appear he intended to carry it out. New attendants have to resort to violence to the patients at times." Emeline Richards and Anna Wilson, who worked among the most difficult females, tried to manage patients without resorting to violence but soon gave up the experiment: "[The patients] got so that they drove us and tried to put the muff on us." Imagine what it must have been like for Eliza Giesken, who was sixteen when she began work on the middle ward. Even five years later, as the most experienced of the female attendants, she was still fighting for her life: "Sometimes [the women] pitch into us and we have to defend ourselves."[46]

The most common technique was a choke hold. Usually attendants worked together, one gripping the patient by the throat while
the other tripped him to the floor. The goal was to end up with your
knees on his chest, your hands around his throat. Such methods were
neither authorized nor reported. Typically only two attendants were
assigned to each ward of thirty or more patients, several of whom
might spiral out of control more or less simultaneously while others
stood by calculating their own opportunities. No wonder workers
felt they had to strike first. But to patients it seemed that certain
attendants were always looking for an excuse to bully and humiliate
the most vulnerable among them.[47]

Van Norstrand took much of this in stride as "the usual little jar-
rings in the ward." In fact, survival of the fittest seems to have been
a basic rule of hospital life. He acknowledged that at times a patient
might become the de facto ruler of his ward—through reputation,
size, cunning, and occasionally, possession of a knife. Certainly some
attendants were bullies and thieves who feasted upon the frightened
and the demented. But others caught off guard were beaten and
sometimes crippled by rogue patients, as were other patients. To bring
a bloody terror under control, staff often had no choice but to swarm
and smother, strapping him into a muff and locking him away.[48]

How all this would be remembered later was in the eye, and
the intentions, of the beholder. As Van Norstrand reminded fellow
superintendents at one national convention, "We all have a class of
patients who are ready to make trouble for us if they can, and those
of us who are also positive men will have enemies ready to assist
these people in making trouble."[49]

TWELVE

A Critical and Searching Examination

There was no turning back from the course charted by the "brethren," as the first members of the Association of Medical Superintendents of American Institutions for the Insane liked to call themselves.[1] Thirty-six state hospitals opened their doors between 1824 and 1860, most based on the Kirkbride plan.[2] The patient population roughly doubled every decade for much of the century, from 2,500 in 1840 to 74,000 fifty years later.[3] Hospitals became permanent shelters for the chronically insane, way-stations for the acutely ill, and virtual hospice centers for late-stage syphilitics and other degenerative cases. But by the mid-1860s it was apparent that they did not cure insanity. Sedative medications, rich diets, clean linen, warm rooms, "amusements," and pastoral views from the windows of scientifically arranged, no-expense-spared temples of caring were essentially palliatives, not cures. Many were comforted but few were healed, and by mid-century public optimism had given way to exasperation. What had gone wrong?

So much had been invested, yet so little had changed. Annual reports still celebrated the therapeutic virtues of kindness and caring, of wholesome labor and amusements, but increasingly legislators, newspaper editors, and family members were drawn to darker tales from other sources. Disillusionment bred a search for scapegoats.

The demon haunting every superintendent's dreams—the crusading former patient who is both credible and persistent—emerged just over the border in Illinois during the early years of Van Norstrand's tenure at the Wisconsin hospital. Elizabeth Packard had been committed to the state hospital at Jacksonville by her clergyman husband. It took her years to fight her way out through the courts. She came out angry and stayed that way, writing, speaking, and confronting legislators. Her anger was contagious and spread across state lines. She became the most famous of many former patients whose revelations inflamed the public and sparked reform movements well into the twentieth century. The superintendent at the Illinois hospital lost his job and eventually killed himself. He was not the only one. Suicide, physical or mental breakdown, death at the hands of a patient: such were the occupational hazards of those who assumed absolute authority over public hospitals for the insane.[4]

Each of Van Norstrand's three predecessors had stumbled early, lost the confidence of the board, and been forced out under humiliating circumstances. Similar dramas were played out in state after state. Careers and reputations were ruined by scandal, by disgruntled legislatures, by the hounding of the press. At annual conventions and in some annual reports, superintendents expressed bewilderment and anger, seeing themselves as martyrs to an unenlightened citizenry and grudge-poisoned patients. Yet for nearly four years, as unlikely a candidate for sainthood as Abraham Van Norstrand remained at the helm, unchallenged and virtually unquestioned. How did he do it? Independent to the point of surliness, he nonetheless alternately charmed and browbeat a variety of constituencies—legislators, trustees, the medical community, county officials, and patients' families. Although essentially pragmatic and authoritarian, he convinced reformers that he was an enlightened practitioner of moral treatment. Above all, he satisfied hard-headed trustees and legislators concerned primarily with economy and good order. Under Van Norstrand, the hospital finally came together as an enterprise and flourished.

"The Dr. looks as though his duties agree with him and [he] has years of usefulness before him," the editor of the *Jefferson Banner* observed.[5] "We are not disposed to dispute the superintendent's anti-utopian views in regard to the treatment of the insane," key legislators reported two years later. "He is well posted in regard to all such theories and selects from them such as his judgment recommends, feeling that the treatment of the insane has advanced as rapidly as any other science for the last half century [and that] chains, perpetual solitary confinement, cold, hunger, filth and neglect [have been replaced by] kindness, proper medicine, warm rooms, good beds, good food and plenty of it, books, lectures, singing, riding, boating [and] cheerful care with quiet and unfatiguing agricultural labor."[6]

Again and again the trustees boasted that in Van Norstrand they had finally found their man. In the spring of 1865, with the uproar over Reverend Kellogg's death still ringing in their ears, they concluded that it was an "unavoidable accident," and they applauded "the present harmony and good feeling that exists between officers, patients and attendants" at the hospital.[7] This sentiment was repeated in the report of the Visiting Committee: "Neatness and good order have uniformly prevailed, respect and friendly greetings interchanged, and the most agreeable harmony has been plainly exhibited. Our confidence in the medical, sanitary and moral arrangements of the institution by the officers in charge has been increased and strengthened."[8] Under Van Norstrand, they asserted, their hospital ranked among the best in the country.[9]

Yet if they admired him as a professional, the best they could muster in the way of personal praise was to acknowledge his "tact and energy."[10] It is as though they did not feel completely comfortable with him, unlike his assistant, Doctor John Sawyer, whom they extolled for his "energy, firmness and untiring zeal. . . . Always at his post, always courteous, affable and gentlemanly."[11] When Sawyer resigned to become superintendent at prestigious Butler Hospital in Providence, Rhode Island, they sent him off with a resolution of thanks for his "constant devotion to the service, and his many attractive [traits] of character."[12] For the superintendent they expressed respect and support; for his assistant, affection and trust.

Whether or not they warmed to Van Norstrand, they had confidence in him and he knew it. With the Kellogg scandal behind him he wasted no time petitioning for a raise. He was being paid only three-quarters of the salary offered to eastern doctors who had turned down the job. Pay up or cut me loose; that was the challenge buried in the deferential prose of his letter. They promptly increased his salary.

He felt even more confident dealing with legislators. Word got around that if they showed up on the morning steamer, chilled by the autumn mist, he would welcome them into the family quarters and warm them with hospital whiskey and friendly repartee before personally taking them on tour.[13] The war had taught him a lesson in public relations, having been seduced himself by good food, fine drink, and flattery. Barely six weeks after Kellogg's death he put that lesson to use, bringing sixty members of the legislature through a snowstorm to party at the hospital. It was an elaborate affair for his staff to pull off, with music and "tableaux" enacted by patients and attendants followed by a late supper. "The hours passed on flying feet," a correspondent wrote. "Observers were struck with the good judgment of Dr. Van Norstrand in allowing his harmless patients to witness and participate in the festivities."[14] Several days later the legislature's Committee on Benevolent Institutions issued a glowing report on the condition of the hospital and introduced a bill to provide funds for the purchase of more land and the construction of two more wings.[15]

Van Norstrand became the state's acknowledged expert on diseases of the mind. With the blessing of the trustees he spent months visiting eastern hospitals and meeting with leaders of the hospital movement. He attended conventions of the association of superintendents and spoke up like an old hand. In 1868 he was asked to address the state medical society. He made a great occasion of it, bringing the members across Lake Mendota on sleighs provided by Governor Fairchild, touring them through the hospital, including a creepy trek down the engine house tunnel. They sat for a "splendid collation" in the patients' dining room. After dinner he professed deep humility at standing before such a distinguished body—the usual fawning disclaimers with which he stoked his boiler and brought his mental engine to life. His topic was the origins of insanity. He made passing reference to the research and theories of acknowledged experts but concluded that no one had any answers yet. The absence of lesions on the brain continued to confound them. If the brain was the seat of the disease, where was the evidence? Would advanced instruments like the microscope find it, or were they looking in the wrong place? "The more we study this disease, the less are we disposed to believe that the mind itself is subject to disease, but only manifests a corporeal disorder, or more properly the corporeal disease manifests its existence through the mind."

He was uncomfortable with this chicken-and-egg dilemma, as well he should have been. No one knew what caused insanity or even how to define it. But they knew it when they saw it. He was on firmer ground in urging early intervention, one of the tenets of the association of superintendents. It was essential for the family doctor to get his patient to the hospital as soon as he detected symptoms—"[He] sleeps not, walks about the house at all hours of the night, does not seem to notice or enjoy the children, has lost all sexual desire or taken an unreasonable dislike to his wife or other friends, charging them with various improper acts. You see [him] before permanent organic changes have taken place. It is then that the best skill and appliances in medical science is available in establishing a favorable prognosis." In other words, get him to the hospital while treatment can still be effective. Don't expect him to get better at home. "You have no facilities for moral treatment, you cannot separate him from the scenes causing or accompanying his insanity—domestic affliction, connubial infelicity, business disaster, overwork. If he is filthy, you have no bath tub or properly tempered water or trained attendants to see that he is clean."

He recited formulaic cure rates: 80 percent for those hospitalized during the first month of their first "attack," 75 percent for those brought in within the first three months, 45 percent if admission is delayed up to one year, and 20 percent at best for all others. His message boiled down to this: an admission delayed is a life destroyed.

Fuzzy theory, standard advice, and boiler-plate statistics: it was a conventional presentation until the very end, when he spoke with rare candor. He might have been talking about himself:

"The universal ambition for public station, power, wealth and social position is telling fearfully on the present generation. We have cut loose from the pastoral simplicity of the ancients and are rioting in all manner of excesses. The well balanced, non-excitable brain can bear the disappointment of defeat, but the unbalanced, sensitive brain gives way to shock. Mental ruin is the result. Let us constitute ourselves the psychological guardians of our less fortunate fellow beings. It is for them we toil today. It may be for one of ourselves tomorrow."

The doctors returned to the city, "highly pleased with their trip, and all speaking in the highest terms of the condition of the Wisconsin Insane Asylum."[16]

Woe be to anyone who dared tread on his toes. In the spring of 1866 the Visiting Committee turned in a report that began with the usual bromides—"Conditions uniformly found good. . . . [Patients] appear contented, without complaint of being ill-used. . . . Economy in fuel by burning in the furnace all brush, grubs and stumps,"—but then took an unexpected turn. Out of these placid waters leaps sharptoothed criticism, aimed directly at Dr. Van Norstrand. It appears to have been a parting shot from Dr. J. J. Brown, the physician whose term on the committee was about to expire. "Medical treatment is the most important [function of the hospital] and the most likely to be neglected. Care should be taken to make [the institution] what it purports to be, a Hospital for the Insane."[17] No specifics were given. For a committee whose reports traditionally tended to smooth feathers rather than ruffle them, this was strong language.

Van Norstrand waited six months to respond, using the annual report as his forum. Was he being accused of shortchanging patients to spend time on other matters—the farm, construction of the new wings, and so on? If so, his accuser had no conception of the enormity of a superintendent's responsibilities.

"The man who takes his text books on Anatomy, Therapeutics and Practice and shuts himself up in his study, only leaving it to visit his patients, will become very deep and mysterious on page, chapter, verse, pennyweights and grains, but what he acquires in depth will be at the expense of breadth and comprehensiveness. Our superintendents are not only expected to superintend the Medical Departments of the Hospital but to be competent to superintend construction and repairs about his Hospital; direct in conducting the farm; management of domestic animals; the intelligent and economical expenditure of appropriations for the support of his house; to conduct or direct large correspondence with the friends of his patients; to make the proper discrimination as to who shall be admitted and who discharged."[18]

In characterizing a superintendent as much more than a narrow specialist, he echoed the position of the association. Their unique calling elevated superintendents high atop the hospital hierarchy—literally "living over a volcano"[19]—with unprecedented responsibilities. At such heights, a balanced, grounded sense of self could easily give way to something dangerously grand. Van Norstrand's rebuttal smacks of such grandiosity and begs the down-to-earth question that Brown raised: were patients receiving adequate medical care, and if not, what should be done about it?

Members of his extended family began to appear on the payroll. Sister-in-law Augusta Hebard started in the sewing room but was soon distributing medications and supervising female attendants. Father-in-law George Hebard, the former hotel keeper in Aztalan, drew a salary as an odd jobs man, maintaining flower gardens around the hospital and doling out tobacco to patients. Troubled young Fred Van Norstrand dropped out of Beloit College and soon combined the role of apprentice attendant, at eighteen dollars a month, with that of privileged son, to the chagrin of patients stung by his heavy-handedness and immaturity. Although not on the payroll, Mrs. Van Norstrand was the official hostess at parties held for patients and a frequent visitor to the female wards. Attendants were convinced that she favored the more genteel class of patients, confining her visits to the rooms of a select few. Van Norstrand occasionally bought livestock from his brother, Elias, personally estimating each animal's weight and value, an exchange that invariably fattened Elias's purse, though whether the hospital also benefited was in dispute.[20]

In every annual report Dr. Van Norstrand reminded his audience of the enormity of his responsibilities. The range of topics he covered was exhaustive: the status of the wings under construction; crop yields from wheat to rutabagas; statistical tables listing the origins, occupations, and mental status of patients present and past; physical plant and security issues such as boiler repairs and the need for safety bars over the windows of the new wings; the type and cost of replacement furnishings required from the state prison workshop and surplus blankets purchased by the hundreds from the army. . . . He boasted of prizes awarded hospital animals and produce at the state fair, complained about drinking establishments in nearby Westport and young sightseers who larked through the halls taunting patients. He dwelled on favored themes: the importance of early hospitalization and the pernicious effects of lying to the sick as a ploy to gain their cooperation. It made life easier for the deputy if his passenger was expecting an audience with the governor, but it was hell for the doctors and attendants when instead he was dragged into the hospital.*

Year after year he attributed the absence of epidemic disease and the relatively low death rate to a healthful location and an abundance of nutritious food. He rated Dr. Sawyer as the best assistant physician anywhere. He even praised Miss Dorothea Dix, "that great philanthropist, friend of the unfortunate and accomplished lady," for her donation of books to the hospital library, confining his reflections about her "excess of desire for notoriety and lack of Christian

---

* What those who argued for early admission failed to acknowledge was that family members and sometimes family doctors tended to recognize the severity of the sickness they were dealing with only gradually and reluctantly. They would argue, plead, pamper, and punish in hopes of influencing a return to normalcy. It made no sense to rush a wife or a father to the hospital because of screwy thoughts or a bout of the blues. Who could afford to part with the man who kept the farm going or the woman who kept the house? Except in cases of violence or frightening dementia, hospitalization tended to be their last resort, not the first as superintendents urged.

humility" to his private papers.[21]

But nowhere does he address the concern raised by Dr. Brown. It is as though the medical treatment he provided spoke for itself. Proper treatment was a given; it was what hospitals did. Brown was not the only official visitor with concerns, but he appears to have been the only one to make his public. Officials faced a hard choice. Suppose a trustee or a member of the legislature arrived without warning, intent on getting candid impressions of hospital life, only to be intercepted by the superintendent and entertained in his family quarters for an hour or two while the morning cleanup was underway on the wards. During that time he was likely to discover that he and the superintendent had much in common, being ambitious transplants from New England with similar views on the topics of the day.

And if on subsequent visits he was led through the same three or four wards but never other, noisier and more chaotic ones, well, he could understand from the superintendent's frank explanations why impromptu visits to certain areas might be upsetting to patients. If he encountered the same attendants again and again but never had a word with others, well, once again, who was he to second-guess the superintendent or his much-admired assistant? The food was plentiful if repetitive and plain, the floors were clean, the laborers went off to their chores, the attendants had plenty to do without passing the time of day with well-meaning outsiders. No one claimed perfection. The officers were the first to admit deficiencies both as to physical plant and activities for patients. Hallways were barren and dark; female patients suffered for lack of regular outdoor vocations. But all that was freely admitted, and more experienced minds than his were devising solutions. It was true that strong odors seeped from under certain doors and chilling cries came from certain iron-covered windows, but who was he to demand access to that particular ward, that troubled patient, that specific attendant, and thus risk confrontation, unpleasantness, or worse—exposure to some abomination that he was utterly unprepared to deal with? Why risk hard feelings between honorable men who enjoyed a comradely relationship?[22]

* * *

The bylaws the trustees had adopted were virtually identical to those recommended by the Association of Medical Superintendents of American Institutions for the Insane. One specified that the superintendent was to pay "strict and daily attention to all patients," but it appears that Van Norstrand gradually yielded much of that responsibility to his assistants, Dr. Sawyer through 1866, and thereafter Dr. John Wilson, the son of his former subordinate in the Fourth Wisconsin. The assistant was required to make rounds twice daily. His duties were largely confined to patient care, whereas the superintendent was spread over the whole hospital and beyond. Daily rounds could thus evolve into a tedious and redundant activity when construction issues, farm crises, and letters from anguished relatives begged for attention. One can imagine Van Norstrand at first deciding as a matter of clinical judgment *not* to subject himself to daily abuse from certain patients until they had come down from their mania or up from their funk. How often should he have to contend with the maniac who demanded immediate release because enemies were stealing his treasure and poisoning his herd? How often must he attempt to elicit a civilized utterance from an evil-smelling wretch hibernating under her skirt? And once he began to avoid certain patients, it was easy to skip the wards where they lived or to fly through in a few minutes. He was the best judge of which ones benefited from his presence and which did not. Let bylaws be a guide, not a straitjacket.[23]

It also appears that over time, unspecified business in Madison increasingly demanded his attention, sometimes two or three days a week. Eventually it was revealed that Dr. Van Norstrand was back in the retail business. In the summer of 1867 he had bought into a grocery store, becoming, in effect, a hidden partner in "J. W. Sumner & Co." For years Sumner had been a major supplier of staple goods to the hospital, often amounting to hundreds of dollars of business per month. The new partners bought out a competitor, Pardee and Clark, and moved to the Pardee and Clark location next to the post office. In newspaper advertisements Sumner & Co. boasted "a First Class Stock of Groceries of every description . . . , the most complete stock of goods ever brought to Madison," in particular "Fresh Drugs and Medicines and all the Principal Patent Medicines" plus "Choice Brandy, Wines and Liquors." Van Norstrand's name is nowhere to be found in the ads.[24]

One day in August, just after Sumner & Co. had taken possession of its former competitor, the hospital teamster returned from his daily trip to town and carted an old coffee sack into the kitchen. It smelled to high heaven but not of coffee. Inside were over a hundred pounds of smoked halibut. He also delivered a batch of overripe eggs, a large amount of foul tobacco, and "dirty black sugar." Pardee and Clark had set the tobacco aside for use as sheep-dip and designated the other goods for the garbage heap, but Van Norstrand had looked it over and decided it was good enough for the hospital.[25] Over the next six months, Superintendent Van Norstrand purchased nearly all the hospital's groceries, drugs, and even paint from Mr. Van Norstrand, storekeeper. Had he found another way to enrich himself on the sly? To some people it certainly looked that way.[26]

A troubling letter awaited the trustees when they gathered in the spring of 1867: "Having been in the employ of your Institution about three years it would seem natural that I should take some interest in its welfare. Hoping and trusting that our institution may become second to none other in the land, I think it is necessary to Purge it from Dr. Van Norstrand and his relatives." The writer listed six reasons why Van Norstrand should go, including "Abuse of patients, Extravagant management of the public funds, making himself and family principle recipients of said funds, Lack of Moral character. . . ." It ended, "Hoping Gentlemen that you will give the above a careful investigation," and was signed, "Levi Decker."

They had been down this road before. Similar charges were leveled against Van Norstrand's predecessor, J. P. Clement. Then they had done their duty as they saw it, embarking on an investigation that exonerated Clement but also destroyed him. The process energized those who wished to harm him and undermined his own fragile confidence and ultimately the confidence of the trustees in him. Since then the board had become thick-skinned. Patients complained, families complained, and God knew that disgruntled former employees complained. Still, Decker's charges could not be ignored, and a committee of three volunteered to look into them.[27]

But it seems that Decker had gotten cold feet. He was merely a citizen who had heard some things that might interest them, he told the committee. He refused to give sworn testimony. If the trustees were happy with Van Norstrand, so be it. He had nothing more to say. The committee concluded, "As a whole, the charges complained of were decided improvements." A false alarm, or so it seemed at the time.[28]

One of the signers of that report was Samuel Hastings, the well-known social crusader and former state treasurer. Hastings was a newcomer to the board, having been appointed the previous year by Governor Lucius Fairchild.[29] With his reputation for integrity and financial wizardry, Hastings had been showered with job offers when he left public office. He became president of a local insurance company and a petroleum company, proprietor of an agricultural equipment factory, and treasurer of three firms including a railroad.[30] No wonder he did not immediately warm to this new responsibility thrust upon him by the governor. During his first year on the board he was virtually invisible. He would have known of the concerns raised by Dr. Brown, and he was on the committee that looked into Decker's charges, but his name rarely appeared in the trustees' journal that year. But at the board's annual meeting in October he became very visible indeed.

Even among the Codfish Aristocracy where family trees were like mighty English oaks, Samuel Dexter Hastings's pedigree stood taller than most. He traced his ancestors back to the age of legend, from Danish raiders who fathered the intimates of English kings, to proud dissenters seeking religious freedom in the new world. The family motto, "In Truth Is Victory," sailed through the generations like an arrow from a long bow to animate young Samuel Dexter Hastings, described by one writer as a man "who will do right though heavens fall." At fourteen he left Boston for Philadelphia, eager to begin a mercantile career and improve himself through "self-drill and self-dependence." Soon he was active in the abolitionist Liberty Party. An early settler in La Crosse ("little more than a succession of sand heaps," he recalled in old age), on the Mississippi River, he established a general store and was the town librarian. He authored the city charter, was town clerk, served in the first state legislature, ran for governor (on the Prohibition ticket), and was named Right Worthy Grand Templar of the Good Templars and Grand Worthy Patriarch of the Sons of Temperance. An admirer wrote: "He was as pure in thought, word and deed as the purest woman." In the early years of Wisconsin's statehood he visited nearly every county, exhorting audiences on the evils of slavery. Later in life it was the evils of drink he crusaded against, lecturing from Ireland to Tasmania and throughout the United States. He would have become a rich man, friends believed, but for his devotion to "the reformatory and philanthropic movements of the times."[31]

Since 1861 Hastings had also served on the board of trustees of the Northwestern Mutual Life Insurance Company, soon to become the "largest moneyed interest" in the northwest. There was considerable cross-pollination between the hospital and Northwestern Mutual. Simeon Mills, a long-time Madison banker, was an early and long-serving trustee of the hospital as well as the insurance company. Leonard Farwell, the former governor upon whose land the hospital had been built, was one of the founders of the company. Other hospital trustees also had connections to Northwestern Mutual.[32]

During the war, Hastings's "purity in thought, word and deed" had been sorely tested by simultaneous allegiances to the state and the insurance company. As state treasurer he spoke out in support of a recently passed law under attack from many in the insurance industry. The *Wisconsin State Journal* printed his letter in full, although at several thousand words it filled three columns. He insisted on the integrity of legislators who supported the law and attacked insurance agents who tried to discredit it. No doubt, as he claimed, the law protected consumers by requiring insurance companies to make deposits with the state to prove their viability. But nowhere in the letter did Hastings disclose his own association with Northwestern Mutual, which stood to benefit from the law by thinning out the competition.[33]

His association with the company would have brought him into contact with Amherst Kellogg, one of its longest-serving officers and also a member of its board. By 1867 Amherst was a prosperous man. His salary was twice that of Superintendent Van Norstrand. No doubt his brother's death at the hospital two years earlier, and the manner in which Dr. Van Norstrand had dealt with it, were still very much on his mind. Like Hastings he was a crusading Protestant, a stout supporter of moral uplift and social reform, and keenly alert to the scent of impropriety. And like Hastings he was self-made. It is not difficult to imagine them falling into easy conversation over many shared interests, the hospital in particular. In his new position as a hospital trustee, Hastings would have been especially receptive to Amherst's long-standing grievances against Dr. Van Norstrand. He would have known about the Packard scandal in Illinois, which had people across the country wondering what *really* went on in their own state hospital. So it may well have been Amherst who forced his hand. Here from the lips of a trustworthy colleague was a horror story about the institution he had sworn to serve. Maybe he could dismiss the Decker letter in good conscience, and the Packard affair was not his worry, but this bloody death at his own hospital, with its unsatisfactory resolution and the self-serving explanations of the superintendent, was something he could not shrug off. When he accepted a seat on the board he may have hoped that the hospital would remain a sleeping giant so that he could devote his energies to more profitable pursuits, but when trustees assembled for their annual meeting in October he was a changed man, a hunter who had caught a scent.

Did Van Norstrand detect an emergent note of coolness, even mistrust, from certain quarters over the summer of 1867? If so, it did not dampen his outspokenness. The annual report he read to the board on October 22 bristled with frustration. Some members wanted more emphasis on "moral treatment" and more outdoor activities for women. These things were all well and good, but medical treatment was paramount, and a superintendent could not in good conscience divert time and resources to lesser priorities. Medical treatment was worth "more than either [moral or occupational treatment] in the acute stage of the disease. . . . I find much more use for certain classes of medicines than when in private practice. Stimulants, tonics, sedatives, deobstruents [*sic*], anaphrodisiacs, emenagogues, and anti-periodics are in daily use here; thereby shortening the period of excitement and recovery, and if recovery is not affected, improving the bodily health and diminishing the per cent of mortality."[34]

In this he reflected the attitude of most superintendents. Why should doctors run these places if medical care was not the primary consideration?[35] Yet he complained too much. When Dr. Brown found fault with the medical care he provided, Van Norstrand countered that a good superintendent must be a generalist, manipulating the many nonmedical facets of hospital life to the patients' advantage, not an ivory tower specialist. But when trustees tweaked him for not being enough of a generalist to provide activities consistent with the moral treatment model, he argued that he was accomplishing far more for his patients by devoting resources to medical care than they would ever get out of moral treatment. He was a prickly man.

As for those idle women they were so concerned about, he tossed the problem back to them: "I have thought much on this subject, and see by the memoranda of our visiting committee that they bravely recommend [out-of-door employment for females]. Public sentiment will not allow us to send them to pick up stones, pull weeds, or hoe among the corn, potatoes, or root crops because they have been educated from infancy to avoid out-of-door air and sunlight as vulgar and damaging to the complexion. Cannot you assist, by your advice and influence, American superintendents in this matter—to afford some rational out-of-door employment to convalescent and incurable insane females? I sincerely hope your deliberations will assist me in this matter." In other words, if you think it's such a problem, you figure out what to do about it.[36]

But if there was friction with some trustees on some issues, for the most part he and they were too preoccupied with practical matters to battle over theory. Plastering and flooring in the new wings had to be accelerated and furnishings delivered if the patient population was to be doubled on schedule. As instructed by the board he had transferred a number of veterans to the government hospital in Washington. Nearby taverns were still a headache, as were belligerent young visitors who came to taunt and sneer. "The farm has yielded abundantly, and well repaid our labor. . . ." Mattress ticking, sheets and cured hair for the new beds had been acquired; the state prison was manufacturing frames. In closing he acknowledged "the many unexpected expressions of confidence manifested towards me by your Honorable Board." Hardly the thoughts of someone worried that he might be on thin ice with his bosses.[37]

If his own report was mostly routine, the same cannot be said of the one put together by the board's executive committee. The reading opened with the usual litany of chronic problems, and this may have lulled him—defaulting contractors, delays in construction, the high cost of heating—but then came two recommendations that would have set off alarms. There were problems in the acquisition of supplies for the hospital. Store owners complained that they had been denied "a share of trade [with the hospital], and [they] are too apt to charge its officers with dishonesty in participating in the profits thereof." No sooner had he caught his breath from that surprise than they came at him from another direction, declaring that routine visits by of members of the Visiting Committee and other trustees "cannot give more than a superficial glance at [the hospital's] workings." That was a departure. Year after year they had assured him and the public that those visits provided all the evidence they needed to reaffirm their confidence in the hospital and its administration. Now, suddenly, such visits had been deemed irrelevant. Why? "Your committee would call the attention of the Board to the fact that the Hospital has been in operation upwards of seven years, during which time nothing like a critical and searching examination has been made in its internal economy, its expenditures, its general habits, and the doings of its officers."[38]

"A critical and searching examination." Words to echo through a superintendent's sleepless nights.

On day two of the annual meeting Samuel Hastings was appointed to the Visiting Committee. Hastings also read a response to the executive committee's recommendations and offered several resolutions, all of which were passed. From now on the superintendent was to publicly invite bids on groceries, medicines, and other regular purchases. Also, a committee of three was to be appointed, at three dollars a day each, to undertake that "critical and searching examination." It was to report back in six months, at the next spring meeting. One of the three volunteers was Samuel Hastings.[39]

If Van Norstrand had gone to the annual meeting confident that he was still the engineer and that the trustees expected the same old milk run with stops at Concern, Deference, and Reassurance, those two resolutions and the unseen forces that precipitated them must have shaken him deeply. His hands were still on the levers, but someone outside had pulled a switch, cogs had been engaged, the train rerouted onto an unfamiliar track leading God knows where. Their faces, presumably, were as friendly as ever, their voices as genial, but suddenly they had set themselves apart. It was a sleight of hand facilitated by *Jefferson's Manual* or some other legislatively sanctioned alternative calculus for the redistribution of authority within governing bodies; it had happened in front of his eyes but it felt like something done behind his back. What had they found out? Who was behind this?*

Maybe he started sniffing around. Had some of his people been talking to trustees behind his back? Had anyone seen him administering necessary discipline without understanding the seriousness of the infraction or the salutary effect of stern measures promptly

---

* Jefferson's Manual was the basis for The Legislative Manual of the State of Wisconsin.

applied? Neither attendants nor patients ever saw the full picture. Few understood that sometimes decisive action was required for the good of the house, the maintenance of order, and respect for authority. Superintendents made enemies. Enemies made trouble. Sooner or later every superintendent found himself in trouble. That was the cross those in his overly scrutinized but under-appreciated calling had to bear. Meanwhile, he must carry on like a hardworking public servant with nothing to hide.

THIRTEEN

Patients that Manifested a Dislike to Dr. Van Norstrand

Did Samuel Hastings know what he was getting into? If he had been talking to Amherst Kellogg and others with grievances, he probably did. Done right, this project would inflict wounds and ignite controversy. At any rate, he was destined to earn those three dollars a day, as would the other members of the special commit-tee, John Chassell Sherwood and Franklin Sheldon Lawrence. As young pioneers from Herkimer County, New York, Sherwood and his brother had built a sawmill and a gristmill in the wilderness near Green Lake. Later he added a resort and called it "Sherwood Forest." It was the first playground in the area to cater to the well-heeled.[1] Lawrence, a Vermonter, had farmed near Madison for some years before settling in Janesville and pursuing a more certain livelihood clerking at insurance, banking, and municipal offices, where he could utilize his gift for figures and record-keeping.[2]

Of all the paperwork the investigation must have generated—memos, schedules, meeting minutes, drafts of various kinds—only transcripts of interviews remain, plus a handful of letters from Hastings to Van Norstrand. There is no paper trail to shed light on how the investigators went about their business, no record of a gentlemen's agreement regarding their access to employees, case-books, financial records, and so on. Was Van Norstrand standoffish? Did he yield only grudgingly? Or did he let these outsiders search his files and interview employees at will? All the activity would have been a grand distraction for them and thus a test of his self-control whenever he came across attendants in hushed conversation. He managed to elicit from the committee an acknowledgement that he had been "courteous and gentlemanly," providing all documents requested and making every effort to assist, "save perhaps in the case of some matters connected with [Sumner & Co.]."[3] It would not have been easy for him. The first letters from Hastings arrived a few months after the fall meeting, and how they must have grated. Hastings's handwriting was like lacework, prim and symmetrical, with only an occasional flamboyant capital letter to hint at the depth of his passion. Line after precise line marched past Van Norstrand's eyes like Christian soldiers. It was a hand blissfully in step with the mind that guided it: "We find in examining the books of the Treasurer [Simeon Mills] that he acknowledges the receipt of various sums of money from you at different times, and upon inquiry of him as to the sources from which this money came, he is unable to inform us, stating that he has never received the information from you. Will you have the kindness to send us a statement in detail at your earliest convenience showing from what sources this money was received? Will you also have the kindness to furnish us with a copy of the rules and regulations adopted for the government of employees and the internal management of the hospital?"[4]

Will you have the kindness? In letter after letter the phrase pecks at his brain, now after accounting records, another time personnel lists, the return of transcripts of interviews. Van Norstrand's writing was an imperious scrawl, a cry of impatience. For all the lightning flashes, ink splashes, and exploding capitals, his hand could not keep up with his thoughts. He was furious to get on to the next item of business. Hastings's fastidiousness must have rubbed him raw: the scratching of a teetotal bookkeeper and stay-at-home do-gooder. As for Hastings, the deeper he dug, the more alert to deception and omission he became. Impatience began to leak through his frosty politeness: "I am led to think you are putting a construction upon one clause of my letter of the 25th different from what was intended. . . . We hardly supposed the items making up this large amount would be regarded as 'driblets.'"[5]

It must have occurred to Van Norstrand that the hospital was not the real object of the investigation. That was mere pretext. They were investigating him. Discovering another of Hastings's missives on his desk, or watching from his window as the former treasurer huddled in the yard with a farm hand or a cook or a teen-aged attendant, he must have known how Gulliver felt, roped down and probed by Lilliputians.

The commencement of a "critical and searching examination" set a great millstone in motion, grinding away toward what end no one could tell. After spending months reviewing records and interviewing patients and employees, Samuel Hastings asked the legislature for authority to convene formal hearings. These in turn took on a life of their own. New witnesses were forever being discovered and called, and former witnesses were called back for cross-examination or amplification. Weeks of testimony overlapped weeks of report writing. A majority report triggered requests from Van Norstrand for time to prepare a response, all of which culminated in the presentation of charges and countercharges before the trustees gathered for their spring meeting, when they in turn authorized further delays so that still more witnesses could be called and statements prepared.

The first round of interviews was held at the hospital. The investigating committee had compiled an extensive list of witnesses to call, beginning with hospital staff, including all thirteen attendants and each of the officers. The superintendent had to grit his teeth through petty indignities like setting aside a room for the committee and making employees available to testify, at which time they would no doubt be given every opportunity to stab him in the back.

On Monday, February 24, 1868, he was the first to be sworn in and take the stand. Among those present were the three committee members, a court commissioner, and someone to transcribe the testimony. Sherwood started the questioning, but it was Hastings who kept Van Norstrand on the stand for several days. Whatever their feelings for one another, the former treasurer and the superintendent conducted a civil dialogue. Van Norstrand was well prepared and forthcoming. He did not sound like a man on the hot seat, nor did committee members go at him like prosecuting attorneys. He was lightly pressed once or twice and lightly parried back. An observer might conclude that not much was at stake, though to Van Norstrand it might have seemed that they were simply handing him more and more rope.

There was much back and forth about procurement issues. When a grocer fills an order, how do you know you're getting an accurate weight? Does the state provide clothing for patients, and if so, how is it acquired? If this was rope, so be it. He reeled it in, responding to all such questions with apparent candor and at considerable length. As for the weights, that was a judgment call. He could not weigh everything. But certain storekeepers were more reliable than others, and certain items were more likely to be short-weighted. Eggs were counted; barrels less than full he sometimes weighed. As for clothing, the ladies in the sewing room made garments for women from calico and flannel, hard-wearing but far from fancy; low cost items were purchased for male patients in need. Above all, he pressed the patients' families to send clothes. The hospital was the last resource. Thus were a relatively few state dollars stretched for maximum benefit to all.

No one asked the obvious questions: Where do you buy most of your groceries? Are you not the majority owner of that store? Isn't that a conflict of interest?

Sherwood asked how Van Norstrand treated patients who arrived "highly excited, disposed to be noisy, moving restlessly to and fro." Again he responded in detail—observation, warm baths, a period of isolation if necessary, sedative tonics, redirection through conversation, and so on—which in turn led to the topic of physical restraint. Expecting this, he had brought some devices and he described the circumstances under which each might be put to use:

"A patient who is not very violent, moving about the wards, picking up straw, hair, buttons or other matters and putting them in the mouth and makes effort to swallow them [or who] undresses himself or other patients or pulls their hair, we use the continuing sleeves [straitjacket] upon. The strap and wristers we use where a patient has a strong propensity to strike attendants or others upon sudden impulse. These leave the hands at liberty, except they cannot raise them to strike."

The muff was used on strong, aggressive patients. The bed strap held down the suicidal or those too frantic to stay put voluntarily. Aggressive patients might be buckled into a chair with a seat strap. None of these devices could be used without his consent, although in emergencies consent was sought after the patient had already been restrained.[6]

Hastings: "In what cases do you employ isolation or solitary confinement?"

"In cases of persistent excitement. Also where they manifest willful violence toward the attendants, officers or other patients."

Hastings: "Do the attendants ever shut up a patient [in the strong room] without orders from an officer?"

"Yes sir, and report it at once to the officers. This is done where a patient strikes an attendant or other patient and is violent, and shows persistency in it. Very little of this [is] required among males, but more among females."

"Under what circumstances are the shuttered rooms in the fourth story used?"

"They are used when it becomes necessary to seclude a patient belonging to the upper ward. They are used for the same purpose [as] the strong rooms below, but are for a better class of patient."

"What is done for the amusement of patients?"

This was old business. Hastings had read the annual reports. He had questioned staff and patients, and he had recently attended a Friday night dance. But that did not keep him from asking the question or Van Norstrand, who obviously expected it, from answering in all the usual detail: "Divine service [on Sunday]. Sometimes a walk. Also, riding, skating, ball playing, quoits, swings, parties in the open air, picnics, boating." And indoors: "billiards, checkers, chess, backgammon, dominoes, bagatelle, matron's parties, theatricals," etc. He estimated how many patients participated in the various activities and how often.

This in turn led to an examination of the division of labor at the hospital—which jobs were done by employees and which were safe enough for the patients. The "safe" jobs also tended to be the most arduous, from stoking boilers to building roads to picking hops for neighboring farmers. Van Norstrand talked about how hard it was to recruit attendants. It was the same lament expressed by counterparts across the country: "We cannot keep a supply of attendants such as we desire. We find it difficult to get a first-class attendant to accept a position in the lower ward[s]. My two best attendants are between 19 and 22 years old," evidence, apparently, that much as he desired maturity and "mental ingenuity" in his caregivers, physical stamina was the first requirement.

Hastings asked about guests entertained at state expense and about the amount of whiskey consumed annually. Family members or deputies arriving with a new patient late in the day were invited to stay over, the superintendent answered, although "If they are not cleanly we send them to the hotel across the way." Visiting legislators and other VIPs sometimes asked for liquor "to keep them warm in crossing the lake. I let them have it."

Several potentially explosive topics were raised during his last two days of testimony. Hastings asked if he had ever administered punishment to a patient. Yes he had, but only once. A vicious and incorrigible Irishman had attacked another patient with the blade of a sheep shears. Van Norstrand ordered a cold bath, but far from dreading it, the Irishman dove in and frolicked about. "I thought it so good a joke that I left him and came upstairs." Two years later the Irishman struck again, tripping up an attendant and bludgeoning him. Again he got the cold bath: "The method is to seat him in the tub with his feet out, and then to put his head under water till he begins to look red in the face. I do not think the patient suffers much, but the punishment is in the fact that he feels he is completely in the power of another." The Irishman was dunked twice and learned his lesson: "He has not offered to injure anyone since. That is the only case that I call punishment that I have used since I have been here."

How did he discipline patients who behaved viciously? "Patients are first talked to." A repeat offender in the upper ward might be sent to the lower ward. "We sometimes shut them up and let them go without their dinners. We try to inculcate kindness in all parts of the house. Kindness will win in the end, and especially after you have had to resort to restraint."

Hastings asked why carpets in the central building, principally in the superintendent's quarters, had been replaced after just several years of use. The original carpets reeked of urine from the previous superintendent's children, Van Norstrand explained. He had planned to economize by delaying replacement, but Dr. Sawyer and Mrs. Halliday, the matron, urged him to replace all the carpets right away, "and [they] being officers of the house I did not feel like saying 'no' peremptorily." In other words, it was done out of consideration for his subordinates.

In response to questions from Hastings about bookkeeping, he said he had consulted Simeon Mills, the board's treasurer, and other trustees about bookkeeping procedures. He was covered. His testimony ended on the 26th, Ash Wednesday.[*]

Next, the committee called Mrs. Mary Halliday, who had been the matron since the hospital opened. In some respects the matron was the unofficial second in command. She was also the hospital's de facto switchboard. All kinds of information up and down the chain of command passed through her. She would have known of abuses committed by Van Norstrand or anyone else. But as she talked about her responsibilities, from overseeing the central kitchen and the sewing, laundry, and ironing rooms, to supervising female staff and making sure that wards were clean and sick patients properly cared for, she hewed to the line established by her boss. She was a team player. Hastings gave her plenty of opportunities to unburden herself of any long-festering concerns, but she refused the bait: "I

---

[*]   The committee added to the official transcript of Van Norstrand's testimony a pair of exhibits they had labeled A and B, consisting of the casebook entries covering Romulus Kellogg's brief and tragic stay and his admission form.

have never *witnessed* cruel treatment to a patient by an attendant. I have *heard* of such a case, and [Dr. Van Norstrand] discharged the attendant for it." She said that the superintendent visited every patient every day, "spending sometimes more and sometimes less time with them. These visits are seldom ever omitted." She defended the purchase of the additional carpets and said she had personally cut up and washed the old ones for use in patient rooms. Nothing was wasted; frugality reigned; activities flourished. It was true that few patients had attended the Friday night dance that Hastings had come to see, but that was not typical. Once in a while the fiddler was second rate, and on severe winter days the hall could not be adequately heated, but usually the dance was a great success, as were the tea parties, card parties, masquerades, and so on.

The next day John Mooney took the stand, the first of six male attendants. At 22, Mooney was already an old hand, having spent the past three years at the hospital. He had started on the third floor among the least disturbed patients. He had also worked the middle ward, and recently he had been sent to the first floor, which was the hardest to staff because patients there were the most hopelessly demented and filthy.

Like every employee called, Mooney understood the delicacy of his situation. He had sworn to tell the truth, but when he went back to work his boss would still be Dr. Van Norstrand. It would have crossed his mind that an excess of candor on the witness stand could come back to haunt him. But he must also have known that he was not without leverage. People who could stomach this line of work were too valuable to treat badly. As it turned out, none of the attendants exhibited Mrs. Halliday's reflexive loyalty to the superintendent, but there is no evidence that Mooney or any of the males were out to torpedo him either. If they did not volunteer information, neither did they feel compelled to conceal it when asked directly.

By now it may have been obvious to Van Norstrand that Hastings and Sherwood were working hand in hand. Over and over they circled back to the same topics, as though looking for patterns of behavior that, if confirmed through constant repetition, could be held up for examination. Is this how a hospital should be run? They elicited the following from Mooney: "If I could not keep [patients] in fear of me, I could not do anything with them. They test every new attendant." This was the heart of the issue for Hastings and Sherwood. The superintendent talked kindness; his attendants talked control.

"When [patients got] ugly and wicked we sometimes struck them. We shut them up. If they pitched into me to fight I choked them. A patient will usually give up when we shut off their wind. I do not remember how many times I have knocked patients down. When I first went in [I] had to use a good deal of force; when the patients got acquainted with me I had to use very little force."

These lines are lifted from a paragraph that fills nearly two pages. The impression is of a witness eager to tell everything he knows. What is missing is the interrogator's side of the exchange. It seems that from time to time the court reporter could not keep up and so ignored questions to concentrate on answers, unwittingly converting a series of simple, brief responses on the stand into a rambling monologue on the page. "Do not remember how many patients I have had to choke," Mooney said, "should say twenty or twenty-five, more or less. . . . Choked them till they gave up; would sometimes change color in the face when choked."[7]

As for recreational opportunities: "There is nothing particular done to amuse the patients on the ward. It takes the attendants about all the time to do the work, so that they cannot sit down to play with the patients." Hastings or Sherwood asked about activities. Mooney did not leap to the challenge as had the superintendent. He came up with a dance every other week, a rare party ("Last one was last fall"), no more than two or three picnics throughout the summer, several sleigh rides over the course of the long winter, plus skating parties attended by no more than four or five patients from his ward. Work was the primary activity: "Those that were unwilling to go we made go." He acknowledged that dances were well attended and a real lift to the patients, but otherwise the social calendar he laid out was bleak indeed.[8]

They asked how often the doctors visited Mooney's ward. "Superintendent and assistant physician visit the wards most every day together." And if the superintendent is gone? "The assistant physician visits when the superintendent has other business." How regularly did the superintendent visit last fall? "Pretty regularly last September and October, more than half the time I think."

This was a topic of special interest to Hastings and Sherwood. How often was the superintendent on the wards, and how much time did he spend with patients? Another was R. O. Kellogg. What had attendants heard about this affair from former co-workers Lowe and Guppy? The formal investigations into Kellogg's death conducted by the trustees and the legislature had been completed years ago and the results made public. What Hastings and Sherwood seemed to be after was inside information that might tell a different story. If so, Mooney disappointed them. Last he had heard, Guppy was in Boston, and Lowe was dead. Neither had told him anything that was not already in the record.[9]

At nine A.M. Monday, March 2, eighteen-year-old Herbert Bird took the witness chair. The hospital was a family affair for the Birds, employing his father, mother, and a sister.

He was asked about former attendants, and this gave Bird an opportunity to put in a word for his friend Mooney: "I regard Mooney as a good attendant, one of the best. I regard him as kind to the patients." They were curious about K. J. Smith, a former supervisor with a reputation for being quick with his fists. Bird confirmed that impression. He told of the time Smith threw an unresisting steamboat captain to the floor and "pounded" him. He did the same to a wild-eyed German who had kicked him. On this occasion Smith had called Bird for help. Bird helped to pin the man to the floor while Smith knelt on his chest. "We can conquer them easier by choking than by striking," Bird said. "The superintendent knows this is the common way of dealing with patients."*

Hastings and Sherwood seemed to be to compiling an alternate version of the hospital to set against the official version depicted in annual reports and the utterances of its leaders, including the trustees. Exploring the use of violence as a control measure was one way to heighten this contrast. Among the unrecorded questions to Bird: Have you seen patients struck?

"I have seen patients' ears boxed, though not often. I have done that." A man named Oster had been a hot-tempered wheeler-dealer on the outside, but inside the hospital he became a vicious sneak who set patients against one another, flooded the water closet, and assaulted attendants whose vulnerabilities he had carefully measured. "We have an old, feeble man on one ward who has a rocking chair. I have seen Oster take the chair away from him. The Doctor has instructed me that when I saw that to box his ears."

Do you know of patients being given what's called "a cold bath"? If so, on whose authority was it administered?

"I was present once when Berkman was put into a bath. He stole a knife from the dining room and hid it. I think the doctor ordered the bath."

Describe the procedure.

"The clothes are first removed and the patient is put into the water and held down. His head and body about to his hips are immersed. His knees hang out of the tub and his head is down in the tub. One of the attendants or supervisor is generally at the head of the tub and holds the patient's head under. Another has his hand on his breast. Another is at [his] feet. I do not remember how long a patient's head was ever kept under water. I should say about a minute. The patient did not strangle very much."

The next witness was Frank Clifford, 23, who had worked at asylums in Michigan and Indiana and had been at the Wisconsin

---

* Van Norstrand fired Smith after discovering the steamboat captain's black eye. Smith had not reported the incident and made excuses when Van Norstrand questioned him about it; pp. 270–271.

hospital for a year.

How do you control patients?

"We shut off their wind and shut them up in the strong room. They dread choking more than striking. I have had occasion I think a dozen times to attack patients. They sometimes go for me, and I have to interfere." He gave three examples. A man came at him with a chair: "I warded the blow off and threw him down and choked him a little, and took him down to the bath room and made him bathe." Another attacked while Clifford was trying to coax a depressed patient to eat: "I took him down and choked him. I had no difficulty getting him up to the strong room." The third, an intermittently violent bachelor farmer being blistered for masturbation, took hold of Mrs. Van Norstrand's arm when she passed through his ward. "I took hold of him and locked him up in his room. He came against the door with his foot and broke the lock, and he came at me. I took him down and choked him a little and took him up to the strong room."

Clifford had accompanied former soldiers being transferred to the federal hospital in Washington. He was asked who else went along to help with the patients.

Van Norstrand had sent five men, but Clifford was the only experienced attendant. The others were the superintendent's son, Fred, just 16; his father-in-law, George Hebard, who was 70; and two "civilians"—his lawyer and his business partner, J. W. Sumner. "Two of the patients were bad," Clifford said. One was an infamous feces-smearer nicknamed "Thunderbolt." "[Ideally], they required an attendant each. The others were melancholy cases. We used no restraint. I think it would have required three attendants to have taken those patients safely to Washington." The implication was that instead of sending an adequate number of capable attendants Van Norstrand had treated family members and business associates to a vacation at state expense.

Next on the stand was the supervisor on the male side of the building, 23-year-old Farrington Redford, an Englishman. He was asked about his responsibilities, which were considerable. He directed the work of the male attendants, cared for the sick, sorted and marked clothes, prepared the dead for burial, and made sure patients took their medicine. "Patients as a general thing are willing to take their medicine, but if they refuse, we generally give it to them by use of a wedge to open their mouth. Am hardly ever obliged to do this more than once. When the medicine is poured they do not strangle much."

Did the superintendent authorize this method?

"I cannot say that I ever got orders from him to give medicine in this way, but he knows we do it. He has sometimes assisted me."

Why the constant turnover of male attendants? Redford could only tell of those he knew personally: "Stenchfield left of his own accord after two weeks. Warren, who stayed two months, left to get married. Edwin Bush was discharged [after] about a month. He did not attend properly to his duties. He lost his keys and told a lie about it. He was a fiddler and used to play for the dances. Miller left of his own accord. He thought he could do better. Denning was discharged. I believe one reason was that he was hard on the patients. Richard Palmer left yesterday and went to painting on the new wings. Bird and Mooney are the most experienced and best attendants here," he said of an 18- year-old and a 22- year-old.

What orders had attendants been given regarding punishment?

"I think not any."

How do you punish patients?

"They are sometimes shut up in a room. They are sometimes given a cold bath, but very seldom. They sometimes wear the muff. Generally, when an attendant has trouble with a patient he informs me, and unless it is some trifling matter that happens every day, I report it to the superintendent."

Describe the cold bath.

"The patient is stripped, hands tied behind his back, and put into the tub partly filled with cold water, and his head held under at the bottom of the tub. He is on his back. His feet generally hang over the end of the tub. It generally takes three or four to do it. I think they generally dread it very much." He was asked for examples and provided several. A big fellow who had assaulted another patient was overcome and manhandled into the tub. "Neither physician was present. I asked no questions. I do not know whether the case was reported to the superintendent." A repeat offender was submerged twice for beating up patients and once for assaulting an attendant. Another fellow was bathed for tearing his clothes and "rubbing manure about." Then there was the notorious Thunderbolt, bathed repeatedly for the same reason. Sometimes a doctor was present, sometimes not.

Regarding Reverend Kellogg, had Lowe and Guppy, the last attendants to see him alive, ever talked to him about that night? Guppy rarely had anything to say, Redford said: "He was very sour and morose—the most so of any man I ever had any dealings with."[10] Lowe had talked about putting Kellogg in the strong room and finding him dead the next morning. These were hardly revelations.

Every attendant was asked how much time the superintendent spent with patients. Did he visit all the wards every day? Their answers tended to support the superintendent. Yes he did, and each morning the assistant physician was at his side. Dr. Wilson came around again in the afternoon, sometimes more than once. Whenever the superintendent failed to make morning rounds, he made up for it in the evening. If Hastings and Sherman considered Van Norstrand vulnerable on this issue they did not get much help from the male attendants.

At 28, Richard Palmer was by far the oldest of them. An army veteran, a former sailor, and a self-described "painter by trade," Palmer was a man of the world, or at least played the part, and thus perhaps too outspoken to remain for long in Van Norstrand's good graces. Redford had been promoted to supervisor after a little over a year on the job, yet Palmer worked two years on the upper ward without a promotion or a raise. To escape the wards he had recently taken a job painting the new wings. He considered himself a skilled and fearless attendant and thus worth more than he was paid: "If the right kind of attendants are employed there need be no knocking down or choking of patients. No punishments have ever been inflicted on patients in my ward since I have been here, [but] it requires skill to handle them. I never struck a crazy man with my fist and never would," he boasted. "They may strike me, but I am cool enough not to strike back." He described how he handled one who ran amok with a chair, driving other patients out of the sitting room and then turning on Palmer. "I met him and took the chair away and shoved him into the bedroom and locked him up. I put the muff on him. I think when they get a good man in such a place they had better raise wages and keep him. Good attendants have left because they did not get wages enough to suit them."[11]

Unfortunately for Van Norstrand, it was Palmer—and not Bird, Mooney, or Redford—who had worked alongside young Fred. Hastings and Sherwood were eager to know how Fred Van Norstrand had fared as a state employee, and the undervalued Palmer was eager to tell them: "If he had any trouble he generally came to me. He never went where there was turbulent patients or where there was any danger without me. I do not think boys like Fred could get along with patients. [But] he is a good boy." Richard Palmer: savvy veteran and protector of the inept but well-connected. One can imagine his smile as he spoke the words, "a good boy."[12]

The last of the male attendants was young Henry Norton, a newcomer who worked the middle ward. No, he had not been given any orders about punishing patients, but yes, he had choked one, slapped another, and helped to hold down and choke a filthy "Scotchman" who would not take his medication.

Van Norstrand was present for some of this, but most of the time he kept himself informed by reviewing transcripts. His blood must have run cold as he sat at his desk turning pages night after night, encountering little else but variations on the themes of Cold Bath, Violence, and Neglect. But so far he had no reason to feel cornered. The attendants had not turned on him, much as they had been nudged to do so. If some of what Hastings and Sherwood had evoked was damning, that was because it lacked perspective, an omission that he and Franklin Lawrence, his one ally on the special committee, could correct by putting the attendants back on the stand. His opponents painted a picture of naught but bullying and abuse. Together, he and Lawrence would have to draw the other side of the story out of his workers, the corked-up violence and mayhem that would explode through the wards but for their firm hand on that cork.

Thomas Kirkbride's biographer described the dilemma confronting even the most admired superintendents, the need to reconcile "the inevitable disparity between therapeutic ideal and hospital reality."[13] Van Norstrand had this burden to bear plus additional baggage of his own making. His one advantage over other embattled superintendents was that the investigation had been kept out of the newspapers. Fortunately for him, the board of trustees dreaded public disclosure as much as he did.

Meanwhile, he could only sit tight as Hastings and Sherwood finished with the men and started on the females. On March 3, Eliza Giesken was called. Three days later, after her six colleagues had taken their turns on the stand, she was brought back to clarify some things, and the first round of testimony from the attendants was over. It was Van Norstrand's turn to ask the questions Hastings and Sherwood had avoided.

But those three days had changed everything. With the reticent males, Hastings and Sherwood had succeeded in generating only a vague and shadowy alternative version of hospital life. But the females had been eager to shed light into every nook and cranny. They pounded Van Norstrand. The men had refused to get personal; the women could not wait. As he poured over the transcripts, their voices—normally so tactful and obliging—reproached him like an angry chorus. Spiteful employees, hopeless patients, and intoxicated crusaders of one stripe or another had discharged similar volleys of mutinous gossip at his predecessors and others in his position around the country. Such was the nature of this lonely vigil. Nichols, at the government hospital in Washington, had it right: this calling was indeed like a seat over a volcano. Scant comfort as each evening another stack of transcripts appeared on his desk.

At 21, Eliza Giesken was already a five-year veteran of life on the women's middle ward. "I have known patients to be put into the tub for punishment. We call it the *cold bath*. They are put in and their heads held under the water. I cannot tell how many times I have known it to be done—a great many. I do not know of any attendant that has given the cold bath without orders since Dr. Van Norstrand has been here. The cold bath is more effective than putting them in the strong room. They all dread it.

"There is a woman by the name of Murray. I have not had much trouble with her. She has taken a liking to me. She liked Dr. Van Norstrand at first, but not now. He was going through the ward and she spit at him, and he struck her, and after he struck her she spit at him again and kept on spitting at him, and he kept on striking her, and they had quite a time. He got her up against the window and got hold of her hair and jammed her head against the wall. She is a very small woman, and one would not think she could be so ugly. I have known a great many times of the doctor striking the patients if they did not behave.

"I do not know of any patients but what speak well of Dr. Sawyer. I think he was less impulsive than Dr. Van Norstrand. He was not as quick and was more mild.

"The superintendent, when at home, generally comes through the wards daily. He sometimes fails to come once a week, and sometimes when absent he does not visit the wards for three or four days."

The next day, March 4, Emeline Richards was called. Emeline was 20 and had worked the lower ward for nine months. "I think that I have struck fifteen patients, perhaps more and perhaps not as many. I never choked a patient. I have held their hands while others choked them. When they are choked we do not throw them down but trip their feet and lay them down on their backs. It is always necessary to do that when we choke them, because otherwise we are afraid of hurting them unnecessarily.

"Miss Hebard [the superintendent's sister-in-law, Augusta] sometimes visits our ward more and sometimes less. Sometimes she comes through with medicine twice a day and sometimes not at all.

I have seen her strike three or four patients.

"We have had patients that manifested a dislike to Dr. Van Norstrand. They think he might let them go home, and dislike him because he does not. The patients like Dr. Wilson because he has not been here as long. One said he had not been here long enough to learn to be ugly."

Next came 21-year-old Anna Wilson, who worked the middle ward with Eliza Giesken. "Last Friday [when Hastings and other committee members attended the dance] we were told we were going to have company, and were told to take only those that would behave and be quiet. [Miss Hebard] told me not to take some that I had all ready [to go].

"Miss Vance [a former attendant] was a very tough case with patients and very often left marks on them. I think I have seen Miss Richards leave marks on a patient. I think she struck one with her keys. I think I struck one with my keys and left a mark. I struck [the patient] on the head with my keys. It brought a little blood. I think the doctor said I ought not to use my keys, but I am not positive. [For] a while the attendants were in the habit of taking the muff strap and striking patients with it. I think I used the strap to strike patients.

"I have assisted to give two cold baths. The first patient was Mrs. Winthrop. She had a spite toward Miss Hebard. She struck Miss Hebard as she was passing around medicine and gave her a bad bruise. She was put into the bath right away. We fill the tub about half full of cold water, then tie the patient's hands and feet—the hands behind them. Then we hold them under water just as long as we can hold our breath. We raise up their heads and let them breathe. If they are as bad as ever we put them under again. In the case of Mrs. Winthrop, we put her head under three times. The other case was Mrs. Jason. She was put in the dark room for being very noisy and raving. She was the most excited patient I ever saw. She was mad, would scold and act as though she wanted to kill us, but was harmless. The doctor came to get her out [of the dark room]. They had to take her by force. She was undressed and put in the bath. I could not tell how many times she was ducked under, not over four, I think. Dr. Wilson held her head. Miss Hebard [was present]. She was supervisor at the time.

"Attendants are not allowed to tell of these things outside of the wards. When Dr. Van Norstrand passed the ward, we tell him what patients have done. He would sometimes say, 'Why did you not box her ears?' Once a patient was at the window nude, and the doctor told me to [strike her with a strap]. I told him I did not use the strap."

Rebecca Griner, 25, had begun work as a domestic in the Van Norstrand family kitchen and dining room. A year later she was transferred to the lower ward. Because patients there were especially difficult, three attendants were assigned. Working with Griner were Emeline Richards and Lizzy Leuty.

"The superintendent, as a general thing, visits our ward every morning, [but] sometimes fails to come through oftener than twice a week. I think once, when off on a visit, he was not in for three days. On his morning visits I do not think I have known him to stay over ten minutes, usually not as long as that. [As for Miss Hebard], the supervisor visits our ward twice or three times a day, [but] I have not known her to spend any length of time in the ward—perhaps ten minutes. Sometimes the distribution of the medicine is missed, perhaps two or three times a week. When it was not brought round [patients] had to go without.

"We have to use rough means [to] conquer violent patients. I think I have struck about seven patients. I do not approve of striking patients on the head. I do not often box their ears. I have done so lightly. I did use my keys once to make a patient let go of Miss Richard's hair. [The patient] had my partner on the floor and well under her own charge. I first loosened her hands from Miss Richards' hair, and next I choked her." Another time she tripped up and choked a patient who had attacked her. "The next day she came to me and asked my forgiveness, and I of course asked hers. I did not report the case to Dr. Van Norstrand. He was not at home that evening. Miss Hebard was not at home. I think Dr. Wilson was not at home. It seems as though no one was at home but Mrs. Halliday that evening."

Anna Sunville, 24, had worked on all three female wards during her three years at the hospital. "I have seen Dr. Van Norstrand box a patient's ears. One night in the dining room a patient was threatening to put a knife through us. He came and took her by the arm and slapped her on both sides of her face. [This was the woman who claimed to be Mrs. Fremont.] I have seen him box a patient's ears in taking her down from one ward to the other. Also there was Mrs. Ebert. She refused to go to bed. Dr. Van Norstrand came and told her she must mind the girls. He boxed her ears once or twice, and she went to bed willingly. Mrs. Eggleston said Dr. Van Norstrand boxed her ears and pulled her hair. Another case, as I was informed by Rebecca Griner, was that of Mrs. Neighbors. Dr. Van Norstrand boxed her ears. The next was Mrs. Zimmerman. She was strapped to the seat and had the muff on. She spit in his face and he boxed her ears. Another case was that of Mrs. Keating. I think she spit in the attendant's face, and Dr. Van Norstrand saw it and came up and boxed her.

"I never saw Dr. Sawyer strike or abuse a patient and never heard of it. I never saw Dr. Wilson strike a patient. If Dr. Sawyer was obliged to take hold of a patient he managed her in a different way.

"I have seen Miss Hebard strike patients, not more than half of forty times. Miss Hebard sometimes strikes a patient because they speak saucy and are cross, sometimes because they would not mind, and sometimes because they refuse to take their medicine. Some days she will walk through one end of the hall and not stop to see or inquire for patients. The reason that she did not visit more was that she was fixing to go to parties. We have eight or ten patients that take medicine daily. It is Miss Hebard's duty to take the medicine to them. She does not do it regularly. We oftener get the medicine [for some patients] than Miss Hebard does. I think there are more patients that dislike than like Miss Hebard. It was otherwise with Miss Lewis. Miss Lewis always took the medicine around. It was never neglected while she was [the supervisor]. She spent most of her time in the wards. I do not think Miss Hebard spends more than half the time in the wards.

"I think Mrs. Van Norstrand dictates and interferes too much with the attendants, especially in my ward. I think the patients would do better if she would not interfere. I think she gives more attention to those patients who have friends than to those who have none.

"Frequently the doctor's family has company, and they are furnished ice cream [while] the patients and attendants have to take skim milk, or go without any. I do not think we ever had ice cream except some that was left after company."

Nineteen-year-old Marietta Richards, Emeline's sister, had worked at the hospital off and on for the past year and a half. Like Rebecca Griner, she had started as a domestic but was later assigned to the lower ward. On both sides of the house the lower ward was a black hole, usually drawing the newest and most vulnerable staff. Some quit. Others held out until there was an opening upstairs. Only a precious few were willing to stick it out for years. "We had considerable trouble to manage patients in the lower ward," Marietta testified. "We used to lock patients in dark rooms, put straight jackets on them, strap them to seats and use the bed strap to strap them to their beds. We had occasion to use some of these restraints pretty often—almost every day." As for herself, she had recently transferred to an upper ward.

"Mrs. Van Norstrand was in the habit of coming into the ward and giving orders, even if it was contrary to what the doctor had said. [And] it made no difference what the supervisor had said. She was older than the supervisor and myself, and she wished me to do as she said. She sometimes goes through the ward in the morning and again in the afternoon, and sometimes not at all. She sometimes spends an hour or two. Sometimes she looks out the windows and sometimes interferes with the work. She has favorites among the patients, especially those that have wealthy friends or are wealthy themselves. She brings them coffee, ice cream, cake and fruit. Other patients [even] when unwell do not have as much attention and as many delicacies as Mrs. Van Norstrand's favorites.

"The patients do not generally like Miss Hebard. They prefer to stay in their rooms to staying where Miss Hebard is when she comes into the ward. I should think I have seen her strike patients as many as fifteen times. I have seen her shake them a good many times. She would box the patients as hard as she could on the side of their head. I consider her very passionate.

"The patients do not generally like Dr. Van Norstrand. I know of patients that will go to their rooms rather than stay in the hall when Dr. Van Norstrand comes through. He struck Miss Martin for spitting at him. She was strapped to a bench and had on a jacket at the time. I cannot say how many times he struck her. Her face was black and blue after. I was about a yard from him when he struck her. I thought at the time he was striking her very hard.

"The cold bath was given to Mrs. Gunther for being filthy. The doctor told me to take the scrubbing brush and scrub her. We did not put her head down more than three times. She is about fifty years old. She is sick now and has been for seven weeks. I heard one of the girls say that neither doctor has visited her in that time.

"There is another patient in our ward, Miss Lennox, that the doctors do not visit unless we ask them. She is sick. She told me she is sixty years old. She is in her own room in the fourth story, and she has to have quieting medicine twice every day. Miss Lennox stays all the time night and day in the fourth story and is up there days alone. I can say pretty positively that it is more than a week sometimes that neither doctor visits her. I think she is gradually failing. She was sick with dysentery last summer, and since then has been confined to her bed. I think the last visit of Dr. Van Norstrand to Miss Lennox was as long as three weeks ago. He went at my request. I told him I thought it was cold up there. One day last summer Mrs. Van Norstrand ordered Anna Sunville and myself to dress Miss Lennox and carry her downstairs. We put her into a rocking chair and a pillow to her back. Miss Lennox groaned and rolled her head constantly. She said she could hardly breathe while sitting up. Mrs. Van Norstrand stayed long enough to see how weak she was and how difficult it was to sit in her chair. She said, 'Mercy, Miss Lennox, why don't you try to sit up?' Miss Lennox appeared relieved when taken back to her room.

"Another case of neglect is that of Mrs. Baker. She is seventy years. Her scrofula is broken out in sores and is very painful. No medicine has been given to her since the fore part of winter. She spoke to the doctors about doing something for it and they paid no attention. She is very industrious and goes into the sewing room every day.

"I have known cases when both doctors were away from the building and could not be had if wanted. They were both away at the time of the medical convention in Madison, and at the time of the governor's party, and at the time of the hook and ladder party. The supervisor, Miss Hebard, was absent at the time of the hook and ladder party. Both doctors and Miss Hebard were also absent at the time of the state fair. There may have been other times they were all absent, but I cannot call them to mind at present."

At 28, Lizzie Leuty was the oldest female attendant but had been on the job only seven weeks. "I saw Dr. Van Norstrand strike Mrs. Zimmerman. He was passing through the ward and she spit on his coat. She had the muff on and was strapped to her seat. He slapped her on the face, raised the color, but left no other mark. I saw Dr. Wilson strike Mrs. Kohl. She used improper, obscene language to him, and he struck her on the side of the face three or four times so that it was black afterwards. Neither doctor has visited Mrs. Gunther since I have been here. She has been sick and confined to her room. She is not American and we cannot understand all she says. She moans all the time. She looks very pale—always keeps her head covered. [The doctors] do not enquire after her. Neither has been through our ward more than once a day."

On March 6, Eliza Giesken was called back to elaborate on some of her testimony. Yes, Dr. Van Norstrand struck the infamous Mrs. Hazel Roach as he manhandled her downstairs, demoting her to a lower ward. And when she cussed him out, he pulled her hair. He also struck Mrs. Jason, among others, knocking her to the floor, and hit her again while she was down. "I cannot tell how many times exactly. I think three or four. I should think he struck her pretty hard." It was Eliza's impression that the superintendent was careful about witnesses. One day while he was touring visitors a demented female launched a chamber pot at him. Normally he would have dealt with her then and there, but this time he simply ducked and guided his party to safety.

And yes, she did often deliver medications when Miss Hebard was unavailable, "sometimes two or three days at a time. Sometimes she would be going to town and sometimes she had company and was fixed up a little and did not like to go in the lower ward. Not long ago she was making a garment to wear to a party, and I carried the medicine quite a number of times, answered the [door] bell, sorted the clothes [from the laundry], and did little chores for her. When Miss Lewis was supervisor she spent most of her time in the wards. She devoted all her time to her duties as supervisor."

Finally Hastings and Sherwood called the assistant physician, Dr. John S. Wilson. Van Norstrand trusted neither Wilson's loyalty nor his competence. Whereas Sawyer had been a colleague, Wilson was a subordinate, just as his father had been. In his memoirs Van Norstrand depicted Wilson senior—his assistant surgeon in the old Fourth Wisconsin—as a bit of a buffoon. Judging from hospital pay records, he considered Wilson junior worth only half the salary of the man he had replaced. But he proved to be a good soldier, at least this time around.

Wilson testified that it had always been understood that staff could not punish patients willy-nilly but had to report infractions to the superintendent and inflict punishment only if he ordered it. He said he had never seen an attendant shake a patient, but it was common knowledge that a new employee was more likely to be attacked than his seasoned partner, and sometimes getting physical with a hostile patient was the only way to prove you had the backbone for the job.

As for the impression given by some attendants that the doctors rushed through certain wards or avoided them altogether, that too was misleading: "I go through the wards as many as six or seven times every day," he said, and often the attendants were unaware that he had come and gone. In fact, he and Van Norstrand made a point of showing up at odd hours to make sure attendants were on the job and had not snuck off to their rooms. "[They] are more apt to be attentive at the times they expect us to visit the ward. I sometimes catch them in their rooms, writing. They may have been negligent under such circumstances."

Lawrence asked about the unfortunate Mrs. Gunther. Had he and Van Norstrand been avoiding her as the attendants claimed? Wilson blamed the attendants. If a patient needed attention, it was their job to alert the doctors: "We always make it a point to see patients that we are giving medicine to, or that are sick with an acute disease, every day. We discontinued Mrs. Gunther's medication about two months ago. She is just as well as she ever was since she has been here. [Hers] is a case of chronic dementia. She is one of those patients that sits on the floor with her knees up to her chin, her arms over her head and her skirts over all. It is understood that if there is any new [problem], the attendant will call our attention to it."

Hastings: "Have you ever known of a patient being choked?"

Wilson: "Yes sir. It was reported by the attendant who did it. He was attacked by a patient and had to choke him off."

Hastings: "Do you understand that this process is sanctioned in the discipline of this institution?"

Wilson: "It is not, sir."

Van Norstrand intervened with a procedural question about medications. Wilson took the opportunity to dispute those who depicted the superintendent as hot-headed and quick with his hands: "I do not think many of the patients dislike the superintendent. I do not think him, as a general thing, austere, but otherwise. I have never seen him strike a patient except with the flat of his hand, and only three times in that way." One of the patients, Wilson claimed, even considered the slap therapeutic! "He said, 'Doctor, I am glad you did it.' He has never repeated the abuse [though] he swears and talks vulgar still."

Van Norstrand questioned him about the females that some attendants alleged were being neglected. Wilson recited a list of palliative medications and treatments attempted with each of them, and he emphasized the hopelessness of their conditions. The best we can do, he said of one, was "to see that she is kept clean, provided with food and with medicine for recurring bad symptoms. It is not a rule of the house to take as much professional interest in utterly hopeless cases as it is those we hope to benefit."

Finally, Wilson insisted that he and Van Norstrand had been off grounds together only twice, for the hook and ladder party and the state fair. Pushed by Sherwood, he acknowledged that there may have been other occasions over the past year and a half but insisted that whenever both were gone, "Squire Hebard or the supervisor" was left in charge. Thus did Wilson's testimony come to an end, with a vision of Van Norstrand's father-in-law—the odd-job man—at the helm of the ship while the doctors partied across the lake. Except for that parting image he had put up a good defense.*

But only the superintendent himself could counterattack. Employees had been tricked into depicting the hospital as a jungle where each day, outnumbered and virtually abandoned by their leaders, they battled for survival, where bored, vicious, delusional patients idled their lives away while the ruling family and its retainers skimmed off the cream of hospital resources; where the superintendent played the bully, his wife the busybody, his sister-in-law the wicked stepsister— and his father-in-law the town fool; and where the most desperately ill patients were abandoned to a slow death. Such was the malicious mischief stirred up by Hastings and Sherwood in all their months of probing and prying. Now at least he knew for certain what they had been up to. Suspicions confirmed!

---

* A few years later Wilson left the hospital, married, and purchased a drug store in town. In the fall of 1871 he went sailing with friends. A wind came up and the others urged caution, but Wilson insisted on heading across open water for the hospital. The "Lady of the Lake" capsized. Staff from the hospital rescued two of the four, but Wilson had already gone under. The superintendent rode to town to break the news to his young widow. *A Biographical Guide to Forest Hills Cemetery* (Madison, WI, 2002), p. 357.

FOURTEEN

Little Short of Murderous Neglect

Van Norstrand faced not only the credibility dilemma shared by every superintendent—that enormous gap between expectation and reality—but real problems of his own making. He *was* impulsive. He *did* attack patients. Unlike Thomas Kirkbride in Philadelphia and John Butler at the Hartford Retreat in Connecticut, he seems not to have evaluated patient progress based upon searching one-to-one conversations but upon more general perceptions of appropriateness and compliance.[1] Those who toed the line got better. Those who made themselves disagreeable did not. And it was true, his sister-in-law was no Florence Nightingale, his wife no Dorothea Dix. Thank God for that! Of course they were not always equal to the occasion. Who would be? And what ruler's idiosyncrasies did not appear outrageous through the eyes of disgruntled underlings?

Smoldering below all this was the Kellogg affair. Hastings was certain to fan it back to life. Along with God knew what else.

On March 12, Van Norstrand would have a chance to set things right. By artfully bullying and charming naive attendants, his opponents on the committee had isolated examples of necessary discipline from the volatile ebb and flow of daily life on the wards and turned them into something monstrous. Through cross-examination he must deflate these misrepresentations and put them in perspective. For one thing, few insane were the wounded pets Hastings and Sherwood were so intent on depicting. Many were shameless, vicious, and conniving. Attendants must be made to shed light on how dangerous ward life could be, how deceptively peaceful it all appeared to outsiders, the order and symmetry of long quiet hallways lit from ranks of open doorways on each side, the sedate sitting rooms, the enormity of the physical plant imbuing the visitor with a false sense of security when in fact only stern rules promptly enforced kept the lid on.

He got his first witness, John Mooney, to clarify his earlier remarks about choking. This was done only "to keep them off of me and to conquer them," not to injure. The same had been true when he knocked people down. He had not hit them with his fists but had "thrown them down; tripped them up."

But what Van Norstrand had failed to anticipate was that every such effort at damage control gave Hastings and Sherwood an opportunity to turn his witness against him, thereby wreaking even more havoc. Hastings asked Mooney if he knew of cases of "cruel or harsh" treatment. Mooney—one of those who had angered the superintendent by coming back drunk from the nearby tavern—responded with an account of how the superintendent dealt with the infamous Thunderbolt: "[Thunderbolt] was shut in the strong room [where] he plastered his manure over the walls and door. The doctor [told us] to make him eat it or stick his nose in it. Me and Miller made him do it." During the cold bath that followed, his head was submerged "until he gave up."

Van Norstrand rose to protest: "The patient smeared the hand hold of the door with his manure. The attendant could not reach through the door and give the patient a cup of water without soiling his clothes."

Hastings asked for more examples of the superintendent's aggressiveness. Mooney recalled three incidents when Van Norstrand slapped, kicked, or otherwise assaulted patients.

Again the superintendent protested: "J_____ and H_____ were both exceedingly violent when they were excited. They were excited at these times. Violent and abusive."

Next came Herbert Bird, who explained that by "knee to the chest" he did not mean that he intended to hurt the patient with the point of his knee but only to restrain him, using his leg to pin the person to the floor. Van Norstrand pressed Bird to acknowledge that the incidents of choking had occurred without his knowledge but ran into unexpected resistance. "You never caught us at it, [but] you knew it was commonly done because I reported two cases to you, and I supposed others had."

Sherwood asked Bird about attendants who drank on the job. The only person Bird identified by name was young Fred Van Norstrand. Sherwood asked for examples of "cruel or harsh" treatment of patients, and Bird described how the superintendent had "cuffed very severely" several patients, grabbed one by the hair and pulled him to his feet, kicked others and used "abusive language." In addition, the superintendent had been avoiding an epileptic man—"quite wild, crazy"—confined in a strong room the past two weeks. "I do not think the superintendent spends time enough in the wards to inquire after all the patients," Bird volunteered. "Five minutes will carry him through my ward the way he has been in the habit of visiting."

After a break for supper Van Norstrand called his son to the stand. Fred admitted drinking wine on the job but only once. "I think it was rhubarb or currant wine. It was some that was used for medicinal purposes. I have not had a drop of whiskey in the ward since I have been there."

Either Sherwood or Hastings pounced on him. He had dropped out of Beloit College. Why? "Because I was not very well suited and they were not very well suited with me."

"Explain what you mean by 'they were not suited with me and I was not suited with them.'" Dr. Van Norstrand objected, and Fred said simply, "My father knows why I left Beloit College."

Even the Englishman, Farrington Redford, supervisor of the male attendants, was a disaster his second time on the stand. Once again things got off to a decent start for the superintendent. Yes, whenever he told the doctors about a sick patient they responded promptly with medication or appropriate treatment. And the wedge was used to force open a patient's mouth for medicine only as a last resort. Force-feeding was also a last resort. Every effort was made to coax a person to eat.

Then Sherwood intervened with a question about a certain Mr. Frazier. Redford said that Frazier had been prowling his room one night yelling bloody murder. Van Norstrand heard the noise and came to investigate. When he opened Frazier's door, out flew the chamber pot, which caromed off the superintendent's head, drawing blood. Van Norstrand and Guppy, the supervisor at the time, overpowered Frazier and dragged him to a strong room. While Guppy unlocked the door, Redford recalled, "The doctor raised Frazier by the hair with one hand and slapped his ears with the other." The beating continued. The next day while bathing Frazier, Redford found bruises all over his face and body: "He was pretty well marked up."

Sherwood asked his usual question about "cruel or harsh treatment," and this elicited a keen observation. Redford described being attacked by three men in the upper ward. Two attendants came to his rescue, and once the men were under control they were hauled off to strong rooms and given what Redford called "a good choking." "We have been obliged to use harsh treatment a great many times. I think anyone looking on would perhaps consider it abuse or ill treatment, but if they were engaged in it and excited they would not stop to think." It was one thing to stand outside the mayhem and cast judgment, quite another to be in the middle of it fighting for your life.

This man who had been so discrete during his first appearance then took aim at the superintendent's in-laws: "I see things that do not meet my views exactly here, whether I am a good judge or not I do not know. I have always thought that things would go off much better if Mr. Hebard's family was not here. They can do things, everyone knows, that any other employee could not do. In the first place it is not generally believed among the employees that they earn the wages that they get, and this creates dissatisfaction. I have heard all the female attendants complain of Mrs. Van Norstrand. They think the old lady, Miss [Augusta] Hebard, watches and dogs their movements, that she is a sort of spy among them. They complain that Squire Hebard interferes and that it does not matter whether he does anything or not. I cannot tell what Squire Hebard's duties are. I don't think anyone can." In other words, the superintendent's father-in-law was paid for doing next to nothing, "while Mr. Bird, an old man, has to work for his twenty-five dollars a month." Redford acknowledged that Squire Hebard was in charge of the flower gardens and the house plants and the fountain, "but I think the patients have done a good share of the work." As for the plugs Hebard fashioned from the tobacco supplied by Sumner and Company, "I cannot call to mind a time when I would chew [it] even if I had no other. The patients complain bitterly of the tobacco." And no wonder. This was the stuff Pardee and Clark had written off as sheep-dip before Van Norstrand and his partner found a more profitable use for it.

What had come over Mooney, Bird, and Redford? Had the female attendants shamed them into doing this?

The superintendent may still have been shell-shocked next morning when he called his sister-in-law to the stand. Perhaps she had demanded an opportunity to strike back at all those snippy girls.

Augusta Hebard was on duty, she claimed, for over sixteen hours a day, beginning at five or six when she unlocked the doors of the iron stairway and went onto the wards to check up on "particular cases," arrange for special breakfasts for those with certain needs, visit the sick, and so on. At nine she made rounds with the doctors. Afterward, she sewed garments for patients, or took them on walks, or covered a ward so the girls could take patients outside. "If a new patient comes I have to see to the bathing. If I have nothing to do in the afternoon I generally take my sewing and go into the upper ward and sew or play cards. I give medicines again at five PM, and at that time I look to see if the rooms are warm and if not, I see that the heat is put on." And so on. Even during her private time she left her door open for patients to drop in, although they "sometimes bother me exceedingly."

She believed she worked harder than her esteemed predecessor,

Miss Lewis. She filled in when Mrs. Halliday was away and helped sort bedding and supervise in the kitchen, and so it was no wonder that sometimes she had to let an attendant dole out medications. It was her sensitivity to the needs of patients and her concern about the laziness and neglect of certain attendants that drove her to do double duty—fetching special foods, looking in on patients, making sure the ladies were warm and comfortable. Her duties were so exhaustive, her devotion to the patients so complete, her expectations of subordinates so uncompromising, that she was an easy target for their spitefulness and chicanery. "I do not believe it possible for a supervisor to do her duty, to look after attendants, upbraid them and follow them closely to see that they do their duty, and still be popular with them."

Hastings and Sherwood didn't bother with her. She was not the one they were after.

* * *

By mid-March, heavy storms had turned roads to slurry and washed away railroad tracks west of Madison, but the lakes were still solid enough to support team-drawn sleds and wagon traffic, which is probably how Van Norstrand got to town the morning of March 17. The next phase of the hearings was to begin in the Agriculture Rooms of the new capitol. In months to come its surrounding oaks would shade the meandering walkways where cannons had boomed and torch-lit revelers had celebrated the election of Abraham Lincoln seven long years ago. Still lacking the long-anticipated dome after years of intermittent construction, the new building of Prairie du Chien stone provided roomier and more elegant hearing space than the hospital but also brought the proceedings into the habitat of capital newspapermen. For Van Norstrand that hour or so spent rumbling through the fog beside the hospital teamster must have passed slowly indeed. Geese pecked at honeycombed ice along the shoreline; a bluebird sighting had been reported in the *State Journal;* but the doctor had other things on his mind. Today, R. O. Kellogg's brief, fatal confinement was to be revisited. The superintendent's enemies were calling witnesses from as far away as Chicago. Anything to breathe life back into a scandal long ago laid to rest.[2]

The first to be sworn was A. J. McKindley, the fellow sent by Amherst Kellogg to retrieve his brother's body on that terrible Friday in late January, 1865.[3] On the stand McKindley read a statement describing that earlier journey. Over a century later it reads like a chapter from a gothic novel: intrigue, deception, a terrible secret.

Upon reaching Madison in late afternoon he rented a wagon and team and then located an undertaker and a minister friend of the Kellogg family. An empty coffin rattled behind them as they crossed the lake toward the darkening woods. The superintendent met them. Out of sight of patients and staff he led them up to the second floor. He told them that patients were not to learn of Kellogg's death: "He wished great care used in moving the body from the asylum, and in no event could it be done till it was quite dark."[4]

He took them to a back room. "[The body] was laid out in plain black clothes. It appeared the body of a man who had come to his death by violence. On his breast were large bruises, with the blood settled under the skin. Hands and arms [were] black in places [from] injuries. The head and face were severely cut and jammed, the result of blows inflicted by someone or caused by being thrown heavily against some hard substance."

They lifted the body into the coffin and removed it to the sleigh. Then McKindley and Reverend Bardwell came back and insisted on an explanation. Van Norstrand took them to his office. "[He] made some general statements, but referred us to the assistant superintendent, Dr. Sawyer, who also said some things in a general way." Sawyer then called in the attendant, Lowe, the last man to see Kellogg alive, to do the burden of explaining. Lowe was wretched in this role, and Sawyer was obliged to interrupt from time to time, guiding and correcting. "I think Dr. Van Norstrand came into the office once or twice. Possibly he joined Dr. Sawyer in some suggestions to Lowe. Lowe appeared a little disconcerted. His statements [appeared] considerably 'doctored' in some way. It occurred to us that he had given his statement before, either to Dr. Sawyer or Dr. Van Norstrand. He appeared to be somewhat at a loss to make the same statement to us, judging from the corrections that [the doctors] were obliged to make." But he managed to describe Kellogg's two nights at the hospital and his shock upon opening the door that fatal morning: a room swept by arctic wind, shutters torn open, window shattered, chamber pot in fragments, walls smeared with blood, and Kellogg's naked body sprawled near the mattress, "not yet cold."

Hastings asked what McKindley made of Van Norstrand's "excessively kind and attentive" behavior.

"We were impressed that there was an object behind to divert our minds and screen the institution and relieve the sadness of the case by over-politeness to us. That is the way we looked at it."

Hastings: "Was there any reason assigned by Dr. Van Norstrand why he wished this matter kept quiet?"

McKindley: "I understood [that] he thought it best owing to the excitability of patients. The idea was to impress me with what was a common practice in asylums, that all such deaths should be kept quiet from the patients."

Sherwood pursued another angle. The superintendent identified "self-violence" as the cause of death. But if Kellogg had intended to kill himself with shards from the chamber pot, wouldn't the cuts on his face and body have been deeper, more penetrating, instead of mere gashes? And if he had dashed his head against the shutters, wouldn't the injuries to his skull have been more substantial? Sherwood seemed to be assembling a more sinister scenario: wounds inflicted by someone else, death by abuse, exposure, neglect.

McKindley equivocated: all that might be true, but he was no expert. Van Norstrand countered: weren't the bruises over the eye, on the hipbones, and elsewhere to be expected of someone who had thrown himself violently on his face? Yes, McKindley conceded, that was also true, but he did not back down from his claim "that Mr. Kellogg was not well cared for."

Reverend Kellogg's wife followed McKindley to the stand. Mrs. Kellogg rejected the superintendent's assertion that the family had withheld information. She denied that her husband had ever been suicidal or inclined to hurt others. His "manifestation of insanity" typically occurred once a day, "early in the morning, about two A.M. He talked very loudly, prophesied what he thought would happen. These spells lasted perhaps two hours but [gradually] increased in length. He was usually much exhausted after these paroxysms. He would lay on the lounge very quietly, then would appear natural and walk about the room." The morning he ran off in his nightshirt she was taken to the house where neighbors were holding him down. "We immediately got his feet in hot water, bathed his head in snow, and after a few minutes he seemed to know where he was and that he had done something wrong. His first remark was, 'Forgive me.' It was addressed to me."

Van Norstrand tried to get her to acknowledge outbursts of extreme combativeness but she refused. She said a neighbor who had put in long hours as volunteer caregiver, Mr. Ebenezer Frisell, also denied witnessing any homicidal or suicidal behaviors.

Long after these events she had tracked down Lowe, who had left the hospital and was living in Jefferson County. She summarized what he told her. "When Mr. Kellogg became noisy the first night they forced medicine into his mouth and removed him to the fourth story. Mr. Lowe left him there, locked in the room, pounding on the door and calling for the superintendent. The next night the same thing was repeated, and in the morning he found him on the floor dead and cold. I asked why Mr. Kellogg had not had an attendant as they had promised. He replied it was impossible, as there were forty persons in his ward and but two attendants."[5]

After lunch, Amherst Kellogg was called. Like McKindley, he brought a written statement to enter into the record. In it he recalled the night of his brother's disappearance, the efforts of neighbors and friends to confine R. O. as he thrashed and flailed, doctors coming and going, the journey to Madison and consultation with Dr. Favill, lengthy interviews at the hospital with Van Norstrand and Sawyer, all three doctors agreeing that "a speedy recovery" was almost certain but only if R. O. was admitted without delay. Both asylum doctors had repeatedly assured him that his brother's needs would be met, that requests from the family would be honored, that they understood that "morphine or opium in any form would be deleterious" and so would *not* be given, and that if R. O. required constant attention, the hospital would provide it.

And then, the next day, the "cruel and utterly heartless" telegram: "Your brother committed suicide last night. We will expect you on the four p.m. train."

"I have always felt," Amherst Kellogg's statement concluded, "that [my brother's] treatment—giving him morphine, locking him up in a [strong] room, leaving him alone and out of hearing while raving and screaming for help, falls very little short of *murderous neglect*."

Hastings: "Did you conceal any fact that could have any bearing upon your brother or his case?"

Kellogg: "Not to my knowledge or intention, and that is evidenced by the fact that I went [to the hospital] for advice. I never heard or saw anything that impressed me that [my brother] was homicidal or suicidal."

Why Van Norstrand took the stand next is not explained. He may have asked for a chance to respond. Legislators and trustees had once found his side of the story convincing enough to exonerate the hospital of blame, but those investigators had not been exposed to Amherst's indignation, Mrs. Kellogg's bewilderment and hurt, and McKindley's edgy contempt. He stood accused of lying about the availability of attendants to care for Reverend Kellogg, lying about the nature of the care Kellogg would be provided, and promising not to give morphine while secretly intending to force it down Kellogg's throat, if necessary. "Murderous neglect," as Amherst put it; "heartless."

"The theory of myself and Dr. Sawyer was that Reverend Kellogg became quiet after he went into [the strong room], the room being warm and comfortable; that after lying quiet two or three hours he became excited again, jarred the shutters open, broke the sash and glass with his vessel* and thereby broke [the vessel]; [and] that he bruised his hands and perhaps his head in trying to get out the window. Failing in this he threw himself upon the floor, perhaps both backwards and forward, until, finally, he threw himself on his face so hard as to produce unconsciousness, resulting in death very near daylight in the morning. I might add here that I do not regard this as premeditated suicide as there was broken glass within his reach which he could have taken to cut himself with if he had desired to."

Lawrence: "Why did you call it suicide?"

Van Norstrand: "I was somewhat excited by the occurrence and did not distinguish perhaps as closely as I ought to in making the distinction between death from self-violence and intentional suicide. No other case like this ever happened in the hospital."

He denied that Kellogg had been abandoned while calling for help and cited the good Dr. Sawyer as his authority. "I had been told that Dr. Sawyer was the last one at Mr. Kellogg's room and sat down on the step and listened. My wife told me that Dr. Sawyer said so. [His] sitting down on the steps is very much like what a physician would have done knowing all about the habits of the insane. Many violent, noisy persons when first put in a room will make a good deal of noise, but when left alone and find that no one is interfering with them, will become quiet and lie down. I wish to add that I believe every word of the record made in this case after Mr. Kellogg's death. It was made by Dr. Sawyer and is in his handwriting."

To support his charge that information had been withheld he once again turned the spotlight onto poor Lowe. He said that some time after quitting his hospital job Lowe came by to describe an encounter he'd had with Ebenezer Frisell, the most constant of Reverend Kellogg's volunteer caregivers in the crisis days of late January, 1865. Lowe got the impression from Frisell that Kellogg would have killed himself or anyone else if he had the chance. "I asked Mr. Lowe why Mr. Frisell [had] not informed me of the fact. He replied that

---

* The chamber pot.

Mr. Frisell said he did not know it was of any importance, or that he did not think of it. I am not sure which." Frisell also told Lowe that Kellogg had attacked someone with an axe. If only he had known all this from the beginning, Van Norstrand insisted, things would have turned out differently for Kellogg at the hospital.

He also claimed to have been in the dark about Kellogg's tendency to lapse into a stupor after a period of extreme excitement. "Had I know of these insensible spells succeeding his violence I would have put him in a bed strap until the violence and succeeding exhaustion had passed, and directed an attendant to have observed him."

That evening a telegram reached Dr. John Sawyer at the Butler State Hospital in Providence, Rhode Island: "Did you accompany R. O. Kellogg to the strong room on the night of his death and go up afterward that night?" It was signed by Hastings and Sherwood.

First on the stand next morning was Ebenezer Frisell, who refuted everything Van Norstrand had attributed to Lowe: "I never saw any signs of suicidal or homicidal tendencies in [Reverend Kellogg]. I never saw any signs of his injuring himself or others. I never told Mr. Lowe that he was homicidal or suicidal. This interview of mine with Lowe may have been a week or ten days after Mr. Kellogg's death. He came when I was weighing hay and I did not have time to say much to him. [He] was a little excited. I do not know but he had been drinking. I thought he had. Lowe was a young man that was a little mite reckless I think, sometimes. He would sometimes have sprees. I formed the impression that he went to saloons sometimes."

In the afternoon Samuel Hastings read Dr. Sawyer's telegraphed response into the record: "No, was in the office, was aware the change was made and remained up till all was arranged." This directly contradicted what Van Norstrand said his wife had told him. Sawyer had *not* been on the scene, monitoring Kellogg's behavior. The unfortunate, excitable—and apparently not very reliable—Mr. Lowe *was* the last man to see Kellogg alive. For all anyone knew, Kellogg *had* been crying out for help for God knows how long, with no one nearby to hear.

Hastings and Sherwood called a succession of physicians to the stand. John Favill was one of the first doctors to settle in Madison and had been practicing for twenty years. He was no stranger to the field of asylum medicine, having served for eight months under high-strung Dr. Clement. Favill had reviewed testimony and documents regarding the Kellogg case, and Hastings asked his opinion about the treatment that Kellogg received.

"The shortest way I can express it is, the case was neglected."

Hastings asked about the cold bath. Did Favill regard this as a safe practice?

"I do not, because I should be afraid of killing my patient."

Van Norstrand: "Was it not administered in the hospital while you were there?"

Favill: "I never saw it administered. I have reason to believe it was administered, and I became aware of it accidentally. I made a great row about it and reported it to the trustees."

Van Norstrand: "You think there was neglect in the case Mr. Kellogg. What different care would you have administered if you had the same information that I had from Mr. Kellogg's brother and the [admission] papers?"

Favill: "Well, doctor, I do not know as I should have done differently, but if I had done rightly I should have watched my patient with more care."

Dr. Lyman Barrows had worked two years at the state hospital at Utica, New York. He was well acquainted with the Wisconsin hospital and its superintendent, having served a term on the Visiting Committee.

Hastings asked him about the Kellogg case.

"The medical treatment I approve. The fact that he was left that night without a watch I object to."

Hastings: "Do you know of any reason why he would not have recovered with proper treatment?"

Barrows: "I should regard the chances for the recovery better than for a fatal result."

What about the cold bath? Did Barrows consider this a safe process?

Barrows: "I do not. I should be afraid of killing my patient. This process was not used at Utica while I was there to my knowledge."

Van Norstrand: Would the superintendent of the state hospital in Utica have paid more attention to Kellogg given the same limited information?*

Barrows: "Mr. Kellogg [appears to have] received more personal attention from the superintendent than I have ever known patients to receive in the same length of time from the superintendent at Utica." At last: score one for Dr. Van Norstrand!

Lawrence asked Barrows to characterize "the general management" of the hospital.

Again Van Norstrand had the satisfaction of hearing at least a qualified endorsement: "Since the present administration, under the circumstances and with[in] the means [provided], it has seemed to me well-managed. I never notify the superintendent or any of the officers of the time of my visits. We [members of the Visiting Committee] have sometimes thought that there was an unnecessary delay in the morning on the plea that the building was not cleaned and ready for visitors, but whenever we have pressed, the doctor has readily yielded."

The remaining two doctors, James J. Brown and A. J. Ward, were also asked whether the cold bath was safe. Both echoed their colleagues: it was a dangerous, potentially fatal procedure.

---

* Barrows may have worked at Utica during the 1840s, when the superintendent was Dr. Amariah Brigham, one of the original thirteen members of the superintendents' association and a well-known writer on health issues. Most of those present would have associated Dr. Brigham with Utica, and so in effect Van Norstrand was asking Barrows whether even the highly regarded Brigham would have done a better job with Kellogg (Hall, pp. 56–57).

FIFTEEN

Rotten Eggs

The implications were troubling. If the superintendent approved of disciplinary procedures as dangerous as the cold bath, what else was he hiding under that confident, genial manner? The question must have occurred to Hastings and Sherwood in the course of their investigation, and what they had uncovered led to a new line of inquiry.

They called William Lohmiller, a bookkeeper for Pardee and Clark who had continued in that capacity under Sumner and Van Norstrand until his resignation a few weeks earlier. He was a reluctant witness. He did not want to make trouble for Sumner and had met with him to discuss what he might be expected to reveal.

Hastings opened the questioning: "Do you know of goods having been charged to the hospital in larger quantities and greater weights than were delivered?"

Yes. Often the hospital was charged not only for the product—butter, sugar, tea—but also for the weight of the crock, barrel or wooden chest it came in. A container's weight was called a "tare." Failure to subtract the tare from a product's gross weight resulted in an inflated charge to the hospital.

The superintendent objected, and Lohmiller acknowledged that he had not brought the practice to his attention because he assumed Van Norstrand already knew.

Van Norstrand: "Did you ever see anything in my conduct, directly or indirectly, to induce you to believe that I knew of this?"

Lohmiller explained why he thought so. He had expressed his concern about the practice to Sumner, who told him it was all right. Also, Van Norstrand had never complained, nor had he ever asked that the amount charged to the hospital be reduced by the weight of the containers. Finally, he had once seen Van Norstrand pay close attention as a shipment of tea was weighed and the bill calculated—nearly sixty pounds including the crate—without objecting.

James W. Sumner was called. "Dr. Van Norstrand asked me if the boys had made any mistakes of over-charged goods sold to the hospital. This was last Monday morning, I think. I told him I thought there was a couple of mistakes, where the tea was charged. [He] said that I better see the boys and see if anything was wrong." He added, interestingly, "I believe he also asked me to ask them what they would swear to."

He was questioned about the new bidding process, and he gave an example of how it worked. One Friday he went to the hospital to submit bids on a list of items. "There was a dance there that evening. Some of the other bids were in. I saw a few of the bids open on the table." No one else had submitted a bid on tea. Sumner had come prepared to offer tea at $1.18 a pound, but since there were no competitors, he raised his bid to $1.20.

Hastings: "Did Dr. Van Norstrand suggest upon what articles you should advance your bid?"

Sumner: "We talked it over a little." Sumner was awarded the contract, which amounted to eleven or twelve hundred dollars, but he insisted that his profit was small, "somewhere from fifty to a hundred dollars."

Van Norstrand asked if the amount billed to the hospital had ever been inflated by failure to deduct the tare. Sumner could not deny this had happened but said he couldn't recall it. Van Norstrand: Had the hospital been reimbursed, as he demanded?

Sumner: "[You] told me Wednesday night last what Lohmiller had sworn to. Since then I have given the hospital credit for the tare on the jars of butter, barrel of sugar, and tare on the chest of tea."

Van Norstrand: "Have you any reason to think that I suspected anything wrong, or that any mistake occurred that I did not ask to have corrected at once?"

Sumner: "All [you] ever found out, or if any mistake did occur, [you] had it corrected, whether for or against [the hospital]."

Van Norstrand: "When you commenced business did I tell you to be very particular about asylum sales and accounts, that it was not only necessary to be perfectly honest but to seem so and be able to show it at all times?"

Sumner: "Yes sir, you did. [You] would tell me [you] had been to other stores and priced articles and then come and priced them at my store and found I was the cheapest and took them. Our agreement was to sell things to the hospital as low as we sold them to others at wholesale."

Van Norstrand: "Have I always been as careful in my purchases for the asylum as Simeon Mills, Judge Vilas, Judge Braley, Mr. Bird or other businessmen of this city who have dealt with you in making purchases for their own families?"

Sumner: "I say yes. [You] always priced things as much as they do. [You] always cautioned me to put things down low."

Van Norstrand: "In the four years that I have bought goods of houses with which you have been connected, have you ever seen anything that induced you to believe that I was less close in purchases for the Asylum than if I had been conducting my private affairs?"

Sumner: "I do not know as I have."

Van Norstrand: "Have you noticed me more careless about the prices since I have had an interest in that store than I was before?"

Sumner: "I have seen no difference."

Sherwood interrupted. If the superintendent was so particular about getting a good deal for the hospital and so diligent about checking in goods as they arrived from the store, didn't it seem "a little singular" that he did not demand that the bills be adjusted as soon as he detected a discrepancy rather than waiting until the investigation had put the store under scrutiny?

Sumner: "As you put it, I must say yes."

Sherwood: "Did you not [tell Lohmiller] that he could have told much more, and thank him for not doing it?"

Sumner: "No sir. I asked him what he had sworn to. I do not think I told him he might have told a good deal more. I did not want him to tell anything else but the truth."

Hastings asked if Fred Van Norstrand had worked at the store.

Sumner: "I employed Fred Van Norstrand and discharged him because he did not attend to his duty and did things he ought not to have done. His habits were bad while in my employ. He drank."

Over the following week other witnesses were called, but Hastings and Sherwood were not done with Lohmiller. Apparently they learned that he did indeed know more than he had testified to earlier, and they summoned him back to the stand.

Lohmiller: "There was a quantity of halibut in the store of Pardee and Clark at the time they sold [out] to J. W. Sumner and Company. I heard Pardee say it was not inventoried [because] it was not worth inventorying. It was not fit to sell. It had lain in the store during the summer. This fish was sold to the asylum a week after J. W. Sumner and Company commenced business. Dr. Van Norstrand ordered this fish sent to the asylum. Mr. Sumner told me to call it codfish on the bill. There were 132 pounds of this fish. I never saw any bill sent back for correction of that fish."

He also recalled a shipment of 65 dozen eggs: "The condition of a good many of the eggs was very bad. They were old, and when broke smelt bad. A good many were what I term 'rotten eggs.'"

A clerk at the store was called to confirm this. Walter Clark and another man had carried the eggs out to the asylum wagon. Van Norstrand was standing by, observing. The eggs smelled so bad, Clark recalled, that he had wondered aloud if they were worth hauling to the hospital.[1]

Van Norstrand might have survived Lohmiller's first appearance on the stand and Sumner's testimony without much damage to his credibility. So what if he had been careless in not detecting an occasional overcharge? So what if his son once again came off as an ass? But these last disclosures were, quite literally, poison. It sounded as though he had fed his patients tainted fish and rotten eggs in order to pocket a few dollars. Certainly these items had not appeared on his own table, although he and his family may not have escaped the smell from the kitchen when they were cooked up for the patients.[2] If Van Norstrand was present when Lohmiller and Clark told this damning tale, he had nothing to say.

Did he send those eggs to the hospital because they were the best he could find at that time of year? Did he send the fish trusting that his cooks would find enough that were palatable to provide the patients a welcome a change from the usual stews and hash? In other words, were his actions consistent with his stated beliefs? During the war he took pains to find fresh meat, milk, and produce for his sick and wounded soldiers. As superintendent he had repeatedly stressed the importance of a rich, varied, and plentiful diet. Purging, bleeding, blistering, and spooning in tepid broth were the discredited old ways. The progressive and humane way was to give nature the resources it needed to work its restorative wonders—good food and plenty of it, plus rest, mild sedatives, and tonics.

Or were the disclosures of Lohmiller and Clark to be taken at face value—proof that under all the high-sounding words lurked a cynical and greedy man and a hypocrite to boot? Was this the work of that other Van Norstrand—the hot-headed teacher, the doctor who strong-armed disciplinary cases into the dead house at Baton Rouge and made a small fortune selling whiskey to soldiers? The one who beat up annoying old women?

He responded to these and other charges in a written statement that he presented to court commissioner J. H. Carpenter on Monday, March 23.

First off, he was "surprised and chagrined" to hear his attendants talk "in plain Anglo-Saxon" of their violence toward patients.[3] It was all news to him. In reporting violent encounters with patients they had always claimed self-defense and minimal laying on of hands. He suspected that it all looked worse on paper than it was. In ferreting out and stringing together stories of mayhem and misery, his adversaries had deliberately set out to create a distorted impression of hospital life. Put in proper context, these occasional "collisions" were common occurrences at any hospital.

Still, he got the point. Some actions on the part of the staff had been made to look bad and so must stop. Therefore he had issued the following order: "Any attendant who strikes or chokes a patient will be arrested for assault and battery, and any attendant seeing and not reporting it will be dealt with as an accomplice." Here was proof that he would not tolerate violence against patients.

Horror tales about cold baths were grossly exaggerated. He had witnessed the procedure only once and decided then and there that it would stop. Female attendants who said he had ordered cold baths for demented old women had misunderstood him. "I simply intended to order them bathed in cold water using a scrubbing brush instead of warm water for persistent filthiness, and did not know that anything else was done until I read the testimony. Cold water and scrubbing brush are more effectual in causing a patient to cease washing himself from head to foot in his own manure than a nice warm bath."

He wrote that he had personally choked only one patient, a woman, "large, stout, and desperate," who tried to bite him when he came to the assistance of a frightened attendant. "I boxed her ears for it. I have boxed the ears of all the cases sworn to by attendants, and perhaps other cases. I have done it in the same manner that I would were I a teacher or father and a large unmannerly child had broken crockery over my head, spit in my face, kicked me, assaulted me with a knife or exceeding[ly] obscene language. I have never seen this do any hurt to the patient, but much good. [It] has changed their malignity and obscenity to respect, kindness and good feeling toward me." His pen emerged from the inkwell dripping bile. "I have no doubt of its utility in the cases in which it was resorted to, but it looks bad on paper, and inasmuch as we are judged from that standpoint by many who have little knowledge of the perplexities of a superintendent and occurring exigencies in his life, and little care for him except to magnify his faults, it is perhaps better for him to have less discipline, and not resort to anything except simpering smiles and meaningless expressions of astonishment at assault, obscenity and other things above referred to."

True, he did send three volunteers to assist two salaried attendants taking ex-soldiers to the veterans' hospital in Washington. Five attendants for the cost of two! And this is called extravagant?[4] Thus were five patients, including two who were "very bad and dangerous and would fight to escape" safely conveyed over eight hundred miles at minimal cost to the state. So what if in return for their services they all took a day or two to see the sights? Who could begrudge them that small reward or himself for authorizing it? To protect hospital funds against extravagance he had entrusted the purse to his father-in-law, George Hebard, "a very careful saving man."

Had he taught attendants how to hit patients without leaving bruises as some had claimed? "I never told any attendant to knock down or strike a patient in my life."

Had a shipment of eggs smelled bad? Indeed it had. There were none on the market that did not. He had taken the best he could find.

He fumed over efforts to make him appear indifferent to the needs of hopelessly demented old women. Of one he wrote, "I considered it folly to go through the formality of climbing the stairs, look[ing] into her room, saying, 'How are you today?' and receiving in reply, 'I am lost, utterly lost!' I have long ceased to look for recovery, as I have many times informed her friends. I do not consider these as cases of neglect," he continued, betraying a sense of powerlessness and disgust at odds with the upbeat tone of his annual reports, "for what good of going to them, pull their dresses off their heads, look into their soulless faces and turn away with a sigh lamenting your inability to see why a good God sees fit to continue life after the soul has fled?"

Throughout his litany of denials, rebuttals, and corrections, Van Norstrand remained confident and unrepentant, his head high. "And now in this solemn manner I wish to say that I have worked harder the last four years than any other four years of my life; that

I have only looked out for the state's interest and the interests of my patients; that I never have encouraged or endured or winked at, officially or privately, anything wrong in dealing with patients or the public; that I have conducted the affairs of this institution as carefully and less generously than I would had they been my own private affairs; that I have never intentionally done, or allowed to be done, a cruel thing to a patient or neglected a patient."

* * *

Mist hanging over the thawing lake, crocuses, daffodils, the sudden greening of the grounds, windows thrown open to vent the accumulated poisons of winter—all the eagerly awaited signs of spring probably left Van Norstrand cold this time around, so preoccupied was he with the storm destined to break over his head when the special committee presented its findings in early May.

April was cruel in a different way for his adversaries on the special committee judging from the exhaustive document that they were compiling—nearly three hundred hand-written legal sheets.[5] Complicating matters for Samuel Hastings, the opportunity of a lifetime had presented itself at the worst possible moment. Samuel Daggett, president of the Northwestern Mutual Life Insurance Company, was dying. At a meeting of company trustees in early April, Madison banker and fellow hospital trustee Simeon Mills nominated Hastings for the position of interim president. He was elected, but just barely—ten votes for, nine against.[6] "No man in our state is more universally respected, or enjoys the confidence of the policy holders and the public generally than Mr. Hastings," declared the *Milwaukee Sentinel*. The *State Journal* urged that his appointment be made permanent when the time was right.[7] Sixteen years after opening his little store in the frontier settlement of LaCrosse, Samuel Hastings was about to take control of one of the biggest financial institutions in the country.

Meanwhile Van Norstrand took pains to strengthen his position. In January he had hosted the state medical society, earning praise from colleagues and press as well. More recently he had either discharged or refused to readmit several of his most hard-core patients, including the belligerent drunk from Stoughton and the periodically murderous half-breed from Prairie du Chien. He had fired Marietta Richards, his most outspoken critic among the attendants. He had issued an order forbidding violence against patients.[8] His sister-in-law, Augusta Hebard, was making a belated effort to control her temper and be more agreeable on the wards.[9] On May 1, just days before the trustees were expected in town, he wrote hasty assessments in the casebook on over thirty female patients: "filthy and disagreeable. . . . Quiet and good. . . . Obscene, vulgar & profane. . . . Quiet and industrious. . . . Willful, obstinate, disagreeable. . . . " Was he hoping to impress the trustees with this fevered, if belated, record-keeping?

He also continued to buy nearly all the hospital's groceries, medications, liquor—even paint and hardware—from his own store, as if thumbing his nose at the board's effort to create a bidding process that was above suspicion. If anything, he abused the system more than ever. Over the previous four years, drugs and groceries had been purchased from many local merchants, although most of the business had been split between three. Only once did a grocer approach three thousand dollars in hospital business in a single year. But in the past *six months* Dr. Van Norstrand had paid out 37 hundred dollars to Mr. Van Norstrand, grocer. For the first time ever, one merchant monopolized the hospital's business, and that merchant was the hospital's superintendent. Maybe he was confident that he would once again emerge from controversy in triumph, or maybe he had decided to make the most of a fading opportunity, propriety be damned. If his buying habits were not provocation enough, in May—the very month his fate hung in the balance—he applied to Treasurer Mills for five hundred dollars in personal reimbursement for "minor incidentals," a category that had rarely exceeded two hundred dollars a month since the hospital opened. Catch me if you dare, he seemed to taunt.[10]

Only a year ago a legislative committee had showered the

hospital with praise. Its accounts were "correct to a cent." Dr. Van Norstrand was the perfect fit for a position that required an "iron constitution and nerve, as well as good professional and business education." He "fully appreciates and faithfully discharges his great responsibility." His recovery rate of "44 ½ per cent" exceeded those of costlier eastern institutions run by famous names.[11]

So much had changed in a year. Misgivings about hospitals for the insane were cropping up across the country. An article in the *Atlantic Monthly* attacked lax commitment laws. Devious relatives, incompetent doctors, and hospital officers loathe to acknowledge mistakes conspired to railroad sane but powerless men and women into "mad-houses" where "abuses are flagrant enough, if the veracity of those who have escaped can be relied upon." "Even as we write there come to us from the State Asylum of Illinois tales of such malign cruelty. . . . Pennsylvania reveals pictures of most wanton neglect and infamous treatment. Massachusetts joins them [in their] bitter cries for reform by her record of the recent death of the son of an eminent clergyman who had been manacled with heavy chains in squalid filth."[12]

Skeletons were being dragged out of closets and hung up for public inspection, to the distress of superintendents in Maine, Vermont, Iowa, Washington, D.C., New York, and eventually even Rhode Island, where Dr. John Sawyer ran the hospital.[13] In Wisconsin, however, the most unsettling revelations were about Mrs. Packard and the asylum in Illinois. The *Chicago Tribune* circulated widely in southern Wisconsin. It had published the complete report of the Illinois investigating committee, and the resulting outrage may have been what prompted the Wisconsin trustees to keep their own findings secret, at least for the time being. But nothing could disperse the cloud of suspicion that hung over their own hospital as the hearings went on, even if the public heard only vague rumors. According to an unsigned letter in the *Tribune* (probably from Hastings or Sherwood), the special committee was not the source of those rumors, but the stories were mostly true.[14] In one form or another the same question was being asked across the country: we created this brave new institution, but do we really know anything about it?

Even the weather added to the drama as the fifteen trustees gathered in the Agriculture Room of the Capitol on Tuesday evening, May 5—heavy rain carried on gusts of unseasonably cold wind.[15] Board president H. H. Giles chaired the meeting. Franklin Lawrence reverted to his role as recording secretary. Routine reports were quickly disposed of before Samuel Hastings took the floor and began to read from a hefty document already being referred to as "The Majority Report." At 8:30 Wednesday morning he picked up where he had left off the night before. After a mid-day break he read on until the last page was turned early in the evening.

One enterprising reporter snuck in for a brief visit. The proceedings looked like "a solemn court of impeachment, even more so than that on exhibition in Washington," he wrote, referring to President Andrew Johnson's ongoing ordeal, and he felt as welcome there as an alligator among bathers in Lake Michigan.[16]

SIXTEEN

A Solemn Court of Impeachment

Hastings had left no stone unturned. Every patient capable of coherent conversation had been interviewed, every attendant and officer had been called to testify, former employees had been contacted by telegraph and letter, experts had been consulted, rumors had been tracked to the source and investigated, annual reports of superintendents throughout the nation had been reviewed, and the prices of everything from allspice to extract of valerian had been compared. In the end, the superintendent stood revealed as a scoundrel and a cheat.[1]

The pattern of the report was a series of contrasts—between theory and reality, between the hospital as depicted and experienced, and above all, between the superintendent as noble public figure and greedy despot.

For guiding principles Hastings and Sherwood had turned to acknowledged experts like Thomas Kirkbride, Pliny Earle, Isaac Ray, and John Gray. They organized selected quotations by topic, assembling a series of gold standards by which to evaluate their own hospital. On the subject of discipline, for instance, their report quoted nine superintendents, from Massachusetts to California, each of whom rejected punishment as barbaric while extolling the therapeutic value of kindness. "Kindness is omnipotent with the insane," wrote Dr. Workman of Toronto. "Punishment can only confirm their malady and transform them into brutes." According to Dr. Isaac Ray, "The feature that characterizes the modern management of the insane is the invariable use of kind and gentle treatment." In an obscure report of the state legislature they found breathless praise to "the still, small and gentle dews of kindness to quench the fires of madness." From the matter-of-fact to the mawkish, the authorities agreed: punishment did not work; kindness did.[2]

"But we must turn from this pleasant picture," Hastings read, "to contemplate the sad and revolting state of the institution under charge of this board." He unleashed a broadside of horrors: chokings, kickings, and beatings with fists, keys, and straps; of belting down, locking away, and near drowning. In Hastings's telling, the bully who emerged most vividly from patients' recollections was young Fred Van Norstrand: "'I have seen Fred take a piece of meat on a fork and put it into a patient's mouth and then take the handle of the fork and attempt to force it down. Have seen him strike the same patient on the head with his keys because he would not eat more. [He] died not long after.'" Fred even attacked a man who beat him at checkers and bragged about it. To see how the strong tyrannized the weak at the Wisconsin Insane Hospital you only had to watch the superintendent's brutal son at work. Hastings posed the fundamental question: "Upon whom rests the responsibility for all this cruelty? We place this responsibility upon the superintendent."

The cold bath was subjected to the same exhaustive scrutiny— the opinions of experts, all of whom rejected it as likely to kill the patient—balanced against the testimony of attendants who recited the same old story: legs hanging over the tub, arms held or tied, the torso pinned, the resisting head plunged, the panic and struggle, the waiting.

Who was responsible? The superintendent "*did know of these abuses* [Hastings's emphasis], and some of the most flagrant wrongs were committed by his express orders."[3] He knew that choking was commonplace; he ordered the cold baths; he boxed ears, battered a woman in restraints until she was black and blue, yanked patients to their feet by the hair, choked, attacked and threw them against the wall. He ordered attendants to feed a man his own excrement and to rub his face in it. Thus did Hastings assemble likenesses of father and son, one a raging tyrant, the other a spiteful thug.

His examination of the Kellogg affair began with another study
in contrasts: the comforting assurances of earlier investigating committees set against the superintendent's lies and evasions. He ended
with a thundering rebuke. No information had been withheld by
the family. Reverend Kellogg had never displayed homicidal or suicidal tendencies. The superintendent's claims to the contrary were
self-serving distortions. The patient almost certainly suffered "kicks
and cuffs, blows and chokings" from the sour-tempered attendants
who dragged him upstairs. The strong room was almost certainly *not*
heated, the shutters were *not* locked, and *no one* stood by to monitor
sounds from the room: "Think of his condition—a highly educated,
intelligent, frail man, with his nervous system unstrung, his mind
wandering from excess of mental labor and religious excitement,
needing kind, tender and soothing care, and such applications to
his body as were so clearly set forth in the communication from his
wife. And then think of the treatment he actually received. Here we
find him on this cold winter's night—the mercury standing below
zero—in this cold, cheerless, desolate, strong room, with nothing
on him but his shirt, with the shutter unfastened, and doubtless
it was but a few moments before in his wild phrenzy the window
was broken, and the cold wind from the north was blowing upon
his naked body! Is it any wonder that he was found dead in the
morning?"

As for the superintendent's professed devotion to duty: had
Dr. Van Norstrand paid "strict and daily attention to all patients" as
the bylaws require? Not according to the attendants. Hastings and
Sherwood had asked them to record the number of minutes he spent
on their wards each day. When combined and averaged these records
showed that the superintendent spent only three to five minutes on
each ward. He avoided especially odious or hopeless patients for
weeks on end. He could not tell one old woman from another, and
he deliberately hid some of them from the Visiting Committee. But
he found plenty of time to lavish rewards on family and friends, to
entertain guests with delicacies that never showed up on the patients'

tables, and to pursue his own business interests.

Were patients kept busy? The superintendent depicted a constant round of diversions, from games and carriage rides to therapeutic labors, but attendants who actually lived with them said they were "confined like prisoners," wasting away for lack of anything to do.

What about tobacco? Half a ton had been purchased over the past two years and doled out as an inducement to get men to work. Yet experts at other hospitals had forbidden tobacco, considering it one of the evils that led to insanity.

Did he try to attract the right sort of employees? Over seventy had come and gone in the preceding four years, including drunks, brutes, and others of "low moral character." Few met the standards specified in the regulations.

Did he protect the state's purse? The hospital was "the largest, most expensive and most important of our public charities." Dr. Van Norstrand had spent nearly one-third of all the money allocated to it by the legislature. He was guardian not only of the patients but of the state's dollars. Had he spent them in the best interests of both his patients and the state?

Hardly. As head of the hospital he received and read bids submitted by merchants, and then as a competing merchant he adjusted his own bids accordingly. When others refused to bid at all, he *raised* his own bid. The hospital paid higher prices at Sumner and Co. than walk-in customers. By Hastings's calculation, the superintendent paid his own store from one-third to one-half *more* for many items than would have been charged by competitors. He routinely included the weight of the crock or the crate and paid his store accordingly. Thus did he transfer state funds for which he was custodian to his own pocket. No wonder he had urged his business partner not to cooperate with those authorized to follow the money trail. He was doubly cursed, first defrauding the state, then attempting to obstruct an investigation into his crime.

Finally, Hastings responded to the written statement Van Norstrand had given the court commissioner in March, a stratagem that had allowed him to evade cross-examination. The doctor argued that he disciplined patients like a teacher or father, that he saved money by sending friends and family members to Washington as attendants, that his critics had no conception of his responsibilities and the arduousness of his job, and that he had never tolerated abuse or neglect and had always been a careful guardian of state funds. "We are constrained to say," Hastings concluded, "that the man who can solemnly make such a declaration in view of the actual facts, shows that his moral perceptions of right and wrong have become so blunted that he is entirely unable to appreciate the high responsibilities of the position he occupies and totally unqualified for the discharge of its important duties." He moved that Dr. Van Norstrand be discharged immediately and that Dr. Wilson be put in charge pending election of a new superintendent.

If he had expected a stampede, he was disappointed. Lawrence rose to protest. He asked for time to prepare a response. Dr. Van Norstrand also insisted on the right to defend himself. The trustees voted nine to four to delay a vote on Hastings's resolution. In an unusual move certain to cause them all a good deal of inconvenience they decided to reassemble on June 2. Lawrence and Van Norstrand had four weeks to put together a minority report. Only after both sides had been heard would they consider Hastings's motion. Hastings and Sherwood had struck the serpent a mighty blow, but it still lived.

Van Norstrand was ordered to bring Mrs. Hazel Roach before the board the next day to be examined by doctors from the community. No good could come of this. Mrs. Roach had been interviewed at length by Hastings and Sherwood, and his own encounters with her had been far from cordial. She had been admitted with a form of epilepsy characterized by verbal and physical aggression, perhaps what are now called psychomotor, or temporal lobe seizures. "Profane, vulgar, obscene and violent," Van Norstrand had written. Her husband thought these spells were related to her periods. Though she had improved on medication she remained on the outs with both the doctor and his wife. It was Mrs. Roach who had tipped off the investigators to Mrs. Van Norstrand's preference for well-connected patients, and as for the superintendent, she would not give him the time of day. Early encounters had been explosive enough—bitter arguments that left them both in a snit. Then one day he pulled her hair, slapped her, and dragged her off to a strong room, and not a word had passed between them since.

Van Norstrand was stymied. Potassium bromide had made her seizures disappear, but they returned when he discontinued the medication. Was she cured, improved, or still sick—the illness masked by the medicine? Should she go or should she stay? It didn't help that he avoided her and that he seemed not to grasp the nature of epilepsy, at least in her case. The note that he wrote about her during his recent day of marathon charting was detailed but ambiguous. "She is still a little unreasonable at times," he concluded, "but I am not certain that is [not] a natural feature in her character. She is very nearly recovered."[4] Perhaps anticipating controversy, he left the door open to either an early discharge or an extended stay.

Lawrence's minutes of the next day's meetings, which were devoted mostly to procedural matters, gave no sense of the frayed nerves and mounting tension. That Van Norstrand still had credibility with most of the trustees is apparent from their response to a petition from the town fathers of Prairie du Chien, who had gotten nowhere with Van Norstrand and so went over his head, appealing directly to the board to readmit the demented, unpredictable Bernard LaRochelle. But the board stood behind the superintendent. For now, La Rochelle was not welcome to return.[*]

Finally it took up the matter of Mrs. Roach. For Hastings, Sherman, and their supporters, her case exemplified Van Norstrand's outrageous behavior toward patients. Though clearly sane she had been treated brutally and held against her will. Two outside doctors who had evaluated her agreed with them. She should go home. This time the board sided with the superintendent's opponents, and a

---

[*] LaRochelle was readmitted in January, 1869, and spent the rest of his life at the hospital. He died in 1891. Male Casebook, pp. 17 and 359.

telegram was sent to her husband to come for her. Citing the case as evidence of Van Norstrand's incompetence, Sherwood again moved that he be fired. But again, no action was taken.

Van Norstrand was not present that evening and played no part in the decision to discharge Mrs. Roach. Something more than the call of duty may have prompted his absence. Like a written statement submitted in lieu of oral testimony, this appears to have been a tactical move. If he was not present he could not be put on the spot. The next day he charted on her for the last time: "Although I fear it is a premature discharge, still in view of the action of the board of trustees I am compelled to put her down as a recovery." If he felt chastened, he wasn't about to admit it.[5] Below his entry, in another hand, appears an implied rebuke: "When is epilepsy cured?"

* * *

Passions did not cool over the next few weeks as Lawrence and Van Norstrand prepared separate rebuttals. A story in the *Chicago Tribune* made light of the whole affair: from the beginning the intention of the investigators had been to bring down the superintendent, their charges amounting to nothing more than "molehills magnified into mountains." The sentiment and the awkward phrasing sounded suspiciously like Van Norstrand.[6]

An angry response from "a member of the investigating committee" appeared nine days later, the writer violating the spirit if not the letter of the board's secrecy ruling by insisting that he had "conclusive evidence of the bad management of the superintendent." If readers could see the evidence, he asserted, they would have to conclude "that your asylum at Jacksonville is pretty well managed after all in comparison to ours."[7]

Hastings and Sherwood had uncovered new information and new witnesses, and on Tuesday, June 2, they squeezed in more testimony in advance of the meeting of the board. Thus at the last moment the hearings resumed. Two former clerks at Sumner & Co. confirmed tales of tainted and diluted commodities—watered whiskey and watered molasses, foul black sugar disguised by grinding it in with a better grade, tobacco good only for "washing sheep," butter unfit to eat, and so on. One claimed to have seen the doctor at the store four or five times a week, the implication being that he could hardly claim to be unaware of what was going on. "We could not have sold [these items] to anyone else," he said.[8]

Three witnesses called back for return engagements were less cooperative. One, John Sumner, ignored the subpoena.[9] Mary Halliday took the stand with obvious reluctance. Hastings and Sherwood pressed her about the tainted food. All they managed to elicit was an admission that things shipped from Sumner and Company did not get the same close scrutiny as goods from other merchants.

If they were trying to drive a wedge between Van Norstrand and his officers, they had better luck with Dr. Wilson. At first Wilson had played the loyal subordinate, but he bristled at some of the things Van Norstrand said on the stand. He was in a thankless position, increasingly at odds with his boss, yet with no fondness for his inquisitors either. But when closely questioned he spoke frankly. "All the cold baths were ordered by the superintendent," just as the superintendent had been well aware of routine violence against patients and had not objected. As for Mrs. Roach, she should have been discharged long ago and likely would have been but for the superintendent's hostility toward her.

Van Norstrand rose to cross-examine. Didn't Wilson agree that epilepsy had damaged Mrs. Roach's mind and that his refusal to bicker with her was proper and enlightened treatment? Wilson stood his ground. She should have been sent home.

Wilson stepped down. At last the hearings were over. In a few hours the trustees would assemble for their second and decisive meeting of the spring. Van Norstrand had never been more exposed and alone. The female attendants had ambushed him, and the males had piled on. Now Wilson had openly turned on him. Even Mrs. Halliday's support was shaky.

Still at his side was Franklin Sheldon Lawrence, the odd man out on the investigating committee. Lawrence had compiled a minority report that added seventy-three handwritten legal pages to the mountain of paper already generated by the investigation, and at 7:30 that unseasonably cold evening, with a heavy rain beating the windows of their hearing room in the capitol, he began to read.[*]

His strategy was to demonstrate that "other motives than those of a purely disinterested and unselfish character" lay behind the attack on the superintendent. From the beginning, the objective of Hastings and Sherwood had been to bring him down. That was at the heart of the report they had patched together from "parts of testimony, wrong deductions and conclusions, and special pleadings." They had snuck behind the superintendent's back, panning for nuggets from grudge-holders and malcontents. They had manipulated information and misrepresented the opinions of the experts—anything to put him in the worst possible light.

Their report was a repudiation not only of the superintendent "but of this board of trustees and its managing committees." Were the choruses of praise echoed by so many reviewing bodies through the years, including the board's own visiting and executive committees, all wrong? Had they all been duped? Had they engaged in a conspiracy to cover the truth? "Who," Lawrence asked, "is to be believed?"

Dr. John Sawyer, now at the Butler Insane Hospital in Rhode Island, emphasized that every hospital community was encumbered with its share of "discharged help, half-recovered patients, and other disturbers of the peace" eager to spread malicious mischief about the man in charge. Such were the sources Hastings and Sherwood had cultivated while ignoring trustworthy witnesses such as recovered patients.

How in good faith could they charge the superintendent with neglect of duty? Lawrence itemized Van Norstrand's accomplishments. Under his guidance two hundred acres of stumps, boulders, and wilderness had been converted to profitable farm land and attractive, shady grounds. Construction of new wings had been

---

[*] The minority report is on pages 131–56 of the appendix.

completed. Sewage and ventilation systems had been economically upgraded using hospital labor. Systemic structural problems in the central building and original wings had been fixed and a barn and other outbuildings erected. "In view of all these duties imposed upon your superintendent, can the majority committee come before you with any grace and charge him with neglect of duty because he failed occasionally to visit a patient or perform his usual visits to the wards?" If patients were neglected, blame the trustees for expecting their man to carry such a burden without bending.

The "abuses" that Dr. Van Norstrand was accused of had been standard practice long before he came to the hospital. Thus Dr. Sawyer was equally guilty, but would anyone dare make such a charge against the revered Sawyer? Did the superintendent succeed in his primary responsibility? A comparison with Dr. Sawyer's hospital in Rhode Island proved that Van Norstrand was doing the better job. His death rate was lower, his recovery rate higher. In a letter dated May 2, Sawyer acknowledged his debt to the man he had assisted for two and a half years: "[Dr. Van Norstrand] always supported and upheld me. By his energy and industry [he] was able to accomplish many improvements which a less earnest man would not have attempted. I thought the Doctor's success was proof of the wisdom of his selection as superintendent, and I am at a loss to imagine a cause for dissatisfaction."

The "animosity and vindictiveness" of Hastings and his partner reached fever pitch in their account of the Kellogg affair. "Every act, every circumstance, every word and saying of your superintendent . . . is construed into acts of cruelty and torture and murderous neglect." Again Lawrence turned to Sawyer, this time as an ethical model by which to judge both the superintendent and his accusers. He quoted from Sawyer's letter—which in all likelihood he had solicited—which refuted Hastings and Sherwood without mentioning them. Kellogg's death, Sawyer wrote, was "one of those accidents which no human skill or foresight can prevent. Every precaution required by the symptoms was taken." Sawyer recalled sitting on the stairs outside Kellogg's strong room, waiting until the attendants had left, "not because I thought it necessary to watch the process, but because I wished to be at hand if my advice was needed."* The men dealing with Kellogg, he recalled, "were long known to be skillful and kind." And when he was called to the room the next morning, Sawyer wrote, "I *distinctly remember* that the body of Mr. K. was warm when I saw it and that the register was open and *warm air coming in.*" (Sawyer's emphasis) Was Van Norstrand neglectful by not personally taking charge? At Sawyer's hospital, subordinates often acted upon their own initiative—including transferring patients to other rooms—without consulting him until later, a degree of independence that was necessary for the welfare of patients and staff alike: "The notion that you would needlessly interfere with the operations of a subordinate seems absurd." On every point, Sawyer's letter refuted Hastings and Sherwood.

Lawrence exhausted himself trying to prove that Van Norstrand had carried out the instructions of the board of trustees "honestly and fairly" when making purchases for the hospital. He insisted that Van Norstrand had resorted to Sumner & Company only as a supplier of last resort when others refused to bid or reneged on their contracts. "It is true that Dr. Van Norstrand is a partner of J. W. Sumner," he said, "but I don't see that the hospital has suffered thereby." He submitted his own list of retail price comparisons—from English soda to turpentine—which proved that the hospital came out ahead by buying from Sumner & Company, and he accused his opponents of using deceptive figures in arguing otherwise. Thus even a topic that seemed immune to obfuscation, the comparative prices of tea, coffee, and eggs, was clouded by charges and countercharges. Further complicating matters, as Van Norstrand later reminded his listeners, were seasonal variations in price, quality, and availability.

Were patients sometimes brutally punished? Lawrence was confident that Dr. Van Norstrand would explain away those charges to the satisfaction of the board. What concerned him were the

---

* This letter seems to contradict the telegram he had sent to Hastings and Sherwood in March in which he stated that he had waited in his office that night, not outside Kellogg's room.

methods and motives of Messrs. Hastings and Sherwood. In their hands, an investigation had become a vendetta. No superintendent anywhere could have survived such hostile scrutiny.

"'By their acts ye shall judge them,'" he concluded.*

---

* Matthew 7:20: "By their fruits ye shall know them."

SEVENTEEN

Abandon Hope

To prevent the superintendent from taking center stage and playing the wounded monarch, Hastings and Sherwood had twice urged that he be fired immediately and twice they had failed. So now Van Norstrand stalked from the wings bearing his own stack of papers. By this time an astute trustee could roughly calculate how long a performance would last by the thickness of that stack. Hastings had taken two days to work through his; Lawrence, several hours. Van Norstrand's manuscript was smaller than Hastings's but thicker than Lawrence's. Two sittings, maybe more.

He opened on a note of sorrow. A shadow had been cast over his administration. Reckless charges had been made. Though he preferred to fix his gaze upon the humanitarian challenges that he and the board had long contemplated together, circumstances compelled him to lower it to the sordid scene contrived by his accusers. He would not shrink from the challenge, however distasteful.

But the trustees must understand that this was an unequal contest. No one should expect his report to match that of his accusers "in literary effort, extended research, or personal bitterness," they being "very capable dealers in gall and wormwood." It had taken them five months of single-minded labor to build their case whereas he had been allowed less than a month—"with an interruption at an average of every ten minutes"—to respond. Above all, he was handicapped by a disinclination to stoop to their level. "It is foreign to my nature," he said, "to deal in personality." Years later, in the opening paragraphs of his memoirs, he would once again strike the pose of a proud man above the fray. Then as now he could not sustain it for long.

He set the scene. For five months he had given the special committee free access to patients, records, and staff. He had never interfered—hardly even paid attention—trusting instead to their sense of fair play. And all that time the sole objective of two of its three members had been to dig up dirt. In this effort they had been joined by male attendants angry at him for threatening to have them arrested if they abused patients. This conspiracy was vouched for by John Mooney, from whose recent affidavit he read: "Redford told us to think up all the difficulties the superintendent had had with patients and swear to them the next day. Redford said he was going over to Hastings or Sherwood and tell them to have us sworn over again, we hadn't told half. He said he would do all he could to get the superintendent removed."

"It was at once plain why there was this unanimous effort to mention every occurrence that could be tortured into wrongdoing," Van Norstrand continued. "Here was a man at the head of my attendants, herding them into his room and giving them their lesson against the superintendent, doubtless rehearsing to them the abuse I had heaped on them—by never inviting them to my table, or introducing them to gentlemen or ladies visiting the wards, or in many cases had misused them by remonstrating with them for neglect or roughness, thus forming them in solid phalanx for the morrow's testimony."

And what did Hastings and Sherwood do when presented with a conspiracy that principled men would have repudiated? They exploited it, even though the attendants intended to punish the superintendent for taking firm measures to *protect patients* from *the attendants'* excesses. In issuing the order threatening legal action he had done what Hastings should applaud and defend. In attempting to circumvent that order by retaliating against the superintendent, the attendants were doing what Hastings should deplore. Yet Hastings cared nothing for their malicious intentions, only that he could use them to further his own.

Not only had the majority members of the committee cynically exploited a conspiracy. They had also tried to coax his business partner into siding with them. Van Norstrand read from a second affidavit, this one sworn to by J. W. Sumner: "John Sherwood told me that he was not after the good management [of the hospital], but was there to find out the bad management of it. Sherwood told me that he had the Doctor tight, and he would protect me, and he wanted me to swear strong and plain, and he would shield me. He said he did not intend to be a whitewashing committee, that if he got after anybody he was bound to fetch them. He said Dr. Van Norstrand would not want to live in Madison after he—Sherwood—got through with him." Samuel Hastings had also paid Sumner a visit: "He said he wanted to see all bills of tea purchased since I had been in business. I told him, why don't you go about to other stores and root up these things. There were other stores where they had imposed on the doctor in weight. Mr. Hastings replied that it was not the stores or me he was after, but he was after the doctor, meaning Dr. Van Norstrand."

As Van Norstrand read on, it became obvious that his report was not the slapdash affair he had described. Frequent interruptions or not, he had found time to pursue witnesses and elicit sworn statements, to scour dozens of reports, to correspond with former employees and to review the writings of eastern authorities, just as Hastings and Sherwood had done.

"With this kind of feeling on the part of the majority of the committee," he continued, "and on the part of the discharged employees, together with those who were in league with them, is it any wonder that they could prove anything their malevolence suggested? Mr. Hastings says to Mr. Sumner that it was not the store or him that he was after, but *he was after the doctor!* How *manly*, how *brotherly*, how *comprehensive* this man's affections—not one grain of practical kindness—all theoretical—his *heart* an *aggregation* of bitterness" (Van Norstrand's emphasis). And as for Sherwood, he had come to Sumner "to pick me and the institution all to pieces, and sow the ill-looking fragments broadcast over the land." Like Hastings, he was "a malevolent man" determined "to fill the mind of Mr. Sumner with the surplus bitterness of his own, breaking up our business connection, and ruin[ing] me pecuniarily as well as socially, to dispossess me of what little I had saved in my professional labors of a quarter century."

Mrs. Roach was another member of their conspiracy. Hastings and Sherwood had shut themselves up with her one day, and afterwards she boasted that they were going to have her sent home soon, "and intimating that the superintendent and his family were going out about the same time." There was one more conspirator, someone especially close to the superintendent—none other than Dr. Wilson, "who, I am informed and believe, has favored Hastings and Sherwood all the way through, and in so doing, I believe, has played the spy on me and my duties."

He defended his refusal to discharge Mrs. Roach sooner, citing her "many relapses" and the advice of Dr. Kirkbride, who had often warned of the dangers of sending patients home too soon. The board had ordered him to discharge her and he had done so, but he was convinced that in time the board would come to regret second-guessing him in this matter.

To what lengths would his accusers go to smear him? They had even dug into his army years, insisting to Sumner that he had been discharged with a bad reputation. "Well, what of it?" Van Norstrand said. "Suppose I was a coward, or indolent, or was fierce with the amputating knife? What has that to do with the 'critical and searching investigation of the Wisconsin State Hospital for the Insane'? Such charges are not made by any man who has honorably worn the blue. They are not made by any member of our late army. They are not made by *any* member of the old Fourth Wisconsin Cavalry, who went out a thousand and ten strong, and who had in the last hours of the forty-two days' fight at Port Hudson but sixty-seven men in the saddle.* I say such charges do not come from men who have bared

---

* He is speaking figuratively. At Port Hudson the regiment was dismounted and fought as infantry.

their breasts to rebel bullets. They are made by men who, in 1861-2-3-4, were stay-at-home *sneaks*, men who were compelled to stay at home to look after pecuniary affairs or were charged with great financial measures." In other words, men like Samuel Hastings.

Who vouches for him? Former Sergeant Clarke, for one. A recent member of the state legislature and Van Norstrand's patient in Baton Rouge, Clarke had rejected overtures from friends of Hastings and Sherwood, telling them, "that I had saved his life, and he was now ready to use it to defend me from slander or any other harm."

He summarized letters of support from a physician-legislator who vouched for his humanity and good conduct, and from Webster Moore, the young man he had recruited into the Fourth Wisconsin who eventually became its commander. Moore cited Van Norstrand's courage in standing up for the men at Ship Island and his success running hospitals under extraordinary wartime conditions. The senior Dr. Wilson, his assistant during the war, wrote that Van Norstrand had exhibited "a capacity and ability and devotion to the service worthy of all commendation. I do not think he has received the credit that is his due." Van Norstrand also submitted a letter presented to him upon his separation from the Fourth Wisconsin which commended him for his "energy and skill," and which bore the signatures of seventeen officers of the regiment.

No doubt he would have welcomed testimonials from other old army friends, but most were beyond reach. Boardman, Bailey, and Bean were dead. Of his closest wartime friends only Halbert Paine survived. Now serving in Congress, Paine would certainly have seen accounts of the hospital controversy in the *Milwaukee Sentinel*, but for whatever reason he chose not to come to the defense of his old comrade.

Why didn't Van Norstrand attack the issue head-on? Why is he so evasive, posing rhetorical questions about courage, energy, and fierceness with the knife? He insists that his army reputation was spotless, but he knew that was not true. Joseph Bailey had told him that officers were saying bad things about him. He must have known that it was not his courage or his skill as a surgeon that was in question but his integrity, and that in linking his army life to his conduct as superintendent, Hastings and Sherwood were asserting that he was a deeply flawed man.

Before the proceedings were suspended for the night Sherwood moved that the letters Van Norstrand had cited in his defense be made available to trustees. The motion failed, a small vote of confidence in the superintendent. All parties emerged from the Capitol into a cool misting rain, the lights of their hotels and rooming houses beckoning through the trees of the surrounding park. It had been a long day.

First thing Wednesday morning, Sherwood again moved that the proceedings be opened to the public. The motion was defeated. He then moved that the governor—presumably in his office nearby—and other state officers be encouraged to come see for themselves what was going on. Again, the motion was defeated. Dr. Van Norstrand rose to continue reading his statement. A few hours rest had not cooled his temper. He insisted that he had always been more stingy with hospital money than with his own purse, whether in transferring veterans to the hospital in Washington, wringing a good price from his brother in the purchase of cattle, or using his leverage with Sumner to underbid other merchants. "I entered into the partnership [with Sumner] to make a place for my son, who had become weary of school. I intended to make the store our headquarters in the city, where people could always find us [and] could leave bundles for patients, and where they could find the Hospital team when they wished to avail themselves of it. I intended to purchase drugs and light articles there, leaving the heavy trade to men who had more means to handle heavy articles, but when these men refused to furnish the goods [they had] bid for, Mr. Sumner was requested to furnish them, and thus he had much of our trade for a few months. I have much regretted this partnership. I found it an improper place for my son. I did not deem it justice to Mr. Sumner to deprive him of all profits from the hospital trade for no reason but that he was my partner, [and] it brought down the animosity of other dealers on me."

As for the committee's insistence on revisiting the Kellogg affair, "Mr. Hastings told me in effect, and I think in these very words, that his reason for making all this expense and trouble was to please [Kellogg's] friends by showing that it was a death from self-violence and not from suicide." In other words, Hastings was simply doing the family a favor. All this renewed anguish and pain over a word. Was the use of the word "suicide" in a telegram evidence of unforgivable insensitivity? "Telegrams are always heartless, using just as few words as possible," he reminded the trustees. He pointed out that in his own annual reports, Dr. Kirkbride routinely referred to deaths by suicide. Was this proof that the impeccable Kirkbride was an insensitive man? Should he have said that these patients "died by self-violence"? Kellogg's wife objected to the use of morphine. So what? "Some old lady in Fort Atkinson did not like its effects in some cases. I have now practiced medicine for twenty-four years and have found it utterly impossible to follow the advice of that class of persons. The whole affair is a sorrowful one. I had hoped that after the thorough investigation given it by a committee of seven honorable men, headed by a minister of the Methodist church, completely exonerating me and my assistants, that these humanitarians would let this poor man's bones lie in peace."

This was not the self-assured executive speaking. This was the "ardent" teacher who frightened his students, the truculent physician who rose to every challenge, slapping demented old women black and blue and locking horns with all manner of knife-wielding, chamber pot-throwing, feces-smearing bullies. Was pain inflicted? Did blood flow? Were displays of submission and mortification extracted? Of course they were. And justice was done. Lessons were learned.

Neglect? If he was guilty, then so was Dr. John Gray of the Utica hospital and other eastern physicians whose reputations so impressed his accusers. They all emphasized how important it was for a superintendent to spend his time with patients who could be cured. It was not as though he had time on his hands, not with his many other responsibilities. Hastings and Sherwood complained that he had neglected Miss Lennox,[1] "a maiden lady of sixty-five years, in poor health, who thinks she has committed 'the unpardonable sin,' and [that] unless she groaned aloud she would choke up and die. She has been in the house nearly two years and has gone through the *whole catalogue* of medication and not benefited." The Visiting Committee thought other patients should be spared her constant loud groaning, and so he sent her up to a fourth floor room that was "large, warm, light, airy and quiet. But Messrs. Hastings and Sherwood seemed to be determined to make a bad case of it, calling [it] a strong room, etc." *This* was what his accusers labeled neglect.

Abuse? Yes, there had been much of it, as he learned from the testimony of the attendants, and he had promptly put a stop to it. As for the cold baths, the whole matter had been blown out of proportion. The cold bath had been given routinely long before his time, the justification being that it was an effective way to control very bad patients. But after he saw it done he had ordered the practice stopped. What his accusers so eagerly represented as cold baths had in fact merely been cold scrubbings which he had ordered administered to feces-smearers and other "persistently filthy" types. Overzealous attendants sometimes got carried away and held the fighting patient's head under, though "not being of a suspicious nature," he had not learned of it until he read the attendants' testimony. "I trust I need not assure you that a recurrence will not take place."

Had he boxed ears? Yes, when anything less would have seemed an abdication of responsibility. "When I came [to] the hospital in April, 1864, the patients were quite clamorous with strangers, complaining of abuse, neglect, etc. They were very abusive in language, occasionally spitting in my face or on my clothes." It was one thing for outsiders to expect the superintendent to hold himself above the fray, but "a different thing to be assailed yourself by a filthy, disgusting creature. It is not part of my intention in this defence to deny that I have boxed the ears of homicidal patients who were flourishing knives to the great terror of attendants, of willfully pugnacious and obscene patients, also of some who have spit in my face, or been willfully guilty of other filthy practices."

He led by example whatever the risk, being "unwilling to ask an attendant to go where [I am] afraid to go [my]self." There was the pugilist issuing ultimatums, the behemoth of a farm wife flailing a blade, the vicious sneak hiding behind his door and crying for help, poised to break his chamber pot over the head of the first person to come to his aid. And of course the notorious Thunderbolt, "a bad man and general thief [who] nearly killed the sheriff with a slung-shot [*sic*]." This man had assaulted attendants and "rubbed his own ordure about the hole in his door, and would then stand back in his room and compel the attendant to reach through it to hand him water or food, thereby spoiling their clothes. I told them to take him and clean the door with his face, nose, mouth and beard, which was gently but faithfully done." Had he resorted to the army's punish-ment in such cases—horse-whipping—"the thunders of Sinai could not have been heard for the groans of the milk and water humanitar-ians." In other words, from the likes of Hastings and Sherwood.

"Whenever I have shaken a patient or boxed ears it has been for a good cause. Still it would have been much better for me person-ally if I had been less energetic, cared less about good order and discipline, and been less ambitious to present a large percent of cures in my annual report to your board. But my nature being otherwise, in the prime of manly energy, I felt that everything ought to come to iron rules, never sparing myself either physically or mentally while a single duty remained unperformed." Thus did his "virtues of com-mission" open him to criticism "from every person who sits by the wayside to malign his betters."

His accusers measured him against the antirestraint theme sounded by so many of the eastern brethren in their annual reports. They especially dwelled "with much unction" on Dr. Kirkbride. Yet, he pointed out, "Dr. Kirkbride is the first man on a list of refer-ences used by a Philadelphia house engaged in making restraining apparatus for insane hospitals. Now, if Dr. Kirkbride does not use these, why does he commend them to others? Gentlemen [the truth is that] Dr. Kirkbride and all other superintendents use them when they think it is necessary. Messrs. Hastings and Sherwood have entirely misapprehended his spirit, or intentionally perverted the facts."

In annual reports he had boasted of the many "amusements" available to patients at the hospital, but now he spoke more frankly. It was true; the hospital could not offer as much in this line as the eastern doctors so lauded by Hastings and Sherwood. However: "I wish to say that aimless amusements have never been favorites of mine; nor do I believe they are appreciated by Western patients; nor do I believe they are as beneficial to Eastern patients as they are in building up the reputations of the superintendents in charge of them." If these great men set such high standards, why were their cure rates lower, their death rates higher, than those at the Wisconsin Hospital?

Yes, some patients under his care had suffered injury and insult, but these were nothing compared to the beatings and humiliations they had endured at home, or in jail, or in the poorhouse. His accusers might conjure milk and honey standards for their fanciful hospital, but in a world of real patients at war with one another and with their keepers, a firm hand was essential, and he did not flinch from using it.

More hard-headed, down-to-earth men than his accusers had passed judgment on him and his management, finding much to praise and little to regret. He quoted from 48 reports submitted by official committees of one kind or another during his years as superintendent. They spoke of "the marked and permanent improvement in management . . ., utmost confidence in the management of the financial affairs of the institution . . ., growing confidence and trust on the part of the inmates . . ., happy improvement in their condition under the regime of the present superintendent . . ., remarkably quiet, contented and cheerful [patients] . . ., a general appearance of cheerfulness and contentment among the patients seldom before observed. . . ." And on and on.

He read letters from discharged patients and their families and testimonials from doctors across the state: "I cannot thank God enough for the kind treatment I have received here.... My wife joins in this expression [of] earnest gratitude, and we both believe that but for your skillful treatment she would have remained hopelessly insane.... Of patients returned to Milwaukee from the asylum, all speak in the highest praise of the kindness received from your hands.... I never will forget your kindness to me as long as I live.... [Dr. Van Norstrand] possesses a *large grand character*, and as compared with our more prominent *best* businessmen, he must rank high, judging from observing his management of this Herculean enterprise.... I [was] impressed with the cordial greeting given to the Doctor by the inmates. There was the freedom, and jocund intimacy, good fellowship and absence of all appearance of absolutism or despotic rule.... [He is] 'the right man in the right place.'"

And yet his accusers had found many who condemned him. Who were they, and what were their motives? Any superintendent worth his salt made enemies—grudge-holding former employees, merchants who lost out on contracts, ex-patients still obsessed and angry, and "renegade attendants," all of them easy prey for "designing persons" like Hastings and Sherwood, whose traps were baited with "artful promises." They had even sent poisonous letters to newspapers, attempting to create a climate of suspicion and hostility toward him.[2] His accusers were like other men, he said: "They do not like to hunt and return with no game. [Their] 'report' is made so manifestly *unjust* as to compel a man of a fair sense of honor to resign."

Resign? The word would have jolted the trustees. He even expressed a degree of remorse: "I have sometimes, much to my regret, carried a part of my very energetic administration of out of door affairs into inside discipline with patients and attendants." Unruly students, slovenly soldiers, willful attendants, even belligerent old women trussed up in canvas and leather—all had been stung by his explosive anger. And some of that he regretted.

Then he was back on the offensive. He compared his death rates to those reported by superintendents his accusers held up as shining examples, and he arrived at a startling conclusion. His vindication was in the numbers: "If neglect or abuse increases the percent of deaths, [my comparison] shows that other superintendents, of whom *their* trustees speak in the highest terms, have neglected or abused their patients, or else that I have not only *not* abused *or* neglected my patients but have given better care and treatment than any other institution in the land. These figures ought to be a sufficient reply to the conspiracy of attendants and the attempted obloquy of the report submitted by Messrs. Hastings and Sherwood. I have proven good care and kindness towards my patients."

But the damage had been done. Once again fired workers and half-cured patients had been recruited for a vendetta; once again trustees refused to stand behind a hard-working superintendent; once again families unable to control their insane at home, "except by the strongest measures," had been encouraged to expect the superintendent to control them "by a kind look alone." His outrage had expanded to include even the board of trustees. And why not? Of them all, only Lawrence had come to his defense while his family and his private life had been trotted out for scrutiny like livestock at auction. He read from a letter sent by a superintendent he refused to name: "The care of the insane in a large state hospital is becoming *so perilous* to the reputation of medical superintendents, especially in the west, that any man who has any reputation to lose may well pause before taking the risks."

He ended with a drumbeat of resentment: "I came to the hospital full of expectation and a hope to succeed where other men had failed. I could not then look back over the paths of similar efforts and see the mental and physical wrecks of those who were willing to give all, even their lives, yea, even lost their reason to restore the same faculty to others. I think the awful lines of Dante should be

---

* The late nineteenth century was a treacherous era for superintendents. Lives and reputations were ruined, often, according to one dismayed colleague, simply on the say-so of "uncured lunatics." Nancy Tomes identified nine who died or were disabled in the line of duty—killed by patients, died of overwork, or their health broken by overwork and scandal. Several committed suicide (Tomes, pp. 277–79). Lawsuits, newspaper accounts of brutality and hell-hole conditions, and widely circulated memoirs of angry former patients all contributed to a wave of investigations across the country that continued for decades. Even the respected dean of superintendents, Thomas Kirkbride, found himself attacked by former patients who charged that they had been kidnapped, choked into submission, and abused generally (Tomes, pp. 256–60).

written over the private room of every superintendent in the land, that he may be constantly warned of the fate of his predecessors." The line he had in mind could only have been: "All hope abandon, ye who enter here."

* * *

For now the trustees could agree on only one thing. Despite the uncertainty hanging over the hospital's future they would listen to *all* the testimony compiled by the investigating committee, nearly a thousand handwritten pages. The reading began at once.

Hastings, meanwhile, was given leave to prepare a rebuttal to the superintendent's statement. A division of labor had evolved between himself and Sherwood. Hastings was the strategist and writer, while Sherwood remained in the trenches firing at targets of opportunity. When the meeting resumed after lunch Sherwood objected to Van Norstrand's continuing presence, arguing that a defendant had no business sitting in on the jury's deliberations. Once again his motion was tabled and the reading resumed.[3]

"It is an imbroglio outsiders cannot understand," the *Chicago Times* said. "Some virulent radicals are after the superintendent."[4]

The reading continued into the night.

* * *

The next day, June 4, dragged by in a tedium of routine matters—a tour of the hospital and a business meeting: the original wards needed to be repainted, more cisterns were needed to store rain water, better accommodations were needed for the chickens and pigs, and so on. The last item of business that afternoon was a motion by Mr. Robinson, the newspaper publisher from Green Bay, authorizing Dr. Van Norstrand to continue to take an active part in the proceedings. The motion passed, another small victory for the superintendent. But a final showdown still loomed.

After supper the board reassembled at the Capitol. Once again thunder rolled and rain lashed the windows as Samuel Hastings took the floor. Listeners may have squirmed to sit through what at first seemed a repetition of arguments and evidence he had already laid before the board in exhaustive detail. But then he turned his sights upon the superintendent's latest statement, targeting every evasion, deception, and cry of wolf. Again and again the superintendent had insinuated that he was the victim of a cruel plot, that the investigation had been a set-up to destroy him. Nonsense! Hastings insisted that public service was his only motive and that in the beginning he had fully expected the superintendent to be vindicated. His hands were clean. The facts spoke for themselves.

As for all those flattering reports and letters recited by the superintendent, so what? So what if trustees and other officials had found much to praise? So what if some patients and families came away well satisfied? The investigating committee had proven that the problems lay elsewhere, often deliberately out of view of official visitors and compliant patients. Nor were all official visitors great admirers of the superintendent as Van Norstrand would have the board believe. A former legislator had written that while leading tours of the hospital Van Norstrand had shown "more fondness for fine horses, cattle and swine than sympathy for the unfortunate human beings in his charge. I am of [the] opinion that he is a cold, heartless, mercenary man."[5]

The superintendent said he had been unaware of systematic abuse, and yet, "He himself has treated the patients with equal if not greater cruelty than has ever been exercised towards them by any of the attendants, thus giving them the sanction of his own example.

"The people have a right to know the facts," Hastings warned his fellow trustees, "and you all understand, gentlemen, *that they will know*. Can you retain as the head of this institution a man who can strike a poor, helpless insane woman, strapped to a bench, with her hands in a muff, until her face is black and blue?"

The superintendent complained that the Kellogg affair had been dredged up only because the family objected to his use of the word "suicide." But in fact the family was convinced that Reverend

Kellogg had not taken his own life at all—"purposely or otherwise." The superintendent blamed the family for withholding information. Yet the superintendent had turned up his nose at the advice and information the family did provide. The superintendent insisted Reverend Kellogg had died from "self-violence" in a warm room. But it had been conclusively proven that no one as ill-clothed as Kellogg was that night could have survived in that room, with the temperature below zero, the window broken, and no heat coming through the register through the early morning hours. Neglect and mistreatment on Dr. Van Norstrand's watch were what killed him.

The superintendent had invested eight thousand dollars of his own money in a store called "Sumner & Company," three thousand more than the man for whom the store was named and about four times his own annual salary. He then purchased nearly all groceries and medicines for the hospital from his own store, billing the state thousands more than other merchants would have charged. He bought food he knew was rotten and pocketed the profits, thereby robbing the state as he poisoned his patients. Knowing what you do, Hastings insinuated, how can you in good conscience continue to entrust the state's most vulnerable and needy citizens to this man's care?

Hastings held the trustees' feet to the fire, confronting them again and again with a damning vision of the all-powerful overseer thrashing trussed up and powerless inmates. Mrs. Roach became a symbol for any number of long-suffering innocents quaking under the superintendent's loutish shadow. Hastings's threat was implicit. Either throw him out now or defend your inaction to an outraged public later.

He took up the superintendent's army record. In his defense Van Norstrand had boasted of his record and denied wrongdoing, thereby making the topic fair game. Hastings had heard from veterans of the old Fourth Wisconsin who saw their old surgeon in altogether different light, and now he laid out their case.

The reader takes heart. At last we are to learn the rumors that damaged Van Norstrand's reputation in Louisiana. Joseph Bailey had warned him of "serious assertions" being spread by hostile officers.[6] What had turned old comrades against him? A New Orleans liquor dealer had promised him "a little fortune" for a liquor license and an outlet in Baton Rouge.[7] In his memoirs Van Norstrand boasted of thousands of dollars tossed in his lap by the owner of a sugar plantation grateful for the delivery of wagonloads of army supplies. Any number of sins was possible, but what precisely had he been *accused* of? Alas, Hastings deleted this passage from the printed version of his report, explaining parenthetically that while the information was of vital interest to the guardians of the hospital, it was not something the public needed to know. For the reader, the curtain falls just before the moment of revelation.

Hastings was convinced that had the board possessed this information four years ago it would not have hired Van Norstrand. The bylaws required that the superintendent be a man of "irreproachable moral character." Dr. Van Norstrand had proven by his behavior in Louisiana that he fell short of that standard. He was an unprincipled man, a guilty man, and it was the duty of the board to throw him out.

Hastings worked his analytical magic on statistics the doctor had cited as evidence of his humanity and effectiveness. Not surprisingly, he arrived at different conclusions: "Wisconsin is the healthiest state in the Union, and hence it should be no wonder that there should be a small number of deaths" at the hospital. No credit to Dr. Van Norstrand on that point. As for the rate of cures, by his calculation it had been higher under doctors Clement and Sawyer, Van Norstrand's predecessors.

He concluded: "I am willing to abide the judgment of those who are deeply interested in this whole matter, the people of the state, when all the facts are laid before them." It was a last warning to the trustees that a flood of indignation was about to break over their heads if they did not do the right thing.

But this was wishful thinking. Hard as Hastings and Sherwood fought to open the process to the public, the board stood firm, and the affair remained under wraps to the bitter end. No flood of revelations ever filled the front pages. No cries of outrage poured in from across the state. The hospital controversy faded from the papers and died a quiet death. A complete transcript of the testimony was eventually published as an appendix to the hospital's annual report, but it appeared too late and in too obscure a manner to reignite controversy.

The debate that followed Hastings's statement was as furious as the weather. His challenge sparked "considerable excitement," according to the *Milwaukee Sentinel*. But the only casualty was Franklin Lawrence, the odd man out on the investigating committee. Lawrence had thrown heart and soul into Van Norstrand's defense. He was on his feet taking a roll call vote when he collapsed headfirst against the edge of the table. Van Norstrand and Dr. Alexander McDill, one of the trustees, stopped the bleeding and nursed him until he was well enough to be taken to his boarding house. The shaken trustees again voted to table the motion to dismiss Van Norstrand, and the meeting was adjourned.[8]

Sherwood and Atwood continued to skirmish in the *State Journal*. Sherwood insisted that Van Norstrand would have been fired if a vote on the motion had not been interrupted, and Atwood struck back with a public scolding. "A clear majority was opposed" to the motion to fire the superintendent, he wrote. One paper attributed Van Norstrand's dilemma to vindictive Republicans: it was "well known that Dr. Van Norstrand ignored all partisan considerations, and this fact inspired the assault upon him."[9]

The next morning Van Norstrand submitted a letter of resignation. Yes, he would have done many things differently if he had come to the job with more experience, but his head was high. The majority of trustees had voted to table the motion to dismiss him, an outcome he interpreted as an implicit vote of confidence. Even so he felt compelled to step down: "Contention between a Superintendent and even a small minority of his board of Trustees [is] so detrimental to an Institution of this kind that I would not wish to occupy the position."[10] He had chosen his moment shrewdly. He had made his case and was getting away without official censure of any kind.

The duties of a superintendent were "laborious and irksome," the *State Journal* acknowledged the next day, and Van Norstrand was to be commended for his "wise and proper" action. As for Franklin Lawrence, his lone ally all these months, the *Journal* said he would be unable to leave his room for weeks, a victim of overwork brought on by the investigation.

EIGHTEEN

A True Gentleman of the Old School

"Dissolved by mutual consent": thus did the former superintendent and the grocer announce the termination of their partnership on the back page of the *Wisconsin State Journal*. Six months after leaving the hospital, Abraham Van Norstrand was a full time storekeeper: "Dr. Van Norstrand will conduct the drug and grocery business as usual, at the old store, where he will be glad to welcome his friends."[1] The flimsies in the business ledger were transformed from page after page of Sumner's neatly squared lists and figures to Van Norstrand's explosive cursive as he skirmished with vendors: "We have tested the coffee & our customers declare it *no* Java but *corn & coffee essence*." Now that the shoe was on the other foot he scrupulously weighed and tested shipments received and paid bills accordingly. The alcohol content of a shipment of whiskey, he discovered, was "7% below what the barrel is marked and at what I was told it would be, making a difference of $8.88."[2] His newspaper ads offered many items "AT COST." With the loss of his biggest customer, Dr. Van Norstrand of the state hospital, did he find his store overstocked? Gradually he began to emphasize more upscale merchandise. Competition in the grocery business was keen, and produce was both perishable and hard work. His ads began to focus on what he called "fancy goods"—toiletries, plus "syringes of all sizes and makes, Drugs, Medicines and Segars."[3]

Still, pacing behind his counter, he had reason to brood. As a young man he had turned his back upon the East with all its constraints, confident that he could wrestle a fortune out of the rough and tumble frontier. Twenty years later he was stocking shelves and waiting on customers. His contemporaries had done well enough. Halbert Paine was Milwaukee's representative in Congress. Hospital trustees were mayors and railroad presidents. They owned major properties in the hearts of their towns; he owned parcels of farm land. They presided over banks and newspapers; he sold liquor and patent medicine, hair brushes and window putty.

But he had not lost his enthusiasm for the big game. He was as ambitious as ever and apparently as energetic. His remaining records are fragmentary, but there is enough in the business ledger to indicate that he was playing for bigger stakes. He owned farm land in several counties, and he may have acquired additional properties in Madison. It appears that he had also gotten back into the loan business. After a bad harvest in 1870 he had trouble collecting and was unable to make payments on a bank debt of thirty-five hundred dollars. He sent out a flurry of notes calling in loans and overdue bills. To a woman who owed fifty dollars plus interest he got right to the point: "Your note has been long past due. I need the money." He was as dogged in pursuit of a few dollars as he was of major debts. A note went to Daniel Lundy seeking "$7.65 plus $.64 interest = 8.29 (-5.00 paid)." He wrote to an attorney about a farmer behind in his payments: "I am real sorry to hear that John [last name unreadable] cannot pay. You know how much I need the money. I suppose it would break the poor fellow up to commence a foreclosure."[4]

On into the next year he continued to call in debts, but by then he was writing from Green Bay, where he was back in the banking business. He also became the proud proprietor of "Van Norstrand and Son," a lumberyard where he sold coal and livestock feed in addition to building materials. If he was unable to pay a few thousand to the Marshall and Isley bank, how had he managed to put down twenty-five thousand for a quarter interest in the National Bank of Commerce of Green Bay?[5] And how did he finance the lumberyard? He sold a farm in Door County, and he was asking five thousand for the house he had moved to in Madison after leaving the hospital. No doubt he also sold the store and perhaps other properties as well, but nothing in his papers explains how, virtually overnight, he transformed himself from a struggling storekeeper, landlord, and small sums lender in Madison into a bank vice president and business owner in Green Bay.

In spite of a prosperous new life in a prospering old town he had not lost touch with developments in the state capital. Upon learning that "God & Humanity Twaddle" Hastings was being considered for a position on the newly created state board of charities, he scribbled letters to Lawrence and other former hospital trustees urging them to support "our mutual friend, E. W. Young," and warning that if Hastings got the job, "[it] would offer him a fine platform to exhibit his penmanship and twaddle."[6]

Not only had he reinvented himself in a city that had been doubly blessed, first as hub of the fur trade and now by the lumber industry, but it appears that son Fred was beginning to shape up. Maybe as a teen-ager Fred had rebelled against a father preoccupied with wealth-seeking, soldiering, and hospital duties, or maybe he did not feel equal to his father's expectations. Whatever the reasons, Fred was a disappointment many times over. He had seldom written to his soldier father, had left college under a cloud, was a loose cannon as an attendant and a drunk as a clerk-in-training at Sumner & Co. He did not have the self-discipline to train for a profession or the backbone for farming, but Abraham stuck by him through all his delinquencies and humiliations, and in Green Bay it paid off. He was co-proprietor of the lumberyard, and this time he apparently pulled his weight. The last we see of Fred, he is twenty years old and well positioned to make a go of it. Years later he moved to Chicago, whether to advance his career or break away from his father we are unable to judge.

These happy developments for the Van Norstrand family occurred just as many lives around them were about to change forever. Months of drought and years of clear-cut timber harvesting had turned surrounding counties into parched and waste-littered tinder. In October, 1871, a firestorm exploded over northeastern Wisconsin.

Some of the nearly two thousand victims were virtually vaporized, while the remains of others were discovered in wells where they had taken shelter, in family heaps on blackened fields, and in skeletal wagons consumed by tornado-like winds of fire. Refugees poured into Green Bay by steamboat, wagon, and on foot—some singed, blistered, and hacking from smoke inhalation, most in shock, and all in despair.[7]

For Dr. Van Norstrand, the Great Peshtigo Fire, as it came to be known, must have brought back memories of Baton Rouge—the dust and smoke of Port Hudson on the horizon and the moaning steam whistles of boats approaching from upriver, bringing ever more wounded to his hospital. Flames licked at the northern fringes of Green Bay as firemen hosed down buildings. The horizon all around glowed eerily, and under a wind-whipped rain of ashes and debris the town became the heart of an enormous relief effort. Old Turners Hall was converted to a makeshift hospital, as were surviving farmhouses in and around the burned-over area. Newspapers identified doctors putting in marathon days and nights at these places, but Van Norstrand's name does not appear. Nor does it show up among citizens prominent in the relief effort. Probably no one in the area had as much experience in emergency medicine and medical administration, but if he pitched in at all during the crisis his contribution went unrecorded. Did he, like other Green Bay doctors, take in some of the sick and burned? The record is mum. All that is certain is that his career in medicine was over. In Green Bay he earned his living as a businessman.[8]

The lumberyard opened for business on October second, and a few weeks later he completed the purchase of three lots on Quincy Street in the exclusive Astor District, where mansions and carriage houses for a new class of high-stakes Yankees were replacing frontier cabins left over from the fur-trading era. He oversaw construction of a magnificent house and settled into the life of a prosperous burgher. He was a booster, a man about town, "a public-spirited citizen and a genial companion."[9] But fate was not entirely kind. Attorney (and future judge) Samuel Dexter Hastings Jr., enjoyed the good life just a few blocks away on Monroe Street.[10]

Success had come late for a man with a history of short-lived ancestors. In 1877 Van Norstrand turned fifty-two. His father had died at fifty-eight. Posterity was on his mind. On his birthday that year he sat at his desk and penned the first sentences of what were to become his memoirs—as far as they went. Chances are he wrote in fits and starts over the next six years, grateful for an occasional free afternoon in which to assemble his personal history of the war years, the most exhilarating period of his life. But in the back of his mind there loomed an even more desperate struggle for survival—an ambush by spiteful accusers, the prospect of official censure, scandal, and public humiliation hanging over his head.

In his mid-fifties he suffered his first stroke but soon returned to his desk at the lumberyard. There was a stove in his office, and he had built the desk to his own specifications. The place was a hideaway from the fussy, female influences of the Astor district. By early May of 1883 he had nearly finished writing about his army years, and the memoirs were about to end in mid-sentence.

The last few pages in his slashing, turbulent hand tell a most unlikely tale. He is on a raid behind enemy lines, out of uniform but not out of the war. The evocation is dark and dreamlike, but the regimental history confirms that these events—or some version of them—did take place.* What is he doing on horseback, risking his neck deep in guerrilla country, two weeks *after* his discharge from the army? And why is he with his old regiment after trying so hard to distance himself from it? Was this Fred Boardman's doing? Boardman had confounded expectations by returning hale and hearty from a long convalescence in the north, and he was living his dream. At long last he commanded the Fourth Wisconsin Cavalry. Had

---

* "'Two expeditions have been to Rosedale on Bayou Grosse Tete. The first commanded by Col. Boardman, started from Baton Rouge Feb. 4th, at 4 o'clock a.m., on steamer Black Hawk, consisting of 86 cavalry and 36 infantry; by daylight landed at Lobdel's Landing and from there took the old plank road crossing the Lake and Bayou Thomas, reaching Rosedale at 11 a.m., routed and captured the rebels there, then crossed Bayou Grosse Tete and proceeded 9 miles up the right bank to Gov. Johnson's Plantation, returning at night to Rosedale; early the 5th, started for Baton Rouge, reached camp at 4 o'clock p.m. with 12 rebel soldiers including 1 Major, 1 Captain and 1 Lieut. and many arms, horses, mules, etc." (*History and Catalogue*, pp. 17–18).

he lured his friend into the saddle for one last adventure? Nothing is explained. It is as though Van Norstrand was drawn in against his will. He carried a gold watch, all of his recently accumulated wealth—ten thousand dollars or more—and his pistols. Boardman weighs heavily on his mind. The new colonel is impulsive and distracted, a big rowdy kid, and Van Norstrand is the scold who keeps him in line.

There is gunfire ahead. Rebel pickets flee a bridge, and horse soldiers in blue clatter across, arriving in the village of Rosedale, where they happen upon abandoned wagons heaped with supplies for the enemy—shoes, rum, quinine. They pounce on the liquor, alarming Van Norstrand, who imagines them sprawled and puking, ripe for rebel cavalry lurking nearby. He orders a sergeant to stave in the casks. It is as though Boardman had abdicated, and he has taken command. A captured major—"furloughed from General Lee's staff," he writes—has Boardman's ear, seducing him with flattery and promises of a home-cooked meal at a nearby plantation. "I objected, but our colonel desired a good drink of the rebel major's liquor. I knew our colonel would be plied with liquor and would be gobbled and most likely all the rest of us [as well]." Van Norstrand insists on coming along and brings half of the horse soldiers with them. The rest remain in town. "We went to the plantation. More than an hour was taken by the folks to get our dinner of hoe-cake, eggs, chicken, and coffee, in fact so long as to make me uneasy, fearing [the major] would send a line to Stuart who would come down like an avalanche with his 1200 [cavalrymen] on our fifty, and gobble us.* The colonel had two or more drinks and felt happy and stout and had no fear."[11]

For months whiskey had been Van Norstrand's life blood. He dispensed it to thousands for palliation and apparently to thousands more for profit. Now, suddenly, it was the bait in a trap about to spring shut upon his fortune and possibly his life. Obvious as the danger was to him, in his telling the others are blissfully unaware, in

---

* Presumably Van Norstrand is referring to the famed rebel cavalry general, Jeb Stuart.

particular their besotted Colonel Boardman.

As soon as Van Norstrand got him mounted and headed back for Rosedale* the captive major, riding alongside Boardman, produced a bottle of brandy from his saddlebag. "I saw at once that the rebel desired delay," Van Norstrand wrote, "and the colonel would be where I could not keep him on his horse if he imbibed again."[12] He spurred his horse between the two drinking buddies, forcing the major aside. The bottle was knocked to the ground.

Van Norstrand's impulse was to gather the troops and beat a hasty retreat to the river where the steamboat Black Hawk and its defending infantryman waited, but Boardman refused to be hurried, insisting that they bed down for the night. "I went with him to a private house where I directed the man to make a bed on the parlor floor, and we both lay down with our horses tied in the yard ready to mount. We did not remove boots, spurs or clothing. I put my heavy cavalry revolver under the blanket where my hand could rest on it."[13]

Their own Major Keith—"every inch a soldier"—sent a messenger to warn that the enemy was crowding his picket line, but Boardman would not be roused. An hour later another messenger; another warning shrugged off by the colonel. A sense of suffocating inertia weighed on Van Norstrand. His every impulse was to rise and mount and flee, but it was as though he had been rendered powerless. In the darkness he gripped his revolver and listened to distant gunfire.

A last warning arrived from Major Keith: With or without you, we're leaving. Spurred by the threat of abandonment, Van Norstrand seized Boardman by the collar, hauled him to his feet, and pushed him outside. At last, a shared sense of urgency, a gathering of voices alert to danger, the snort and tremor of anxious horseflesh. The wounded were left at a farmhouse, unburdening the troopers for a dash to the waiting boat. Van Norstrand lost himself in the thundering stream. He could smell the river dead ahead. His money, pistols,

---

* Van Norstrand calls this town "Rose Hill."

and gold watch were tucked securely around him. Soon he would be safely out of this mess: "We had succeeded in reaching beyond the bridge at which we had. . . ."

There is no more. Over a century later the remaining pages of the journal are still pristine white.

On the afternoon of May 7, 1883, a laborer named Joseph Dhyne found his employer—normally so alert and commanding—stumbling across the lumberyard. Van Norstrand went down on his knees to vomit. He told Dhyne that he could not see. Dhyne helped him back to the office. He said he felt cold, and Dhyne spread a buffalo robe on the floor and started a fire in the stove. He would not let Dhyne go for a doctor, instead sending him off on a scheduled delivery run. Lucy was out East with Flora, a recent bride. Young Fred had long since set off on his own. There was no one at home to come check on him.[14]

Nearly eighty years later a grandson who had inherited the ledger felt compelled to explain the abrupt ending. His lettering is so controlled and formal that the paragraph he entered under those last lines on page 153 looks engraved:

> Abram Harris van Norstrand M.D., my maternal grandfather, died in A.H. van Norstrand & Son's Lumber Company's office, at the very desk he himself built, in Green Bay, Wisconsin, of a stroke of apoplexy on the afternoon of May 7th, 1883, aged 57 years, 8 months & 12 days. He is buried in Woodlawn Cemetery there, where later his wife Lucy Hebard van Norstrand, his son Frederick C. van Norstrand, & his daughter Flora Belle van Norstrand Smith were buried close around him. . . .
> I very much regret that my grandfather's diary is incomplete and can only suppose that the necessary pursuance of his affairs, current events, and one thing and another interrupted its completion. He

was a true gentleman of the old school, all too few
in number, modest, honest, affable and courageous.
God rest him!

Frederic van Norstrand
October 21st, 1962, San Francisco, California

* * *

It is hard to believe that even "the necessary pursuance of his
affairs" could compel a man to put down his pen in mid-sentence of
such a crucial passage, never to pick it up again. More likely it was
a crippling shock to the brain. In the unit history's account of the
Rosedale raid there is no mention of firefights, casualties, a desperate flight from enemy cavalry. Nor does the name Jeb Stuart appear,
and no wonder, since Stuart spent the war with Lee's army in the
east. Furthermore it would have made no sense to send such an outnumbered detachment deep into an area thought to be harboring a
regiment or more of enemy cavalry. It was not Jeb Stuart's horde that
was closing in on Abraham Van Norstrand; it was the hospital years,
Samuel Hastings, and a replay of the fight of his life. No wonder
these last pages are so thick with dread.

Obituaries described a man much like the one his grandson
recalled: "warm-hearted and liberal-minded . . . , an excellent con-
versationalist, a genial companion, and a public-spirited citizen . . . ,
a kind, genial, pleasant man and a good citizen. . . . His friendships
were warm and true." The papers did not mention the investigation
at the hospital or the sins it uncovered, although David Atwood's
Wisconsin State Journal did acknowledge that "some of his acts were
severely criticized." But on balance, the writer concluded, he had
been a good manager and good for the institution.[15]

That opinion appears to have been widely shared. Within days
of Van Norstrand's resignation from the hospital the state medical
society appointed him to its committee on nervous and mental

disease.[16] Governor Fairchild did not mention the hospital controversy in his next annual address to the legislature, though by then he surely knew all about it. Nor would anyone know that anything was amiss at the Wisconsin State Hospital by reading the *American Journal of Insanity* that year. As for state newspapers in mid-1868, their pages were full of developments in Washington—reconstruction legislation, the impeachment of Andrew Johnson, the upcoming political conventions. Items about the hospital were often buried on page three or four and lacked the kind of inflammatory detail that destroyed careers and reputations in other parts of the country. Not only did Van Norstrand escape official or professional rebuke, but in 1874, six years after leaving the hospital, he returned as a newly appointed trustee, the occasion fastidiously noted in the minutes by the secretary, Samuel Hastings. He got right to work, taking positions on the visiting and auditing committees and on another to upgrade hospital livestock.* Hastings resigned from the board a few months later.

It seems that men in important places admired Van Norstrand and were protective in spite of reams of evidence that he had treated some patients viciously, packed the payroll with family members, and enriched himself at the expense of the state and the patients in his care. It was his accuser Hastings who ended up on the defensive while Van Norstrand slipped quietly into private life. Why did he get off easy? Where was the outrage?

It helps to see him as other hard-driving, quick-tempered, self-proclaimed "practical" men might have seen him. A dark side emerges from obituaries and biographical sketches of public figures of the period. There is the community leader as he would like to be remembered, the noble father selfless in his labor for family and friends and in service to the public, a booster, a patriot, a savior to those less fortunate, and there is the private man crippled by a sense of injured pride. Grudges linger, unsettled scores eat at his peace

---

* Ironically, he voted against raising the superintendent's salary to $3,000. *Journal of the Wisconsin State Lunatic Asylum*, January 28, 1875.

of mind. Along the way he has been maimed by undeserved blows and unacknowledged sacrifices. The obituary of former hospital trustee Winchel D. Bacon was uncommonly candid in this regard: "His combative disposition and persistent endeavors to control in matters of politics, religion and local affairs kept him continually in hot conflicts with his neighbors and impaired his usefulness in the community."[17] In his prime, A. J. Noonan, Frederick Boardman's uncle and protector, was a political power broker whose influence transcended party lines and extended throughout the state, but his last years were spent in a hospital for the insane in Milwaukee, "darkened and embittered by misfortune and failure."[18]

It is no wonder that Van Norstrand's understanding of the word "kindness" was very different from our own. For years, superintendents across the country assured the public that in this enlightened era of hospital treatment for the insane, "kindness" was the guiding principle. But "kindness" was invoked by authorities of all kinds in those days, much as "excellence" is today. It was a malleable concept indeed. It suggested sweetness and light, but practical, pugnacious men knew better. Many believed slavery was the kindest system for assuring the welfare of the Negro; unrelenting drill and labor was the kindest way to cure the soldier of homesickness; boxing the ears of an unruly child or a mischievous underling was a firm but kind way to instill discipline. "Kindness" was like "moral treatment," a murky but unassailable concept that, owing to his position, a superintendent or a trustee was obliged to endorse, at least in his official utterances. But among practical men, "kindness" may have been a sort of code, a curtain dropped between unpleasant reality and the sensitive public: trust me, I'll put things right. If so, the trustees may not have liked much of what Hastings made them listen to, but they would have understood.

They liked the doctor's take-charge manner. He *commanded!* He was decisive and severe. His vision was large and his reach was great. Nor was the Wisconsin Hospital the only place where some "treatments" were in truth forms of coercion. To Benjamin Rush and others, discipline *was* therapy: you could not talk sense to someone who was thrashing about like an animal. Like animals, violent patients had to be subdued through hard discipline or fear, and nothing embodied both like being submerged to the point of drowning.[19] In 1881, the *North American Review* denounced the "unparalleled despotism" of hospital leaders, their authority granted by statutes that "assume superintendents to be saints, with whom passion, selfishness, revenge, and neglect are impossible." The writer cast a jaundiced eye upon "the reciprocal compliments between the superintendent and the trustees, so prominent in their reports," which served to smokescreen "all the secrets, the favoritism, the partisan interests, the contracts, sinecures, and profits of asylum management" that neither side wished the public to know about.[20] An Australian who conducted an exhaustive study of American hospitals came to the same conclusion. Collusion between trustees and superintendent was inevitable. Trustees saw what they wanted to see. A typical inspection was a mere "dress parade." "The sad fact is," George Tucker concluded, the "American method of organization and management invites abuses of every form, and in every stage."[21]

While daily labor in barn and fields was therapeutic for many chronic patients, the primary beneficiary was the hospital. Here was a labor pool that was plentiful and cheap. The admirers from Jefferson who had recommended Van Norstrand for the position were right. He was a strong manager who subordinated all elements of the hospital, including the patients, to the welfare of the institution itself. Under him the hospital itself was the primary patient, and he made sure that it prospered and bent to his will. The sick may or may not recover, but the hospital would endure as a tightly controlled social system, a complex physical plant, and a respected institution. For those who spent time there it was at best an oasis, a shelter from an abusive world, a place for some to restore body and soul, but hospital care was no "cure" for mental illness.

As for financial abuses, that was a murkier issue. Van Norstrand may have stepped over the line, but financial self-improvement in office was not unusual among politicians and office holders generally, even among do-gooders like Hastings.

Samuel Hastings no doubt commanded the respect of his fellow trustees. It would have been unwise for them not to take him seriously, but righteous crusaders like him did not invite the sort of comradely regard that at least some bestowed on down-to-earth Dr. Van Norstrand. Best to remain guarded and correct around a man like Samuel Hastings. Where Hastings saw criminal misbehavior, others saw a strong but flawed man grappling with enormous hardships. Where Hastings saw despotism run amuck, they saw the very qualities Van Norstrand had admired in his idol in Louisiana, General Benjamin Butler, "the best specimen of a tyrant."[22] Consciously or not, Van Norstrand had conducted himself at the hospital much as Butler had while commanding the Department of the Gulf, provoking outrage from some, grudging admiration from others. And like Butler at New Orleans, he left office under a cloud of suspicion but made a clean getaway. Whatever people were saying, they could not make it stick. As for the turbulence Hastings and Sherwood had unearthed in their investigation, maybe the majority of trustees convinced themselves that it was a form of kindness to spare the public those details.

Finally, Van Norstrand made his own luck. As he had demonstrated time and again—in his prewar business dealings, his sudden relocations from one community to another, and in the army—he knew when to cut and run. He walked away from the hospital in better shape than those who came before or immediately after him. The three easterners who had preceded him had spent long apprenticeships at well-established hospitals. Only one, Dr. John Sawyer, survived his brief term as temporary superintendent with his reputation intact. The other two were turned out in disgrace. The first to go, Dr. J. Edward Lee, returned to his old job under Thomas Kirkbride in Philadelphia, where he fell into a depression and died a few years later.[23]

After Van Norstrand resigned, Dr. Alexander S. McDill, a trustee, was pressured by the board to fill in pending recruitment of that elusive perfect fit from the East. He held on for five years before resigning to take a seat in Congress. His replacement, Dr. Mark

Ranney, came as a virtual refugee from the hospital in Iowa, where he had served a stormy term as superintendent. The skies did not brighten for him in Wisconsin. He was soon unburdening his woes to one of the eastern brethren, Dr. Isaac Ray, who had recommended him for the post. The staff was in open revolt. He had become an outcast in his own hospital. Even his assistant physician took part in a charade that mocked both him and his wife—to the delight of mutinous attendants. Again the trustees failed to rally around their man. Dr. Van Norstrand, for one, wanted Ranney's resignation. The situation became so hopeless that the board's only option was to clean house. Ranney left, and the officers who had undermined him soon had their walking papers as well.[24] Dr. McDill returned from a term in Congress to find the board again desperate to fill the superintendent's office. Would he step into the breech a second time? He died on the job a few months later.

The trustees tried to lure Dr. Sawyer back from the Butler Hospital in Rhode Island. He graciously declined. Still unable to attract a first-rate candidate, they promoted the assistant physician, Dr. D. F. Boughton. In time, another investigative committee was appointed; a litany of familiar charges was made: "The superintendent has not been in the habit of giving his personal attention to the medical department. . . . Neither the medical nor the business management have been satisfactory . . . sick patients dying alone and unattended . . . looseness and unbusiness-like ways, and extravagant and unauthorized expenditures . . . an entire lack of responsibility and accountability. . . ." The attack went beyond Boughton, beyond the board of trustees, to the heart of the hospital system: "We believe the entire plan of management of insane asylums is too magnificent. From the laying of the cornerstone, each of these institutions is planned, equipped and supported on a scale of grandeur that ill befits a public charity."[25]

Boughton wrote a rebuttal thick as a novel: the absurdity of expecting him to spend all his time with patients when the place reeked of sewer gas, fresh water was so scarce that a half dozen patients had to be run through the same scummy bath, and urine *still* froze on the floor of some rooms "until a warm spell came and thawed it out that it might be cleaned." What sense did it make to probe their minds if they were living in filth? First things first. "It is better to give your patients pure air to breathe, plenty of out door life, clean water for bathing, wholesome food." Sometimes a superintendent must battle a deteriorating physical plant and a penurious bureaucracy before he can afford the luxury of "inquiring daily after each patient's health."[26]

Like many in his position he had been sidetracked by what the historian Gerald Grob called "administrative psychiatry," and this was his downfall. What good was a doctor who said he was too busy to doctor?[27] Boughton was sent on his way.

Through two decades of investigations, smoldering scandal, and the banishment of one superintendent after another, the trustees continued to proudly assert that the Wisconsin hospital ranked with the best in the country. Since hospitals everywhere were falling from grace during the second half of the nineteenth century, maybe their claim was not so extravagant after all.

* * *

Abraham Van Norstrand also fared better than his friends in the old Fourth Wisconsin. Only two survived the war, and only one died of old age. In May of 1863, Sidney Bean, the young scholar ("DeQuincy and the Religion of the Greeks") and professor of mathematics and physics at Carroll College, was shot dead leading the regiment into murderous fire pouring from the crest of Port Hudson. The next year, a few months after the Rosedale raid, Frederick Boardman led another of his periodic incursions into rebel territory. It was not the job of a regimental commander to scout for the enemy, but that did not stop Boardman from roaming well in advance of his troops. Just east of Baton Rouge, near Olive Branch, he spurred his horse toward a bridge over the Comite River intent on flushing out enemy guards. A bullet hit his right arm, and as he spun in the saddle he took a second, fatal ball to the head. His funeral was a front-page event in Milwaukee, but his death came as no surprise to the men with whom he soldiered. It is an open question whether peacetime held any attraction for him anyway.[28]

Of all Van Norstrand's army friends, the one least likely to become a national hero was the land speculator and civil engineer, Joseph Bailey, but hero he became, and in the most unlikely way. In Wisconsin, Bailey had learned from loggers and other frontier-types how to outwit barriers that nature had put between them and the marketplace, and so in Louisiana, when generals gazed upon such obstacles and grew faint of heart, they often turned to Bailey for solutions. During the siege at Port Hudson he engineered hidden gun emplacements and trench systems that burrowed ever closer to the enemy. And he was a relentless taskmaster. That seething gadfly from the Sixth Michigan, Edward Bacon, caustically observed: "Qualified to be Chief Engineer about as he was to be a bishop, he got his position to keep out of danger, and to find play for his abilities as a Negro driver, which gave him the envy and admiration of Creole overseers. No base man ever believed more religiously than Bailey did in the necessity of cruelty and atrocious wickedness to make his importance felt."[29] It must be remembered that Bacon was indiscriminately livid; the higher a man's rank, the greater Bacon's contempt. He was surely wrong in impugning Bailey's courage. Bailey saw far more combat than his critic. But even Van Norstrand had been struck by Bailey's ruthlessness toward blacks, recalling how, during the Battle of Baton Rouge, he had threatened to beat a Negro servant with his sword if he tried to flee. In the heat of battle he thought he heard the man run off. He spun around, sword in hand, only to find "the poor fellow laying at full length minus his head, which had been carried away by a stray cannon ball."[30]

In the spring of 1864 the Union army under General Banks launched an expedition westward up the Red River, deep into Confederate territory. It was supported by a fleet of ironclad gunboats and transports commanded by Admiral David Porter. A coordinating force from the north soon ran into trouble, and gradually the whole enterprise came unraveled. Hungry, underarmed rebel formations swarmed over captured wagon trains and abandoned weapons. Meanwhile, the falling level of the river left Porter's fleet literally high and dry. But Joseph Bailey knew how to move stranded tons of deadweight. He had seen it done to a fleet of logs. Why not a fleet of riverboats? He sold his scheme to skeptical but desperate commanders. They gave him three thousand soldiers, including experienced loggers from Maine and Wisconsin, plus hundreds of teams, and within a week the brown soup fouled by animal carcasses and other wastage of war was slowly crawling up a pair of wing dams, each extending hundreds of feet from shore. One wing was assembled from felled trees that were woven together, the other from demolished buildings and cribs of stone that had been floated downriver on barges. Sailors dumped armor plating, heavy guns, and cotton bales over the side. The boats rose in the water and were soon afloat. One by one they fired back to life and crawled out of the backwaters into the fast-moving central current. They shot the gap between the stressed and rapidly weakening dams and soon reached deep water and safety.

All would have been lost if not for Bailey. Admiral Porter and his officers commissioned a silver bowl from Tiffany's and presented it to him with a commemorative sword. Porter lobbied for his promotion to general, which was soon accomplished. Bailey also received the official thanks of Congress, one of only a handful of soldiers so honored during the war. But wartime glory did not translate into civilian success. He came home sick and exhausted. His old business ties had long ago come undone. A hoped for federal position did not materialize in spite of appeals directly to President Johnson from admirers in high places. He packed up his family and set out by wagon for southwestern Missouri to start life over in the cattle business. There he was pressed into running for sheriff in a county that was still a minefield of wartime passions and vendettas. Three months into the job, the man who snatched a Union fleet from destruction and rose to the rank of major general was shot in the back of the head by a pair of ex-bushwhackers turned pig thieves.[31]

By rights, Halbert Paine should have died at Port Hudson, his shattered leg bent under him, his face to the spiky horizon of enemy gun-barrels overhead. He should have died of shock or bled to death on the boat to New Orleans, or days later when a damaged artery spouted blood, or still later, after the inevitable infection flared over his stump. Instead, like his former subordinate Joseph Bailey, he wore the twin stars of a major general at war's end. But unlike Bailey, Paine's elevation in the world continued in peacetime. A Republican, he served three terms in Congress, supporting the reconstruction agenda of the radical wing of the party and introducing legislation that led to the creation of the weather bureau. Appointed commissioner of the patent office by his old friend Carl Schurz, President Grant's secretary of interior, Paine was responsible for the bizarre aviary din that spread through formerly hushed halls of the federal bureaucracies, as nimble-fingered masters of the QWERTY keyboard revolutionized federal paperwork, the clatter and ping of the typewriter—a Milwaukee invention—a fitting soundtrack to that age of industrial innovation. Of the original band of senior officers and messmates in the Fourth Wisconsin, Paine was the only one to survive into the twentieth century, long enough to assemble in old age a complete record of his military service and to write a definitive treatise on election law.[32]

Expose any of those officers to the white hot scrutiny that Samuel Hastings had fixed upon Abraham Van Norstrand, and all would have appeared morally disfigured: Paine, the commanding officer whose soldiers pillaged Baton Rouge and who ultimately made off with a collection of elegant furnishings himself; Boardman, the reactionary who loathed do-gooders in blue; Bean and Bailey, who played Pied Piper to hundreds of slaves along the Mississippi valley, putting them to work on the fever-plagued lowlands across the river from Vicksburg and then abandoning them there.

Three Percent Hastings

In early 1868, Samuel Hastings would have needed every ounce of his famous self-control and Christian modesty not to yield to the thrilling expectation of a great personal reward. Not only was he poised to bring down the tyrant at the state hospital, but it appeared all but certain that the troubling qualifier "pro tempore" would soon be dropped from his title as president of the Northwestern Mutual Life Insurance Company. He had only to survive another meeting of its board of trustees, one more round of balloting, to secure a position in the business world commensurate with his role as wartime state treasurer and with unlimited potential for financial reward, professional stature, and influence generally.

But by year's end, both pending triumphs had been snatched away. Superintendent Van Norstrand had escaped unpunished. Hastings's catalogue of outrages had not won over his fellow hospital trustees. Months later, a renegade group of Northwestern agents threw their support behind another man. Hastings lost the election for president and his seat on board as well. How greedily Abraham Van Norstrand must have feasted on the news from Milwaukee as he stocked shelves and waited for customers.[1]

But Van Norstrand, the lifelong Democrat, was not around to savor Hastings's final fall from grace. In old age the former state treasurer played a minor role in a trial that was front page news for weeks. Although not a defendant, he was called to testify, and other witnesses were questioned about his actions as a state official. From all of this emerged a dark twin to the tireless and devoted public servant of legend.

In 1891 George W. Peck was sworn in as governor. Like Van Norstrand, Peck had served in Louisiana with the Fourth Wisconsin. He was well-known as the author of *Peck's Bad Boy* and other books of humorous recollection. More importantly, as only the second Democrat to sit at the governor's desk since the Civil War, he came into office with scores to settle. His attorney general immediately initiated a lawsuit to recover, in his words, "all interest misappropriated" by a half dozen or more former state treasurers. At issue was a shadowy custom well-known to capital insiders and tolerated by a succession of Republican governors that permitted treasurers to supplement their salaries by taking pay-offs from "pet" banks. Damaging testimony was elicited from former bank presidents and head cashiers. During the war years bankers had been anxious to tap into the wealth pouring into the treasurer's vault in the form of tax receipts and federal funds. Because the treasurer, Samuel Hastings, took a personal risk in transferring state money into private banks, he was highly selective. A banker so chosen was understandably anxious to remain in the good graces of his patron. A tangible expression of gratitude seemed almost inevitable. Usually it took the form of a percentage of the profit the bank made from loaning this money out. It was alleged that the treasurer in turn shared his bounty with the Republican party. None of this money ever showed up in the books he kept. Thus a precedent was set. For decades, government funds generated fortunes for one political party and a handful of state treasurers.[2]

The trial featured a cast of gilded names—former governors, war heroes, political big shots, and pioneer movers and shakers. To some of these luminaries Samuel Dexter Hastings had been known as "Three Percent Hastings." They believed he had left office a wealthy man. It was rumored that he had cleared $100,000 in what the prosecuting attorney delicately called "gratuities." The *Milwaukee Journal* was not so kind. "Treasury-looters" was how it described those who profited from such practices through the last half of the century.[3]

Under persistent questioning, former governors Fairchild and Hoard acknowledged they had heard that treasurers got rich this way but insisted they had no personal knowledge of the practice. Former bank presidents Van Slyke and Simeon Mills had heard the same stories. Van Slyke went so far as to admit that he had based the size of a treasurer's payoff on the amount of state money deposited in his bank. But as for greenbacks actually changing hands, the former executives retreated behind faulty memory and lack of access to records long stashed in dark cellars. A cashier named James L. Hill testified that Hastings was the first treasurer to deposit state money in the Bank of Madison and that he was rewarded by "loans of money that he wasn't required to repay."[4]

Called to the stand, Hastings denied ever accepting interest money on state deposits but acknowledged that he profited in other ways. There were "loans" from the Bank of Madison, drafts from the Marshal and Isley Bank in Milwaukee, vague "considerations" from the First National Bank, plus sums from "other banks [that] in making up their quarterly accounts would enter something to my credit." How much did it all add up to during his eight years in office? "Not to exceed twenty thousand dollars or twenty-five at the outside," he calculated.[5]

How Van Norstrand would have delighted in these revelations! It hardly mattered if Hastings had actively solicited payoffs or simply took what was offered. He had neither put an end to the practice nor redirected the money back into state accounts where it rightfully belonged. When put to the test, Samuel Hastings—early champion of the abolitionist cause, president of the Wisconsin Sunday-School Assembly, Right Worthy Grand Templar of the Independent Order of Good Templars, Prohibition Party candidate for Congress and later for governor, and all around avenging angel—proved to be as venal as the next man. Slip a bankroll into his pocket, and what did he do? Exactly what Van Norstrand had done in Baton Rouge. He looked the other way and kept his mouth shut. But while Van Norstrand and his comrades were putting their lives on the line for causes Hastings had long championed, that pillar of virtue was using his office in the state capitol to leverage bribes from banks. And now everyone knew. Hallelujah![6]

Two years after the trial, Samuel Hastings left the town in which he had spent nearly half his life. By then he was a snowy-bearded octogenarian. Rooms were added to the stately home of Samuel Jr., judge of the circuit court in Green Bay. There in the Astor district, a few blocks from the former Van Norstrand place, the old crusader spent the last years of his life.

Hastings played a small part in a long and complicated case. The judge ruled that money pocketed by the treasurers belonged to the state and should be repaid—over $600,000 all told—but a new Republican administration came to their rescue. A law was passed. The old men would not have to go to the poorhouse after all, although no law could restore their reputations.[7]

* * *

On young Dr. Van Norstrand's first journey inland from Milwaukee he met a well-established physician named Alfred Castleman. Castleman was fuming mad at his partner, and on the spot he offered Van Norstrand the other man's position. Castleman was about forty. He had been practicing medicine in the area for over a decade. Van Norstrand was a year out of medical school and a virtual babe in the woods. But he rejected the sheltering arm of a veteran practitioner, detecting something off-putting about Castleman, and he was right. Part seer, part crank, Castleman was always agitated about something. An abolitionist, an organizer for the new Republican party, and an avowed enemy of quackery, he threw himself with a fury into all the right causes only to leave the earth scorched in all directions. Newcomers to the sawdust and mud communities around him suffered for lack of medical care or from the wrong kind of care, and so he agitated for a medical school attached to the new university and for a hospital for the insane. His outspokenness won him the presidency of the state medical society and a professorship at the medical school-to-be, but with every lurch forward he bumped heads with the very people whose support he needed. As a regimental surgeon during the war he was the subordinate from hell, alienating his commanding officer with his bullying insistence on proper ventilation and sanitary measures in camp. He detested far-off George McClellan, the general-in-chief ("nothing short of an imbecile, a coward or a traitor—the best retreater in modern warfare") as vehemently as nearby colleagues who suffered, he said, from "gangrene of the mind." Chronically ill and embittered at war's end, he felt unwelcome back home and so resumed his westward pursuit of a better world all the way to in Oakland, California, where he died.[8]

Another pioneer whose mental status declined as the surrounding wilderness gave way to church steeples, factory chimneys, and immigrant voices was Timothy Johnson, the nomadic Connecticut Yankee who planted a handful of seedling communities in what was to become Jefferson County, including Aztalan and Watertown. Like Castleman, Johnson was a lone operator, "tough, sinewy and persistent," a local editor wrote, "retiring and secluded in his habits." With a pitchfork he had faced down "whiskey hungry" Indians; he had welcomed many a lost and desperate traveler into his home, fathered the first white child born in Jefferson County, and managed to provide for a family of nine plus an occasional hired man or two. But he also grew fearful and suspicious as towns and roads and ever more settlers crowded near. He tried to start over in the wilds of northwestern Wisconsin but returned to his grown children in Watertown, a melancholy and remote old man. It is hard to imagine him surviving for long in forced confinement with deranged strangers, but that his how he spent the last years of his life—at the insane hospital in Madison.[9]

In contrast to Castleman and Johnson, Amherst Kellogg was an old settler who thrived on constant change. As a prosperous, city-dwelling senior citizen he celebrated the log house years of the 1830s and '40s, when faith, family, and hard work steeled one through sorrows and reverses—cousins lost to water, poison, fire, and fever;

houses and barns up in flames; close calls with frostbite and summer epidemics; family reverses from bank failures; and opportunities missed or stolen. Pluck *did* lead to luck, luck to good connections, good connections to the affection and confidence of your business companions and the prosperity of your common enterprises. Study hard, work hard, pray hard, master double-entry bookkeeping, take the pledge, give yourself to Jesus. The Kellogg family saga, which he declaimed in biblical detail at a gathering of the clan in 1902, was proof of the power of faith to lift a man up from the plow, the anvil, the plumb line, and the saw, and set him behind the pulpit or the executive desk.

But neither in his reunion oration nor a much longer, printed version of the family's story did Amherst mention the death of his brother at the state hospital. We see Romulus Oscar as a proud young graduate of Wesleyan College, a professor of ancient languages, a business partner, and a young husband: an up and comer. Then he drops from sight. Nor, in the published version of Amherst's recollections, do we see his own dark side as vividly as he wrote of it in his original manuscript. Like Abraham Van Norstrand, Alfred Castleman, and other Yankee pioneers, he had a short fuse. Memories of youthful tantrums troubled him well into old age. He had gone after his brother with an axe "and would have brained him" if R. O. had not gotten away. He "would have killed" a playmate with a rock. In the published version we are told simply that his deepening faith purged him forever of a "violent temper."

A widower, Amherst spent his last years with his daughter in Madison. Louise Phelps Kellogg was a historian and editor with the Wisconsin Historical Society, and in preparing his manuscript for publication she was protective. The image of her father that she wanted to preserve was that of esteemed senior citizen, distinguished guest lecturer to some of her undergraduate classes, and the archetypal "deeply religious and Puritanical New Englander" who had civilized the West—not an axe-wielding kid with blood in his eye.[10]

* * *

Late in life, a cousin of the Kellogg brothers became convinced that the mystery of R. O.'s death had finally been solved. George Kellogg was an arborist in Rock County who had kept a diary for decades. Most entries were shop talk—weather; the number of evergreen plants set out and fruit trees grafted.[11] In January of 1895 he dug out the volume from thirty years earlier and added a note to his original account of the "sickness, derangement and death of our bloved [sic] R. O. Kellogg in the 4th story out of hearing, no one in attendance, locked in. . . ." He had recently learned, he wrote, of the deathbed confession of a former hospital attendant, who had "struck [R. O.] a blow that made him [unreadable] & then pounded him to death."

Dr. Van Norstrand had followed up on a similar rumor a year or two after Kellogg's death, only to be told by the sister of the former attendant named Lowe that her brother was not dead and had nothing to confess.[12]

But thirty years later a deathbed confession, fishy as it sounds, was at least possible. For George and perhaps other Kelloggs, the matter was finally settled.

ACKNOWLEDGMENTS

My thanks to Charles East of Baton Rouge for the many courtesies he showed a stranger, and especially for leading me to the papers of Halbert Paine; to Patrick Brophy of the Bushwhacker Museum in Nevada, Missouri, for information about Joseph Bailey; to Attorney Joe Kryshak for directing me to the early annual reports of the Wisconsin Insane Hospital; to Sue McCutchin of Mendota Mental Health Institute, Kathleen Meenk of Winnebago Mental Health Institute, and Nancy Williams of Madison; and to the staff of the Hoard Museum in Fort Atkinson, Wisconsin, which houses the papers of Lucien Caswell. Mary K. Huelsbeck and other staff at the Neville Public Museum in Green Bay located the papers and photos of Abraham Van Norstrand and went above the call of duty by microfilming his handwritten, unpublished memoirs, thereby providing me with extended access to this essential document. Without the extraordinary collections of the Wisconsin Historical Society and the helpfulness of its staff, especially those of the archives department, it would not have been possible to piece together this story. A requirement of the society, which holds the records of the Wisconsin Insane Hospital, is that patients' names not be used. Therefore the names given patients discussed in the book are fictional but ethnically similar. My wife Alice, daughter Betsy, and brother Jim—the real professional in the family—did their best to help me purge any excesses and inconsistencies. I thank them for their careful reading and suggestions. Thanks also to Joan Strasbaugh, Ellie Wilson, and Jennifer Bottcher for their help preparing the manuscript for publication, although I am responsible for any errors of fact or documentation.

Photographs of Abraham Van Norstrand and his son are courtesy of the Neville Public Museum of Brown County. Those of the Wisconsin Insane Hospital, Sidney Bean, Joseph Bailey, and Halbert Paine are courtesy of the Wisconsin Historical Society.

NOTES

Prologue: A Locked Room, a Battered Body

1   John Wesley, *The Works of John Wesley*, vol. 11 (Grand Rapids, MI, 1958), p. 384.

2   This paragraph and much of what follows is based upon Amherst Kellogg's memoirs and testimony (Louise Phelps Kellogg Papers, Wisconsin Historical Society); also, George Kellogg's diary (George Kellogg Collection, Wisconsin Historical Society); George H. Noyes, George C. Markham, and Frederick C. Winkler, *Semi-Centennial History of the Northwestern Mutual Life Insurance Company* (Milwaukee, WI, 1908); and Harold F. Williamson and Orange Smiley, *Northwestern Mutual Life, A Century of Trusteeship* (New York, 1976). Amherst Kellogg testified that he drove to Madison (Appendix to Annual Report of the State Hospital for the Insane for the Year 1868 [Madison, WI, 1868, p. 342], hereafter referred to as Appendix). He also said that a few days earlier, he and Romulus had taken a sleigh ride through Fort Atkinson. By Monday the snow would have ruled out travel by wagon. The daily train to Madison had already been through town. The only other way to reach Madison was by sleigh, of which there were many types, including some with enclosed one or two-person cabins.

3   *Wisconsin Chief,* Feb. 15, 1865; *Milwaukee Sentinel,* Feb. 2, 1865; Amherst's testimony in Appendix.

4   Frederick A. Norwood, *The Story of American Methodism* (Nashville, TN, 1974), p. 30.

5   From Romulus Kellogg's application for admission to the Wisconsin State Hospital for the Insane, which was filled out by his brother, Male Casebook, Wisconsin State Hospital for the Insane (Wisconsin Historical Society), pp. 273–74; Amherst's testimony in Appendix, p. 341.

6   Admission application; testimony of Amherst and Mrs. R. O. Kellogg in Appendix; *Wisconsin Chief,* Feb. 15, 1865.

7   *Wisconsin State Journal,* Jan. 30, 1865; a note written by Mrs. Kellogg, which was attached to application for admission, described the methods she used to comfort Romulus, testimony of Amherst Kellogg in Appendix, p. 348; Romulus Kellogg's application for admission to the Wisconsin State Hospital for the Insane, which was filled out by his brother, Male Casebook, pp. 273–74; Amherst's testimony in Appendix, p. 341.

8   Testimony of Mrs. R. O. Kellogg, Appendix, pp. 338–39.

9   Testimony of Amherst Kellogg, Mrs. R. O. Kellogg, and Dr. John Favill, Appendix, pp. 338–50.

10   George Kellogg, a cousin of Amherst and Romulus who owned a nursery near Janesville, recorded daily temperatures for January in his diary; distances to the hospital are given on p. 214 of the 1865 Annual Report of the Trustees of the Wisconsin State Hospital for

the Insane (hereafter called Annual Report of the Trustees); costs of buildings are given in Richard N. Current, *The History of Wisconsin*, vol. 2, pp. 297 and 495.

11 Van Norstrand's handwritten memoirs, p. 23 (hereafter called Memoirs). The memoirs and an album Van Norstrand kept of his military orders, letters, and so on, and a folder of his business letters dating from the late 1860s are in the archives of the Neville Public Museum in Green Bay.

12 Louise Phelps Kellogg papers and the George J. Kellogg collection in the archives of the Wisconsin Historical Society. These collections include clippings, family records, and above all copies of character sketches of family members written by Amherst in prose and verse. Also, Stewart H. Holbrook, *The Yankee Exodus* (New York, 1950), p. 119.

13 Williamson and Orange Smalley, *Northwestern Mutual Life*, pp. 334–35.

14 Amherst Kellogg's testimony, Appendix, p. 342.

15 Ibid., p. 343.

16 John Charles Bucknill and Daniel H. Tuke, *A Manual of Psychological Medicine* (London, 1858), p. 180.

17 Ibid., pp. 170, 180.

18 Benjamin Rush, *Medical Inquiries and Observations upon the Diseases of the Mind* (Philadelphia, 1812), pp. 196–99. A justification for this point of view is given in volume 3 of the first edition of the *Encyclopedia Britannica*, published in 1771: "Violent anger will change melancholy into madness; and excessive cold, especially of the lower parts, will force the blood into the lungs, heart and brain; whence oppressive anxieties . . . vertigoes and a sensation of weight in the head, fierceness of the eyes, long watchings, various workings of the fancy intensely fixed upon a single object, are produced by these means" (from the essay, "Melancholy and Madness," vol. 3, pp. 196–99). Conversely, to restore mental balance, that excess of blood must be drawn out of the overheated brain. One way to accomplish this was by cooling the head and warming the body.

19 Male Casebook, pp. 273–74, January 27, 1865.

20 Mrs. R. O. Kellogg's testimony, Appendix, p. 340.

21 Amherst Kellogg's testimony, ibid., p. 343.

22 J. G. McKindley's testimony, ibid., p. 334.

23 Male Casebook, p. 274.

24 Ibid.

25 Ibid.

26 Amherst Kellogg's testimony, p. 343.

27 Annual Report of the Trustees, 1864–1867.

28 "Superintendent's Report," included in Annual Report of the Trustees, 1864, p. 928.

29 The names of all patients except R. O. Kellogg have been changed.

30 Female Casebook, entries for "CR," June 12–22, 1863.

31 Male Casebook, entries for "WP," January 18, 1865–May 20, 1866; letter to Governor Lewis from sister of "WP" dated December 31, 1864; admission application for "WP," January 13, 1865, *American Journal of Insanity*, January, 1865, pp. 462–67.

32 Male Casebook, entries for "WP," dated February 10 and March 17, 1865. Croton oil

acts wickedly on flesh. It was the active ingredient in solutions used by Hollywood "skinners" to peel wrinkles from the stars of the 1920s and 1930s, and it is still used by plastic surgeons. It is also used to induce tumors in laboratory mice. But a century and more ago, in an age of horrific symptoms and harsh remedies, croton oil was prescribed as a drastic, last-ditch laxative (a few drops did the trick; a teaspoonful was lethal), and topically as a counterirritant. Inflammation induced on the body's surface was believed to act somewhat like a poultice, relieving symptoms of internal inflammation caused by diseases like pleurisy and pneumonia, or in Peterson's case, symptoms of pain or dementia, such as severe headaches and/or mania: George P. Hetter, "An Examination of the Phenol-Croton Oil Peel," parts 1 and 2, *Plastic Reconstructive Surgery*, January and February, 2000; also, Bradley and Chester, *From Croton Oil to Isotopes, One Hundred Years of Medicine at Hampton Veterans Administration Center; Encyclopedia Britannica*, 1902, vol. 31, p. 659.

33   Male Casebook, entry for "WP," May 20, 1866.

34   Female Casebook, entries for "JL," dated August 22–September 23, 1865.

35   *Journal of the Wisconsin State Lunatic Asylum*, notes of meeting of trustees April 12, 1864, p. 260.

36   *Milwaukee Sentinel*, February 2, 1865.

37   Journals of the State Senate and State Assembly, February 24, 27, 28, and March 1, 1865.

38   Memoirs, p. 12.

39   Journal of the Senate, April 7, 1865; also, Annual Report of the Trustees, 1865, p. 215.

40   Van Norstrand to trustees, April 11, 1865, Journal of the Wisconsin State Lunatic Asylum.

41   Appendix, p. 133.

42   Journal of the Wisconsin State Lunatic Asylum, 1854–69.

43   Madison City Directory, 1866, pp. 174–75.

1. *"The Fortune I Desired and Expected"*

1   Wisconsin Necrology, Wisconsin Historical Society, vol. 4, pp. 31–32.

2   Memoirs, p. 2.

3   Ibid., p. 2.

4   Ibid., pp. 4–5; also, Jacqueline Van Norstrand, *The Ancestors and Descendants of Frederick van Norstrand & Elizabeth Harris of Cayuga County, New York* (, 1995).

5   Memoirs, p. 6.

6   Ibid., p. 6.

7   Ibid., pp. 6–7.

8   Ibid., p. 5.

9   Frederick Clayton Waite, *The Story of a Country Medical College* (Montpelier, VT, 1945), pp. 98–100.

10 Martin Kaufman, *The University of Vermont College of Medicine* (Hanover, NH, 1979), pp. 33–40.

11 Waite, *Country Medical College*, pp. 23 and 112–115.

12 Memoirs, p. 12.

2. *"I Soon Found My Hands Full"*

1 Elisha Keyes, *History of Dane County* (Madison, WI, 1906), pp. 27–29; also, David V. Mollenhoff, *Madison, A History of the Formative Years* (Dubuque, IA, 1982), pp. 19–27.

2 Meridel LeSuer, *North Star Country* (Minneapolis, MN, 1998), p. 74.

3 John Henry Ott, *Jefferson County Wisconsin and Its People* (Chicago, 1917) pp. 61–63.

4 Ibid., pp. 50–52.

5 Mollenhoff, p. 141.

6 Memoirs, pp. 13–14.

7 Hannah Swart, *Koshkonong Country* (Fort Atkinson, WI, 1975), pp. 108, 156, 162; also, Swart, *Koshkonong Country Revisited*, vol. 1 (Muskego, WI, 1981), p. 37.

8 Memoirs, p. 15.

9 Ibid.

10 Peter T. Harstad, "Sickness and Disease on the Wisconsin Frontier: Malaria, 1820–1850," *Wisconsin Magazine of History*, winter 1959-1960, p. 84.

11 Memoirs, p. 15.

12 Ibid., pp. 15–16.

13 Ibid., p. 16.

14 Ibid., pp. 16–17.

15 Ott, p. 66.

16 Peter T. Harstad, "Sickness and Disease on the Wisconsin Frontier: Smallpox and other Diseases," *Wisconsin Magazine of History*, summer, 1960, p. 260.

17 Peter T. Harstad, "Health in the Upper Mississippi River Valley, 1820–1861," Ph.D. thesis, University of Wisconsin, 1963, p. 302.

18 Ibid., p. 311.

19 Peter Harstad, in *Wisconsin Medicine—Historical Perspectives*, ed. Ronald L. Numbers and Judith Walzer Leavitt, pp. 21–22 (Madison, WI, 1981).

20 Harstad, "Health in the Upper Mississippi," pp. 308–10.

21 Swart, *Koshkonong Country*, p. 267.

22 Chester Verne Easum, *The Americanization of Carl Schurz* (Chicago, 1929), p. 109.

23 Caswell, Lucien B., Reminiscences, Wisconsin Historical Society, p. 30.

24 Harstad, "Sickness and Disease: Malaria," p. 86.

25 Memoirs, p. 3.

26 Ibid., p. 17.

27 Ibid., p. 17.

28 Harstad, p. 21.

29 Memoirs, p. 17.

30 Frederick Merk, *Economic History of Wisconsin During the Civil War Decade* (Madison, WI, 1916), pp. 201–2; Alfons J. Beitzinger, *Edward G. Ryan—Lion of the Law* (Madison, WI, 1960), pp. 16–17; also, Memoirs, p. 17.

31 Memoirs, p. 22.

32 Ibid., p. 26.

33 *Jeffersonian,* November 2, 1854.

34 Memoirs, p. 19.

35 Ibid., p. 19; also Journal of the Assembly, 1852.

36 Ott, p. 219; also, Swart, *Koshkonong Country,* p. 57.

37 Ott, p. 219–24.

38 Easum, p. 111.

39 Memoirs, p. 20. (Reflecting on his tactics twenty years later, Van Norstrand was contrite: "Now that the old gentleman is dead I regret that I worked so diligently against him.") Also, the *Jeffersonian,* October 26 and November 2, 1854.

40 Swart, *Koshkonong Country Revisited,* vol. 1, p. 116. The origins of the Republican Party are in dispute, but Wisconsin Republicans trace their party back to a gathering of Whigs, Free-Soilers, and disaffected Democrats in the town of Ripon in 1854. See Richard N. Current, *The History of Wisconsin, Vol. II, The Civil War Era, 1848–1873,* Madison, 1976, p. 218 and footnote p. 219.

41 Memoirs, p. 20.

42 Ibid., p. 22–23.

43 Caswell, p. 53–54.

44 Memoirs, p. 19. *Jeffersonian,* May–December, 1853, and December 4, 1856.

45 Memoirs, p. 21.

46 Ibid., p. 21.

47 *Jeffersonian,* October 25, 1855.

48 Incorporation papers, Bank of Jefferson, in Wisconsin Historical Society archives, *Defunct Banks, 1853–1873.* Also, Memoirs, p. 24.

49 Swart, *Koshkonong Country Revisited,* photo, p. 138.

50 Memoirs, p. 21.

51 Swart, *Koshkonong Country Revisited,* p. 138–39.

52 In his memoirs, Caswell wrote that they were South Carolina bonds, but records of the Wisconsin bank comptroller indicated that they were issued by North Carolina. *Bank Incorporation Book, 1853–1868,* Wisconsin Historical Society.

53 In his own memoirs, Van Norstrand said the year was 1858. He was wrong. He continued as cashier of the Bank of Jefferson, and Caswell as cashier of the Koshkonong Bank, until December, 1859. Swart, p. 139; Memoirs, p. 24.

54 *Bank Incorporation Book, 1853–1868.*

55 *Jeffersonian,* August 25, 1859.

56 Merk, p. 194.

57 Memoirs, p. 24; also, Swart, *Koshkonong Country Revisited,* p. 139.

58 Ibid., p. 24–25.

59 *Bank Incorporation Book, 1853–1868;* also, Memoirs, p. 25.

60 *Jeffersonian,* May 19, 1859, and March 29, 1860.

61 Easum, p. 108 and 157.

62 *Westernized Yankee—The Story of Cyrus Woodman,* by Larry Gara, Madison, 1956, p. 148.

63 Easum, p. 206–09.

64 Current, p. 258–59; Beitzinger, p. 52; Easum, p. 208–09.

3. *"My Blood Is Up"*

1   Memoirs, p. 22.

2   Ibid., p. 25.

3   Ibid., p. 27. Van Norstrand calls it "a train from the south end of the state," but the only such train stopping in Jefferson originated in Chicago, with several stops in between: *Travelers Official Railway Guide of the United States and Canada,* June, 1868.

4   Memoirs, p. 28; also, Van Norstrand to Randall, April 29, 1861; Randall Papers, Wisconsin Historical Society.

5   Memoirs, pp. 28–29.

6   Ibid., pp. 30–31.

7   Ibid., p. 32; also, Merk, pp. 199–200.

8   Memoirs, p. 32.

9   *Racine Weekly Journal,* July 10, 1861.

10 Memoirs, p. 40. Many opponents of slavery doubted that freed blacks could survive in white society and so advocated relocating them to colonies in Africa or Central America. Hall traveled in Africa and wrote several reports for the American Colonization Society. Also, see David Herbert Donald, *Lincoln* (New York, 1996), pp. 166–67.

11 Memoirs, p. 38.

12 Ibid., p. 39.

13 In this 1814 battle near Niagara Falls, Scott led his troops into an English ambush. His brigade was decimated and he was severely wounded. It was not his finest moment. See John S. D. Eisenhower, *Agent of Destiny—The Life and Times of General Winfield Scott* (New York, 1997), pp. 85–95.

14 Memoirs, p. 38.

15 Ibid., p. 38.

16 Florence Nightingale was a controversial public health advocate in England who organized a battlefield hospital for British soldiers during the Crimean War.

17 Memoirs, p. 41.

18 Ibid., p. 41.

19 Ibid., p. 40.

20 Ibid., p. 42.

21 Ibid., p. 37. Jim is not mentioned again until Van Norstrand is in Louisiana, and so this reference is puzzling and could be out of place. Possibly they met in Louisiana. It seems unlikely that the army would have sent personal servants on military transports already overcrowded with soldiers and even less likely that Jim, if a free man in the north, would have been willing to accompany Van Norstrand into the deep south.

22 Readers may wonder if Jim was an invention, lifted from *Huckleberry Finn*. However, that would not have been possible. Excerpts from Twain's novel first appeared in *Century Magazine* in February, 1885. Van Norstrand died in May of 1883. A very young slave named Jim appears in *Tom Sawyer*, but he has little in common with the much older "Nigger Jim" of *Huckleberry Finn* or with Van Norstrand's enterprising servant.

23 Ibid., pp. 43–44.

24 Halbert Paine, *Manuscripta Minora* (unpublished), Charles East Collection, Hill Memorial Library, Louisiana State University, Baton Rouge, p. 2.

25 *Dictionary of Wisconsin Biography*, p. 278; also, *Milwaukee Evening Wisconsin*, April 17, 1905.

26 Bean was apparently not related to Samuel Bean, Van Norstrand's opponent in the 1856 legislative race.

27 Paine, pp. 3 and 6; Memoirs, p. 48.

28 Papers of Col. Sidney Alfred Bean, Wisconsin Historical Society.

29 Matthew C. Perry, *Narrative of the Expedition of an American Squadron to the China Seas and Japan*, vol. 2 (Washington, DC, 1856), p. 412; Samuel Eliot Morison, *"Old Bruin" Commodore Matthew C. Perry, 1794–1858* (Boston, 1967), p. 274; also Wickham Hoffman, *Camp, Court and Siege* (New York, 1877), p. 44.

30 Papers of Major Frederick Boardman, Wisconsin Historical Society.

31 Boardman to Noonan, November 13, 1861, Boardman papers.

32 Boardman to Noonan, March 1, 1862.

33 Boardman to Noonan, June 11, 1862.

34 Randall to Noonan, April 22, 1861, Randall papers.

35 E. C. Dixon, "Newport, Its Rise and Fall," *Wisconsin Magazine of History*, June, 1942, pp. 444–55.

36 Memoirs, p. 45.

37 Ibid., p. 49.

4. *"The Best Specimen of a Tyrant"*

1 E. B. Quiner scrapbooks, vol. 3, p. 78. During the war, Quiner compiled a series of scrapbooks consisting primarily of soldier letters and correspondents' dispatches clipped

from Wisconsin newspapers and organized by regiment (Wisconsin Historical Society archives).

2   Quiner scrapbooks, vol. 3, p. 82.

3   Paine, p. 6.

4   Quiner scrapbooks, vol. 3, pp. 79–80.

5   Quiner scrapbooks, vol. 3, pp. 79–80.

6   Boardman to Noonan, March 1, 15, and 29, 1862.

7   Memoirs, p. 49.

8   "Letters of General Thomas Williams," *American Historical Review,* vol. 14, 1909, p. 307.

9   Ibid., pp. 307–8.

10   Ibid., p. 309.

11   Quiner scrapbooks, vol. 3, pp. 79–80.

12   The annual report of Wisconsin's adjutant general for 1865 dramatically states: "The hardships of the voyage in a crowded transport, had engendered disease, and many of the regiment found a soldier's grave in the sandy bosom of this ocean solitude," a statement echoed in Quiner's *Military History of Wisconsin: A Record of the Civil and Military Patriotism of the State in the War for the Union* (Chicago, 1866), p. 499. *Wisconsin Losses in the Civil War* (Madison, WI, 1915), a compilation of deaths and injuries by date within each regiment, records two deaths by disease within the Fourth Wisconsin while the *Constitution* was en route to Ship Island, but these could have been soldiers left behind because of illness. Statistics kept by Van Norstrand do not reflect any deaths in March.

13   Boardman to Noonan, March 15, 1862.

14   Quiner scrapbooks, vol. 3, p. 81.

15   Quiner scrapbooks, vol. 3, pp. 81, 84, 85.

16   Memoirs, pp. 50–51; Quiner scrapbooks, vol. 3, pp. 8, 85, 96.

17   Memoirs, p. 51; Quiner scrapbooks, vol. 3, p. 97.

18   Hoffman, p. 52.

19   John William DeForest, *A Volunteers' Adventures* (Baton Rouge, LA, 1996), p. 29.

20   Paine, p. 10.

21   Memoirs; this episode based upon pp. 51–52.

22   The position of general-in-chief was currently vacant, General McClellan—who had replaced Winfield Scott—having been removed from that position in early March. General Halleck would be appointed later that year.

23   Memoirs, pp. 66 and 93.

24   Ibid., p. 55.

25   Bean's diary, April 3, 1862.

26   William DeLoss Love, *Wisconsin in the War of the Rebellion; a History of All Regiments and Batteries the State Has Sent to the Field* (Chicago, 1866), p. 531; also, Quiner scrapbooks, vol. 3, p. 97.

27   Quiner scrapbooks, vol. 3, p. 96.

28 Bean's diary, April 3 and 29, 1862.

29 Paine, p. 14.

30 Edward Bacon, *Among the Cotton Thieves* (Detroit, 1867), pp. 6 and 15.

31 Paine, p. 16; also, Paine to his wife, July 30, 1862, Charles East Collection, Hill Memorial Library, Louisiana State University, Baton Rouge.

32 Memoirs, p. 55.

33 Quiner scrapbooks, vol. 3, p. 96.

34 Memoirs, p. 57.

35 John D. Winters, *The Civil War in Louisiana* (Baton Rouge, LA, 1963), p. 103; Shelby Foote, *The Civil War, A Narrative: Fort Sumter to Perryville*, vol. 1 (New York, 1958), p. 369.

36 Winters, p. 102; Memoirs, p. 57; Norton DeHave to father, May 3, 1862, Wisconsin Historical Society; "Letters of Thomas Williams," May 1, 1862; Quiner scrapbooks, vol. 13, p. 130.

37 Memoirs, p. 55.

38 Ibid., p. 57.

5. *"A Severe Punishment of a Deluded and Spiteful People"*

1 Charles King, *Kitty's Conquest* (Philadelphia, 1891), p. 295. This novel was based on King's experiences as a young lieutenant stationed in New Orleans after the war.

2 DeHave to his father, March 16, 1862.

3 Jefferson Davis Bragg, *Louisiana in the Confederacy* (Baton Rouge, LA, 1941), p. 127.

4 "Letters of General Thomas Williams," July 26, 1862.

5 Boardman to Noonan, July 14, 1862.

6 Nor did Wickham Hoffman have anything good to say about Halbert Paine in his own memoirs, written after an adventurous career as secretary of the American legations in Paris and St. Petersburg. He lauded Boardman and Bailey and expressed fondness for the soldiers of the Fourth Wisconsin, but he never mentioned their colonel by name, nor did he acknowledge Paine's heroism during the Port Hudson campaign the next year. But he did refer to a certain commander at Baton Rouge who enriched himself through illegal cotton deals and was later promoted to brigadier. Paine succeeded Williams as commander at Baton Rouge and later got his first star, but the rest is a smear, which is probably why Hoffman did not name the man he had in mind. It was a slap at an old adversary—enough to sting without provoking a lawsuit. See Hoffman, *Camp, Court, and Siege.* It will come as no surprise that "Nancy" (Paine, p. 19) was slang for homosexual. See Roy Morris Jr., *Ambrose Bierce, Alone in Bad Company* (New York, 1998), p. 169.

7 Paine, p. 19.

8 Quiner scrapbooks, vol. 3, p. 110.

9 Memoirs, p. 59.

10 Ibid., p. 59.

11 DeHave to his father, July 10, 1862.

12 Paine, p. 20.

13 Quiner scrapbooks, vol. 3, p. 110.

14 Memoirs, pp. 61–62; also, Paine, p. 24.

15 Quiner scrapbooks, vol. 3, p. 111.

16 Memoirs, pp. 67–69.

17 Paine, p. 30.

18 Memoirs, p. 68; Quiner scrapbooks, vol. 3, pp. 121–23; also, G. G. Benedict, *Vermont in the Civil War* (Burlington, VT, 1888), pp. 11–12.

19 Newton Culver papers, 1861–1864, Wisconsin Historical Society.

20 Memoirs, p. 69.

21 Norton DeHave to his father, July 10, 1862.

22 Memoirs, p. 69.

23 Love, p. 535; Quiner, *The Military History of Wisconsin*, p. 500; also, *History and Catalogue of the Fourth Wisconsin Regiment of Volunteers from June 1861, to March 1864* (Baton Rouge, LA, 1864), p. 10.

24 The War of Rebellion: A Compilation of the Official Records of the Union and Confederate Armies, War Department, Washington, DC (hereafter called Official Records), series 1, vol. 15, p. 25.

25 Ibid., p. 29.

26 Arthur M. Schlesinger Sr. and Dixon Ryan Fox, *A History of American Life* (New York, 1996), p. 620.

27 Quiner scrapbooks, vol. 3, p. 123.

28 *History and Catalogue*, p. 10.

29 Official Records, series 1, vol. 15, p. 32.

30 Love, 535; also, Quiner, separate folder of Fourth Wisconsin newspaper clippings, Wisconsin Historical Society, p. 4.

31 Winters, pp. 196–197.

32 "Letters of General Thomas Williams," July 2, 1862.

33 Quiner scrapbooks, vol. 3, p. 123.

34 Memoirs, p. 72.

35 Ibid., p. 73.

36 Ibid., p. 74.

37 Ibid., p. 71.

38 Paine, p. 24.

39 Memoirs, p. 63.

40 Paine., p. 23.

41 Quiner, separate folder of Fourth Wisconsin newspaper clippings, p. 7.

42 Official Records, series 1, vol. 15, p. 32.

43 Ibid., p. 31.

44 Ibid., p. 23.

45 Quiner scrapbooks, vol. 3, p. 121.

46 Bacon, p. 15.

47 Quiner scrapbooks, vol. 3, p. 115.

48 Boardman to Noonan, July 17, 1862.

49 Benedict, pp. 15 and 20.

50 Memoirs, pp. 78–79.

51 John Harley Warner, *The Therapeutic Perspective: Medical Practice, Knowledge, and Identity in America, 1820–1885* (Cambridge, MA, 1986), pp. 28–31, 129, and 149.

52 Memoirs, p. 78.

53 Ibid., pp 79–80.

54 Benedict, p. 17.

55 Memoirs, p. 79; Paine, p. 31; also, Winters, p. 110.

6. *"The Whole Camp Still as Death"*

1   Bacon, pp. 6–7.

2   Charles East (ed.), *The Civil War Diary of Sarah Morgan* (Athens, GA, 1991), p. 181.

3   Mark Twain, *Life on the Mississippi* (New York, 1991), p. 252.

4   East, p. 49.

5   Ibid., p. 68.

6   "Letters of General Thomas Williams," July 26, 1862.

7   Sarah A. Dorsey, *Recollections of Henry Watkins Allen* (New York, 1866), p. 140.

8   Richard S. West Jr., *Lincoln's Scapegoat General—A Life of General Benjamin F. Butler* (Boston, 1965), p. 164.

9   Memoirs, pp. 80–81.

10 Ibid., p. 80. Six from the Seventh Vermont died the night the regiment arrived in Baton Rouge (Benedict, p. 20). Also, Charles East, *Baton Rouge: A Civil War Album,* privately printed, 1977, p. 93.

11 East, *The Civil War Diary of Sarah Morgan,* p. 181.

12 Ibid., p. 183.

13 Memoirs, p. 81.

14 Ibid., p. 81. The description of Van Norstrand's instruments is based upon Charles Beneulyn Johnson, M.D., *Muskets and Medicine,* (Philadelphia, 1917), pp. 97–100.

15 Memoirs, p. 64.

16 "Letters of General Thomas Williams," June 2 and June 16, 1862.

17 The Emancipation Proclamation would not take effect until January, 1863, and even then would not apply to slaves in areas already controlled by the Union, such as the lower

Mississippi. Meanwhile, the legal status of blacks seeking Union protection in those areas remained in dispute, a dilemma Butler circumvented by declaring them "contrabands"—illegal goods confiscated by Union forces. He put many to work as laborers.

18   Quiner scrapbooks, vol. 3, p. 126.

19   Ibid., pp. 124 and 126.

20   Paine, p. 26 (Paine to Butler, June 4, 1862).

21   Ibid.; also, Quiner scrapbooks, vol. 3, pp. 116 and 124.

22   Quiner scrapbooks, vol. 3, pp. 116 and 126.

23   Memoirs, p. 65.

24   Paine, p. 27.

25   Ibid., pp. 27–28; also, Quiner scrapbooks, vol. 3, p. 116.

26   Memoirs, p. 64.

27   Quiner scrapbooks, vol. 3, p. 126.

28   Ibid. The collar is on display at the Wisconsin Veterans Museum in Madison. It is hinged at the throat, with a coupling for a padlock at the neck and grooved posts four inches long extending toward each ear, as if to accommodate fittings brought down over the head. The documentation reads: "While our army were [*sic*] at Grand Gulf, Miss., an intelligent contraband gave much valuable information as to the position of the enemy, and otherwise rendered himself very useful to our forces. He finally fell into the hands of the rebels, who administered one hundred and fifty lashes, and placed an iron collar round his neck, riveting it on very strongly. The Negro was captured from the rebels at Baton Rouge, La., by Company F, 4th Wisconsin, who of course immediately released him from the collar." History of the North-Western Soldiers' Fair, "List of Donations and Names of Donors," Chicago, 1864.

29   Boardman to Noonan, June 8, 1862.

30   Paine, p. 72 (Schurz to Paine, February 20, 1862).

31   Bacon, pp. 8–9.

32   Paine, p. 24.

33   Bacon, pp. 27–28.

34   Paine, p. 19.

35   Bacon, p. 28.

36   Paine, p. 33; Bacon, pp. 28–31.

37   Quiner scrapbooks, vol. 3, p. 137; also, Hoffman, p. 53.

38   East, pp. 192–194.

39   Ibid., p. 201.

40   Hoffman, p. 49.

41   Memoirs, p. 81.

42   Memoirs, p. 81; Official Records, series 1, vol. 15, pp. 51–52; also, William C. Davis, *Breckinridge—Statesman, Soldier, Symbol* (Baton Rouge, LA, 1974), p. 319.

43   Memoirs, p. 83.

44   The overview of battle described here is derived primarily from Winters, pp. 113–24, and supplemented by other sources including Union officer after-action reports in Official Records.

45   Eliza McHatton-Ripley, *From Flag to Flag* (New York, 1889), pp. 34–36.

46   Memoirs, p. 81.

47   Ibid., p. 89.

48   Ibid., pp. 82–83.

49   Ibid., p. 84. The early August strength figures for the Fourth Wisconsin are from Paul E. Steiner, *Disease in the Civil War* (Springfield, IL, 1968), p. 204.

50   Memoirs, p. 83.

51   East, *The Civil War Diary of Sarah Morgan*, p. 201.

52   Related by Paine in a letter to his wife, August 31, 1862.

53   Memoirs, p. 84.

54   Ibid., p. 84.

55   Ibid., p. 86.

56   The conviction that one's own regiment ranked at or near the top was nearly universal. John William DeForest of the Twelfth Connecticut Infantry proudly recorded that one insightful general considered his outfit "too highly gifted for infantry.... The most intelligent men I ever commanded." Beware the "peaceable New England farmer and mechanic" when he becomes a hardened warrior; he is smarter, better drilled, better disciplined, etc., etc. DeForest, *A Volunteer's Adventures,* p. 42, and *Miss Ravenel's Conversion from Secession to Loyalty* (Lincoln, NE, 1998) p. 246.

57   Memoirs, pp. 89–90.

7. *"The First Negro Hospital"*

1   Paine, p. 35.

2   Paine to his wife, August 31, 1862.

3   Memoirs, p. 87; also, Paul E. Steiner, *Disease in the Civil War* (Springfield, IL, 1968), p. 205.

4   Quiner scrapbooks, vol. 3, p. 141.

5   Paine, pp. 38–39; also, Butler to Paine, August 19, 1862 in Official Records, series 1, vol. 15, p. 553.

6   Official Records, series 1, vol. 15, pp. 550–51.

7   Memoirs, p. 88; also, Paine, p. 37.

8   Paine, p. 37; Official Records, series 1, vol. 15, p. 551.

9   Paine to his wife, August 31, 1862.

10   Paine to his wife, August 31, 1862. Charles East was the first to point out Paine's about-face from principled self-denial to eager acquisition (Charles East Collection, LSU Special Collections).

11   Memoirs, p. 88.

12   Quiner scrapbooks, vol. 3, p. 141.

13   Edmund Wilson, *Patriotic Gore* (New York, 1962), pp. 270–71; also, Winters, p. 123.

14   Paine, p. 40.

15   Van Norstrand to *Milwaukee Sentinel,* Quiner scrapbooks, vol. 8, p. 49.

16   Annual Report of the State Hospital for the Insane, 1867, p. 271.

17   Warner, Chapter 4, "Therapeutic Change."

18   Memoirs, p. 91.

19   Ibid., p. 46.

20   Henry T. Johns, *Life with the Forty-Ninth Massachusetts* (Washington, DC, 1890), pp. 170–72.

21   Henry Martyn Cross, "A Yankee Soldier Looks at the Negro," ed. William Cullen Bryant II, *Civil War History Magazine,* June 1961, p. 144.

22   Quiner scrapbooks, vol. 3, p. 124.

23   DeForest, *A Volunteer's Adventures,* pp. 9–11 and 39.

24   Memoirs, p. 91. In a few weeks Phelps would resign from the army rather than obey General Butler's order to gather up contrabands and force them to work on Union for-tifications, saying that he "was not fit for slave-driving or slave-catching." Benjamin F. Butler, *Butler's Book* (Boston, 1892), pp. 448–49; also, DeForest, *A Volunteer's Adventures,* p. 43.

25   Memoirs, p. 92.

26   Ibid.

27   Ibid., pp. 94–97; *History and Catalogue, p*p. 11–12; Winters, pp. 156–57.

28   Memoirs, p. 46.

29   Ibid., pp. 98–100.

30   Memoirs, pp. 101-7.

31   Eric T. Dean, *Shook Over Hell—Post-Traumatic Stress, Vietnam and the Civil War* (Cambridge, MA, 1997), Chapter 6, "'Dying of Nostalgia': Official Diagnosis."

32   Bucknill and Tuke, pp. 160–64; also, Albert Deutsch, "Military Psychiatry," in *One Hundred Years of American Psychiatry,* ed. J. K. Hall, p. 375 (New York, 1944).

33   *The Medical and Surgical History of the War of Rebellion,* vol. 6 (Wilmington, NC, 1991) (reprint), pp. 884–86.

34   Ibid., pp. 885–86; also, Austin Flint, M.D., *Contributions Relating to the Causation and Prevention of Disease* (New York, 1867).

35   Memoirs, pp. 103–4.

36   Ibid., p. 106.

37   Letter dated December 26, 1861, in Van Norstrand's records, National Archives. In his memoirs (pp. 107–8) he refers to another request for medical leave made in late 1862. Both were granted.

38   Memoirs, p. 108.

8. *"The Wails of the Wounded"*

1   Quiner scrapbooks, vol. 8, p. 188.

2   Winters, p. 242.

3   Quiner scrapbooks, vol. 8, p.188.

4   *Gazette and Comet,* Baton Rouge, LA, November 12, 1862.

5   Memoirs, p. 117; also, Quiner scrapbooks, vol. 8, p. 189.

6   Richard S. West Jr., *Lincoln's Scapegoat General—A Life of General Benjamin F. Butler* (Boston, 1965), p. 4.

7   Lawrence Less Hewitt and R. Christopher Goodwin, "The Battle of Bisland, Louisiana," *North and South* 1, no. 7: 29.

8   Quiner scrapbooks, vol. 8, p. 251.

9   Memoirs, p. 120; Paine, p. 47; Quiner scrapbooks, vol. 8, p. 251.

10   *History and Catalogue,* pp. 15–16; Winters, p. 237.

11   Halleck to Banks, May 23, 1863, Official Records, series 1, vol. 26, part 1, p. 500.

12   Ibid., p. 105; William B. Stevens, *History of the Fiftieth Regiment of Infantry* (Boston, 1907), pp. 100, 105, 106; Frank M. Flinn, *Campaigning with Banks* (Lynn, MA, 1887), p. 17.

13   Johns, p. 206.

14   Ibid., pp. 200–201, 206, and 216–21.

15   Memoirs, p. 117.

16   Ibid., pp. 117–118; also, Charles Beneulyn Johnson, *Muskets and Medicine* (Philadelphia, 1917), p. 97.

17   Memoirs, p. 119.

18   Ibid., pp. 117–18.

19   Ibid., p. 118.

20   Ibid., p. 121.

21   Johns, p. 206.

22   Memoirs, pp. 121–22.

23   Mark J. Schaadt, *Civil War Medicine* (Quincy, IL, 1998), pp. 70–71.

24   Memoirs, p. 143.

25   Johns, pp. 344–45.

26   Johnson, p. 99; Schaact, pp. 61–63; Charles S. Tripler, M.D., and George C. Blackman, M.D., *Hand-Book for the Military Surgeon* (Cincinnati, 1861), pp. 39–45; Frank Hastings Hamilton, *A Practical Treatise on Military Surgery* (New York, 1861), p. 9.

27   Memoirs, pp. 130–31.

28   John Leobner to Van Norstrand, undated letter in Van Norstrand's military album.

29   Peter Stasse to Van Norstrand, December, 1863, military album.

30   Memoirs, pp. 124–25; Diary of Newton Culver, pp. 115–17.

31   Rice to Van Norstrand, June 29, 1863, in military album.

32   Memoirs, pp. 134–35.

33   D. W. Fish to Van Norstrand, September 1, 1863, in military album.

34   Memoirs, pp. 132–33.

35   Ibid., p. 141.

36   Ibid., p. 124. Craigue survived and eventually commanded the regiment: *Official Army Register of the Volunteer Force of the United States Army*, Adjutant General's Office, Washington, 1865.

37   Maxon died July 16: *Wisconsin Losses in the Civil War*, p. 223.

38   He copied this letter into his memoirs, pp. 135–39.

39   Quiner scrapbooks, vol. 8, p. 246.

40   S. K. Towle, "Notes of Practice in the U.S.A. General Hospital, Baton Rouge, La., During the Year 1863," *The Boston Medical and Surgical Journal* 70, no. 3, February 18, 1864: 49–60.

41   Memoirs, pp. 128, 133, 143–44.

9. *"Friends and Enemies"*

1   Paine, p. 49.

2   Sidney Bean's unfinished letter was printed in the *Wisconsin State Journal*, June 15, 1863; Quiner scrapbooks, vol. 8, pp. 222–23; "Civil War Letters of Knute Nelson," *Norwegian-American Studies* 23, 1967: 38; also, *Memoirs*, p. 122.

3   Paine, p. 51.

4   Quiner scrapbooks, vol. 8, p. 228.

5   Quiner scrapbooks, vol. 8, p. 230.

6   Paine, pp. 51–52. In his memoirs Paine wrote that his wife later toured the battlefield and found the boot he had cut from his mangled leg. She filled it with a pint or so of spent bullets that she found nearby, some of which had almost certainly been fired at him.

7   DeForest, *A Volunteer's Adventures*, p. 143.

8   Memoirs, p. 131; also, letter dated June 18, 1863, Van Norstrand's military album.

9   Memoirs, pp. 131 and 142.

10   Winters, pp. 280–82.

11   Memoirs, p. 146.

12   Obituary, *Wisconsin State Journal*, May 8, 1883 (in Wisconsin Necrology, vol. 4, Wisconsin Historical Society).

13   Jacqueline Van Norstrand.

14   Memoirs, p. 151.

15   Letters from the New Orleans liquor dealer, dated October and November 1863, are in Van Norstrand's military album.

16   Mark T. Carleton, *River Capital, an Illustrated History of Baton Rouge* (Woodland Hills, CA, 1981), p. 96.

17   Goldsmith to Van Norstrand, November 5, 1863, Van Norstrand's military album.

18   DeForest, *A Volunteer's Adventures*, p. 29.

19   Flint, pp. 113–17.

20   Against all expectations Frederick Boardman had returned from the north and assumed command of the Fourth Wisconsin. As Pierce's plantation was in guerrilla country Boardman treated his old friend and protector to a princely escort of 100 cavalrymen.

21   Memoirs, pp. 147–48. An order in his military album dated January 24, 1864 reads, "Guards and pickets will pass Surgeon A. H. Van Norstrand to West Baton Rouge and return." This would have been too late to be the event that Van Norstrand describes but may indicate a visit to a planter named Pipes with whom he also had financial dealings. Pipes had two large spreads in West Baton Rouge according to Joseph Karl Menn in *The Large Slaveholders of Louisiana—1860* (New Orleans, 1964). The rebel colonel, Henry Watkins Allen, later Louisiana's last governor under the Confederacy, spent months recuperating from wounds sustained in the battle of Baton Rouge at the home of a man named Pierce, six miles from Baton Rouge—possibly this same Pierce who wooed Van Norstrand for favors from the Union commissary (Sarah Dorsey, *Recollections of Henry Watkins Allen*, [New York, 1966], p. 144).

22   *Memoirs*, pp. 147–49.

23   Ibid., pp. 148–49.

24   The story of the Louisiana sugar plantations, their seasonal cycles, and the plight of their owners during the war is wonderfully told by Charles P. Roland in *Louisiana Sugar Plantations During the Civil War* (Baton Rouge, LA, 1997). The material for this summary is based on pp. 30–31, 42–47, 74–79, and 87–90.

25   *Memoirs*, p. 149; also, Menn. In Van Norstrand's hand the name looks like Pike, but no one named Pike is listed in Menn. However, a David Pipes is listed. Pipes owned 153 slaves, and his holdings were in West Baton Rouge, on the west side of the Mississippi, which may account for the January 24 order in Van Norstrand's military album.

26   See Fred Harvey Harrington, *Fighting Politician, Major General N. P. Banks* (Philadelphia, 1948).

27   Frederick Boardman's obituary refers to this climate: "In the midst of the temptations and facilities for plunder which surrounded him, his personal integrity has remained as unquestioned . . . as his personal courage." *Milwaukee Sentinel,* May 13, 1864.

28   Also, the first 20 or so pages of his military scrapbook have been torn out. What did he (or his heirs) not want us to see?

29   Bailey to Van Norstrand, March 2, 1864, Van Norstrand's military album.

30   Van Norstrand to Paine, November 18, 1863.

31   Paine to Van Norstrand, January 2, 1864.

32   Van Norstrand to Lewis, March 5, 1864.

33   His discharge was dated January 28, 1864 (Annual Reports of the Adjutant General of the State of Wisconsin).

10. *"A Second Class Man"*

1   Sources for the hospital's historical background include the Journal of the Wisconsin State Lunatic Asylum, 1854–1869, and early annual reports of the superintendent and committees of the Board of Trustees.

2   Robert F. Kraus, M.D., "J. Edward Lee, M.D., and the founding of the Wisconsin State Hospital," *Transactions and Studies of the College of Physicians of Philadelphia* 40, No. 2, October, 1972; also, Journal of the Trustees, pp. 6–8.

3   Between 1825 and 1865 the number of asylums in the United States increased from 9 to 62 according to Norman Dain, in *Concepts of Insanity in the United States, 1789–1865* (New Brunswick, NJ, 1964), p. 55. In *Psychiatry and the Community in Nineteenth Century America* (New York, 1969), Ruth Caplan gives the number of hospitals in 1861 as 47, including 27 run by state governments and 5 by cities, p. 60.

4   Dain, p.120; also, Thomas B. Elliott, M.D., "An Address to the Legislature in Behalf of the Insane of the State of Wisconsin," February 6, 1856, Madison, WI. Elliott was the former assistant physician at the Indiana State Hospital for the Insane.

5   Albert Deutsch, *The Mentally Ill in America, A History of Their Care and Treatment from Colonial Times* (New York 1949), Chapter 8, "The Cult of Curability and the Rise of State Institutions."

6   Deutsch, pp. 209–10; also, "Special Report of the Commissioners of the Lunatic Asylum," Madison, WI, 1855, pp. 14–18.

7   Elliott, "Address to the Legislature."

8   William Malamud, "The History of Psychiatric Therapies," in Hall, pp. 273–94; also, Albert Deutsch, "The History of Mental Hygiene," in same collection, p. 334.

9   1863 "Annual Report of the Board of Trustees of the Wisconsin State Hospital," pp. 442–43.

10 1861 Annual Report, p. 12.

11 Ibid., p. 7, and 1860, p. 12.

12 1863 Annual Report, p. 445.

13 Ibid., p. 447.

14 In the late 1850s the city budgeted $8,000 for fire protection, police, streets, and lighting, according to Mollenhoff, p. 83. Less than a decade later the hospital was spending over $5,000 just for coal (1867 Annual Report, p. 275).

15 1878 Annual Report, p. 15.

16 Undated list of charges written by Dr. John Favill and filed in the Journal of the Wisconsin State Lunatic Asylum.

17 Letter to Board of Trustees from Dr. J. P. Fuchs, M.D., April 14, 1863, Journal of the Wisconsin State Lunatic Asylum.

18 From testimony recorded during the investigation of Dr. Clement during February and March of 1862, Journal of the Wisconsin State Lunatic Asylum. Sawyer's background is given in the annual report of 1861, p. 13.

19 From the superintendent's section of the 1863 Annual Report.

20 Dale Robison, "Wisconsin and the Mentally Ill: a History of the "Wisconsin Plan" of State and County Care, 1860-1915," Ph.D. dissertation, Marquette University, 1976, p. 61. Original source: *American Journal of Insanity* 21, 1864–1865, p. 432.

21 *Milwaukee Sentinel,* Feb. 20, 1864.

22 Col. L. Bunker to Lewis, March 22, 1864 (Correspondence of Governor James T. Lewis, Wisconsin Historical Society).

23 Van Norstrand to Board of Trustees, April 12, 1864 (Records of the State Hospital for the Insane, Wisconsin Historical Society).

24 W. W. Reed to Elisha Keyes, April 11, 1864, and D. T. Weymouth to Keyes, April 8, 1864 (Records of the State Hospital for the Insane).

25 Robert A. Birmingham and Leslie E. Eisenberg, *Indian Mounds of Wisconsin* (Madison, WI, 2000), p. 197. Also, Birmingham and Katherine H. Rankin, *Native American Mounds in Madison and Dane County* (Madison, WI, 1994), pp. 8–10.

26 Description based upon the few nineteenth-century photographs of the hospital interior on file in the Iconography Office of the Wisconsin Historical Society.

27 *Jefferson Banner,* Feb. 25, and April 7, 21, and 28, 1864. The April 21 story had originally appeared in the *Wisconsin State Journal.*

28 1864 Annual Report, pp. 923–29.

29 Male Casebook, p. 56.

30 Female Casebook, pp. 297 and 435.

31 *American Journal of Insanity,* July 1866, pp. 156–57.

32 1864 Annual Report, pp. 928–29.

11. *"The Usual Little Jarrings in the Ward"*

1 Case number 637. Patient names have been changed but their hospital case numbers, which are given in footnotes, have not. In some cases, casebook page numbers may be cited instead of a case number.

2 Male Casebook, p. 260.

3 Case number 588.

4 Case number 430.

5 Case number 776.

6 Case number 557.

7 Case number 576.

8 Female Casebook, p. 91.

9 Case number 787.

10 Case number 783.

11 D.P.W. to Van Norstrand, May 1, 1868.

12 Observations about MW, admitted July 31, 1863, were recorded by a succession of physicians through the years, and show up in several volumes of the Female Casebook.

13 GWS, admitted August 8, 1864. Male Casebook.

14 Case number 682.

15 PJ, p. 95, Female Casebook.

16 Male Casebook, p. 264.

17 Case number 771.

18 Female Casebook, p. 114.

19 SC, admitted June 4, 1863. Female Casebook.

20 Male Casebook, p. 414.

21 SH, admitted February 12, 1867. Male Casebook.

22 Case number 655, Male Casebook.

23 Male Casebook, pp. 385 and 349. The lakes are given their contemporary names. In those years they were still known to many as Third Lake (Monona) and Fourth Lake (Mendota).

24 Case number 535.

25 Letter to the superintendent sent from Princeton, Wisconsin, dated Dec. 26 (year not given), Male Casebook, pp. 279, 291, and 339. George Morris Piersol, M.D. (ed.), *Cyclopedia of Medicine* (Philadelphia, 1935); Spanish fly and croton oil were also used as counterirritants in the treatment of consumptives in the late nineteenth century, according to Barbara Bates in *Bargaining for Life* (Philadelphia, 1994), p. 31.

26 J. F., Female Casebook, p. 316.

27 Female Casebook, p. 4; Male Casebook, p. 262.

28 G. C., Male Casebook, p. 31.

29 T. L., admitted September 4, 1860. Entries about him begin on p. 17, Male Casebook, and appear at intervals throughout several volumes until his death at the hospital in 1891.

30 Testimony of Martin Lyon, Appendix, p. 366.

31 Case numbers 825 and 761.

32 Male Casebook, p. 449.

33 Female Casebook, pp. 118, 229, 327, and 359.

34 From "Rules for the Regulation of the Wisconsin State Hospital for the Insane," October, 1860.

35 Appendix, p. 264; also, Journal of the Wisconsin State Lunatic Asylum, pp. 67 and 92.

36 1872 Annual Report, pp. 15–16.

37 Annual Reports of 1872, pp. 15–16; 1869, p. 6; and 1908, p.1 of the superintendent's statement.

38 Annual Reports of 1876, 1888, and 1906 (superintendent's statements).

39 Appendix, p. 377.

40 Dr. Isaac Ray, superintendent of hospitals in Maine and Rhode Island and a highly regarded writer on hospital topics: quoted in Gerald Grob, *Mental Institutions in America* (New York, 1973), p. 212.

41 Appendix, p. 75.

42 Annual Reports of 1864 and 1865 (treasurer's statements); Appendix, p. 325. Wilson was the son of the Dr. Wilson who served under Van Norstrand with the Fourth Wisconsin.

43 1865 Annual Report, statement of the Visiting Committee.

44 L. N. to Van Norstrand, March 6, 1868; W.J.J. to Mrs. Mary B., September 27, 1868.

45 J. B to Governor James T. Lewis, May, 1864; E. M. to Lewis, August 16, 1864.

46 Appendix, pp. 270, 294, 298–99.

47 A pamphlet written in approximately 1890–1891 by Rose and Barbara Trautman entitled, "Our Experiences as the Victims of a Foul and Cruel Wrong," and addressed to Governor George Peck, charged that beating and other forms of mistreatment were routine and that the doctors allowed the hospital to be used as a dumping ground for sane but troublesome wives.

48 Appendix, pp. 116 and 187–92.

49 *American Journal of Insanity,* July, 1866, p. 88.

12. *"A Critical and Searching Examination"*

1 Nancy Tomes, *The Art of Asylum-Keeping, Thomas Story Kirkbride and the Origins of American Psychiatry* (Philadelphia, 1984), p. 267.

2 Samuel W. Hamilton, "The History of American Mental Hospitals," in Hall, pp. 152–53; Deutsch, p. 208.

3 Deutsch, p. 232.

4 Tomes, pp. 274–79; Caplan, pp. 182–88; Grob, pp. 263-67.

5 *Jefferson Banner,* June 20, 1866.

6 "Report of the Joint Committee on Charitable and Benevolent Institutions," Journal of the Assembly, pp. 402–3, February 13, 1868.

7 1865 Annual Report, pp. 257–58.

8 Ibid., p. 259.

9 Ibid., p. 258.

10 Ibid., p. 211.

11 Ibid., p. 260.

12 1866 Annual Report, pp. 49–50.

13 Appendix, pp. 246–47.

14 *Wisconsin State Journal,* March 9, 1865, p. 1.

15 *Journal of the Senate,* pp. 480–82, March 17, 1865.

16 "Proceedings of the Medical Society of Wisconsin," 1868, pp. 37–42. *Wisconsin Union,* January 31, 1868.

17 Journal of the Wisconsin State Lunatic Asylum, pp. 318–19.

18 1866 Annual Report, pp. 9-10.

19 Dr. Charles Nichols, superintendent of the Government Asylum in Washington, D.C., quoted in Tomes, p. 16.

20 Appendix, pp. 98–99; also, treasurer's section of the annual report for that year.

21 See Van Norstrand's annual reports for 1864 through 1867.

22 Appendix, pp. 72 and 355–57.

23 "The Acts to Provide for the Government of the Wisconsin State Hospital for the Insane," p. 24; also, "By-Laws of the Board of Trustees," 1863.

24 *Madison Daily Union,* September 11, 1867, p. 4.

25 Appendix, pp. 358, 386, and 392–93.

26 See "Statement of current expense accounts" in Annual Reports of 1867 and 1868.

27 Levi Decker to Board of Trustees, April 7, 1867, in Journal of the Wisconsin Lunatic Asylum.

28 See minutes for April and May, 1867, Journal of the Wisconsin State Lunatic Asylum.

29 Hastings to Fairchild, April 4, 1866.

30 Madison City Directory, 1866.

31 Henry Colin Campbell, *Wisconsin in Three Centuries,* New York, 1906, pp. 339–48 of biographical volume; *Biographical Review of Dane County, Wisconsin* (Chicago, 1893), pp. 410–13; Albert H. Sanford and H. J. Hirshheimer, *A History of LaCrosse Wisconsin, 1841–1900* (LaCrosse, 1951), pp. 36, 41, 74, 86; *History of Dane County* (Chicago, 1880), pp. 996–98.

32 *Milwaukee Sentinel,* May 27, 1868; Williamson and Smalley, pp. 334–36; Noyes, Markham, and Winkler, pp. 137–40.

33 *Wisconsin State Journal,* May 23, 1865.

34 1867 Annual Report, pp. 271–72.

35 Tomes, pp. 59, 63, 83–84.

36 1867 Annual Report, pp. 274–75.

37 1867 Annual Report, pp. 274–78.

38 Minutes of the annual meeting of the Board of Trustees, October, 1876, Journal of the Wisconsin State Lunatic Asylum.

39 Ibid.

13. *"Patients that Manifested a Dislike to Dr. Van Norstrand"*

1 *Portrait and Biographical Album of Green Lake, Marquette and Waushara Counties* (Chicago, 1890), pp. 234–35; *United States Biographical Dictionary,* Wisconsin edition, 1877, pp. 550–51.

2 *History of Rock County, Wisconsin* (Chicago, 1879), pp. 709–10; Wisconsin Necrology, vol. 6.

3 Appendix, p. 115.

4 Hastings to Van Norstrand, January 18, 1868.

5   Hastings to Van Norstrand, April 11 and February 1, 1868.

6   All testimony is from the Appendix, pp. 3–393.

7   Appendix, p. 266.

8   Ibid. p. 265.

9   Ibid. p. 266.

10   Ibid., p. 286.

11   Ibid., pp. 291–92.

12   Ibid., pp. 291–93.

13   Tomes, p. 264.

14. "Little Short of Murderous Neglect"

1   Tomes, pp. 213–22; also, Winfred Overholser, "The Founding and Founders of the Association," in Hall, p. 59.

2   The description of the weather is based upon weather reports and anecdotal information in the *Wisconsin State Journal,* March 6 through 14.

3   Appendix, p. 345. Amherst Kellogg saw his brother's body for the first time on Saturday, after it was brought back to Fort Atkinson.

4   See McKindley's statement, Appendix, pp. 333–38.

5   Appendix, pp. 344 and 348–49.

15. "Rotten Eggs"

1   Appendix, p. 376.

2   Mrs. Halliday's testimony, Appendix, p. 386.

3   Based on Van Norstrand's testimony, Appendix, pp. 370–77.

4   He fails to mention that one of the salaried attendants was his son, Fred. Thus only one of the five was an experienced attendant. (See Appendix, pp. 96–98.)

5   *Wisconsin State Journal,* May 6, 1868, and *Chicago Tribune,* May 7.

6   Williamson and Smalley, p. 57.

7   *Wisconsin State Journal,* April 20, 1868. The remarks from the *Milwaukee Sentinel* were quoted in this story.

8   Appendix, p. 290.

9   Ibid. p. 316.

10   These conclusions are based upon an analysis of "warrants," or checks, issued by the treasurer over a four-year period. A list of warrants was printed annually.

11   *Journal of the Assembly,* March 20, 1867.

12   L. Clark Davis, "A Modern Lettre De Cachet," *Atlantic Monthly,* May, 1868, pp. 599–600.

13 Grob, pp. 263–67, in particular the footnotes; also, Caplan, p. 182. For an excellent summary of the dilemmas faced by superintendents of the late nineteenth century see Tomes, pp. 264–310, "The Perils of Asylum Practice."

14 *Chicago Tribune*, May 16, 1868.

15 *Wisconsin State Journal*, May 6, 1868.

16 *Milwaukee Sentinel*, May 7 and 8, 1868.

16. *"A Solemn Court of Impeachment"*

1 The majority report of the Special Committee is on pages 3–130 of the Appendix to the Annual Report of 1868.

2 Appendix, p. 23 re: Workman and legislative report; p. 25. re: Ray.

3 Appendix, p. 42.

4 Appendix, pp. 311, 316, and 323. Also, case number 761, application and entries in Female Casebook.

5 Journal of the Wisconsin State Lunatic Asylum, May 7, 1868; Female Casebook, pp. 374 and 420.

6 *Chicago Tribune*, May 7, 1868.

7 *Chicago Tribune*, May 16, 1868.

8 Appendix, pp. 389–93.

9 Ibid., p. 391.

17. *"Abandon Hope"*

1 Case number 634.

2 *Chicago Tribune*, May 16, 1868.

3 Journal of the Wisconsin State Lunatic Asylum, June 3, 1868.

4 *Chicago Times*, June 3, 1868.

5 "Remarks of Hon. S. D. Hastings, Chairman of the committee appointed to investigate the affairs of the State Hospital for the Insane, Madison, June 4, 1868," p. 3. Hastings's report was later printed in pamphlet form.

6 Bailey to Van Norstrand, March 2, 1864, in Van Norstrand's military scrapbook.

7 Goldsmith to Van Norstrand, November 5, 1863, ibid.

8 *Milwaukee Sentinel*, June 6, 1868; *Chicago Tribune*, June 7; *Wisconsin State Journal*, June 5.

9 *Madison Democrat*, June 8 and 9; *Daily Milwaukee News*, June 6.

10 Van Norstrand to President of the Board of Trustees, quoted in Journal of the Wisconsin State Lunatic Asylum, June 5, 1868.

18. *"A True Gentleman of the Old School"*

1   *Wisconsin State Journal,* January 9, 1869.

2   "J. W. Sumner—store business letters and private correspondence," a ledger book with the Van Norstrand papers, Neville Museum, Green Bay.

3   *Wisconsin State Journal,* February 6, 1869.

4   J.W. Sumner store ledger

5   "Semi-annual Report of Bank of Commerce of Green Bay," Brown County Register of Deeds, Bank Records, 1854–1903.

6   J. W. Sumner store ledger.

7   Denise Gess and William Lutz, *Firestorm at Peshtigo* (New York, 2002), pp. 141–219.

8   *Green Bay Advocate,* October 12 and 26, 1871; *Green Bay Press-Gazette,* July 1934, Ter-centennial Edition, Civic and Social section, p. 22.

9   *Wisconsin State Journal,* May 8, 1883.

10   Sylvia Hall Holubetz and George Nau Burridge, *The Astor Historic District, Its History and Houses* (Green Bay, 1981.)

11   Memoirs, p. 151.

12   Ibid., p. 152.

13   Ibid., p. 152.

14   Obituaries in the *Green Bay Advocate,* May 10, 1883 and *Milwaukee Telegraph,* May 13. The clippings are on p. 31, vol. 4, of Wisconsin Necrology.

15   *Wisconsin State Journal,* May 8, 1883; *Green Bay Advocate,* May 10.

16   *Chicago Times,* June 12, 1868.

17   Wisconsin Necrology, vol. 5; March 20, 1864.

18   *Milwaukee Sentinel,* December 12, 1882.

19   Rush, pp. 175–83; Deutsch, pp. 80–81 and 140–41; Caplan, pp. 182–83.

20   Dorman B. Eaton, "Despotism in Lunatic Asylums," *North American Review,* 1881.

21   George A. Tucker, *Lunacy in Many Lands* (Sydney, 1887), pp. 34–37.

22   Memoirs, p. 66.

23   Tomes, p. 171.

24   Tomes, pp. 273–74; also, Journal of the Wisconsin State Lunatic Asylum, October 24, 1874.

25   "Report of the Investigating Committee, State Hospital for the Insane," Madison, WI, 1880.

26   From Boughton's defense, "Records of the State Hospital for the Insane, 1860–1880."

27   Grob, p. 205.

28   Diary of Richard Folger, 4th Wisconsin Cavalry, in Fyfe Family Papers, Wisconsin Historical Society, entries for 3,4, 5, 1864; also, Love, pp. 909–11, and *Milwaukee Sentinel,* May 13 and 14, 1864.

29   Bacon, p. 188.

30   Memoirs, p. 86. Van Norstrand also included this tale in his letter to the *Milwaukee Sentinel* (Quiner scrapbooks, vol. 8, p. 49).

31   William Riley Brooksher, *War Along the Bayous, The 1864 Red River Campaign in Louisiana* (Dulles, VA, 1998), pp. 209–13; Betty Sperret, *Scenes from the Past*, ([city of publication], 2001), pp. 104–9; Jack D. Welsh, M.D., *Medical Histories of Union Generals*, (Kent, OH, 1996); Patrick Brophy, *Past Perfect: Tales of Town and 'Round* (Vernon County, MO, 1999), pp. 125–28; *The Daily Mail* (Nevada, MO), April 20, 1893; Michael J. Goc, *"The Dells," An Illustrated History of Wisconsin Dells*, (Friendship, WI, 1999), pp. 35–39.

32   Welsh, *Medical Histories of Union Generals*, p. 249; Ezra J. Warner, *Generals in Blue, Lives of Union Commanders* (Baton Rouge, LA, 1964), pp. 356–57; *Dictionary of Wisconsin Biography*, p. 278; Stewart Sifakis, *Who Was Who in the Union*, vol. 1 (New York, 1988), p. 300; *Milwaukee Evening Wisconsin*, April 17, 1905.

Epilogue: "Three Percent Hastings"

1   Williamson and Smalley, pp. 57–58; Noyes, Markham, and Winkler, pp. 137–40.

2   *Wisconsin State Journal*, January 20, 1891; *Milwaukee Journal*, January 18, 1892, and August 28, 1931; Arian Helgeson, "The Wisconsin Treasury Cases," *Wisconsin Magazine of History*, Winter, 1951.

3   *Milwaukee Journal*, January 18, 1892; Helgesen, pp. 129–30; Robert C. Nesbit, *The History of Wisconsin, Industrialization and Urbanization (1873–1893)* (Madison, WI, 1985), pp. 618–19; transcript of testimony, State of Wisconsin vs. Harshaw, et al., p. 153.

4   Testimony, State of Wisconsin vs. Harshaw, et al., p. 114.

5   Testimony, pp. 114 and 151–54.

6   *Dictionary of Wisconsin Biography*, p. 162; biographical sketch of Samuel Dexter Hastings from *The National Cyclopedia of American Biography* (New York, 1900); Campbell, biographical volume, pp. 339–48.

7   *Milwaukee Journal*, February 23, 1892 and August 28, 1931; Arian Helgeson, "The Wisconsin Treasury Cases," *Wisconsin Magazine of History*, Winter, 1951.

8   Donald R. McNeil, "Dr. Alfred J. Castleman, Agitator and Critic," *The Wisconsin Medical Journal*, March, 1952, pp. 291–96; William S. Middleton, "The First Medical Faculty of the University of Wisconsin, Part I," *The Wisconsin Medical Journal*, August 1955, pp. 378–85.

9   *Watertown Chronicle*, January 22, 1851; *Watertown Democrat*, February 2, 1871; *The History of Jefferson County* (Chicago, 1879), pp. 401–2; Swart, *Koshkonong Country*, pp. 108–9 and 162.

10   Amherst Kellogg, "Recollections of Life in Early Wisconsin," *Wisconsin Magazine of History*, June, September, and December, 1924; also, the manuscript version in the Louise Phelps Kellogg Papers, Wisconsin Historical Society; David Kinnett, "Miss Kellogg's Quiet Passion," *Wisconsin Magazine of History*, summer, 1979; "The Kellogg Clan—Paper read by Amherst W. Kellogg, September 1st, 1902, at the Kellogg Klan Klub Piknik, Lincoln Park, Chicago," in the Louise Phelps Kellogg papers.

11   Diary of George Kellogg.

12   Appendix, p. 250.

BIBLIOGRAPHY

Primary Sources

Bank Incorporation Book, 1853–1868. Wisconsin Historical Society (hereafter, WHS).

Bean, Colonel Sidney Alfred, Papers of. WHS.

Blueprints of the State Hospital for the Insane dated 1924 and 1926. (These are the earliest still on file with the Bureau of State Facilities.)

Boardman, Major Frederick, Papers of. WHS.

Brown County Register of Deeds, Bank Records, 1854–1903. WHS.

Canon, James, Diary. WHS.

Caswell, Hon. Lucien B., Reminiscences. WHS.

Culver, Newton H., Papers of. WHS.

Defunct Banks, 1853–1873. WHS.

DeHave, Norton, Papers of. WHS.

Fairchild, Governor Lucius, Papers of. WHS.

Female Casebook, Northern State Hospital (now Winnebago Mental Health Institute, Winnebago, WI).

Fyfe Family Papers, WHS.

Journal of the Wisconsin State Lunatic Asylum (1854–1881). (Consists primarily of minutes of annual and semiannual meetings of the board of trustees and related documents). WHS.

Kellogg, George J., Collection. WHS.

Kellogg, Louise Phelps, Papers of. WHS.

Lewis, Governor James, Papers of. WHS.

Male and Female Casebooks, Wisconsin State Hospital for the Insane (now Mendota Mental Health Institute). WHS.

Paine, Halbert. Manuscripta Minora (unpublished memoirs and related papers). Charles East Collection, Hill Memorial Library, Louisiana State University, Baton Rouge.

Quiner, E. B., Scrapbooks compiled by (soldier letters and correspondents' dispatches clipped from newspapers and organized by regiment). WHS.

Randall, Governor Alexander, Papers of. WHS.

Records of the State Hospital for the Insane, 1860–1880 (includes D. F. Boughton's lengthy, handwritten defense of his tenure as superintendent). WHS.

Sumner, J. W. "Store business letters and private correspondence" (ledger book that includes letters and other entries made by Abraham Van Norstrand). Neville Public Museum, Green Bay.

Van Norstrand, Abraham. *Memoirs* (handwritten ledger). Neville Public Museum, Green Bay.

———. Military file. National Archives, Washington, D.C.

———. Wartime scrapbook. Neville Public Museum, Green Bay (consists of handwritten and printed orders, letters received, copies of letters sent, and other documents).

Books

Bacon, Edward. (1867). *Among the Cotton Thieves*. Detroit, MI.

Bates, Barbara. (1994). *Bargaining for Life*. Philadelphia.

Beitzinger, Alfons J. (1960). *Edward G Ryan—Lion of the Law*. Madison, WI.

Benedict, G. G. (1888). *Vermont in the Civil War*. Burlington, VT.

Bettersworth, John K. (1943). *Confederate Mississippi*. Baton Rouge, LA.

Biographical Guide to Forest Hill Cemetery. (2002). Madison, WI.

Biographical Review of Dane County. (1893). Chicago.

Birmingham, Robert A., and Leslie E. Eisenberg. (2000). *Indian Mounds of Wisconsin*. Madison, WI.

Birmingham, Robert A., and Katherine H. Rankin. (1994). *Native American Mounds in Madison and Dane County*. Madison, WI.

Bockoven, J. Sanbourne, M.D. (1963). *Moral Treatment in American Psychiatry*. New York.

Bradley and Chester. *From Croton Oil to Isotopes, One Hundred Years of Medicine at Hampton Veterans Administration Center*.

Bragg, Jefferson Davis. (1941). *Louisiana in the Confederacy*. Baton Rouge, LA.

Brooksher, William Riley. (1998). *War Along the Bayous, The 1864 Red River*

Campaign in Louisiana. Dulles, VA.

Brophy, Patrick. (1999). *Past Perfect: Tales of Town and 'Round.* Vernon County, MO.

Bucknill, John Charles, and Daniel H. Tuke. (1858). *A Manual of Psychological Medicine.* London. (1968 facsimile edition, New York and London).

Butler, Benjamin F. (1892). *Butler's Book.* Boston.

Campbell, Henry Colin. (1906). *Wisconsin in Three Centuries.* New York.

Caplan, Ruth B. (1969). *Psychiatry and the Community in Nineteenth Century America.* New York.

Carleton, Mark T. (1981). *River Capital, an Illustrated History of Baton Rouge.* Woodland Hills, CA.

Cassidy, Vincent H., and Amos E. Simpson. (1964). *Henry Watkins Allen of Louisiana.* Baton Rouge, LA.

Cunningham, Edward. (1994). *The Port Hudson Campaign, 1862–63.* Baton Rouge, LA.

Current, Richard N. (1976). *The History of Wisconsin.* Vol. 2, *The Civil War Era.* Madison, WI.

Dain, Norman. (1964). *Concepts of Insanity in the United States, 1789–1865.* New Brunswick, NJ.

Davis, William C. (1974). *Breckinridge—Statesman, Soldier, Symbol.* Baton Rouge, LA.

Dean, Eric T. Jr., (1997). *Shook Over Hell—Post-Traumatic Stress, Vietnam and the Civil War.* Cambridge, MA.

DeForest, John William. (1998). *Miss Ravenel's Conversion from Secession to Loyalty.* Lincoln, NE.

———. (1996). *A Volunteer's Adventures.* Baton Rouge, LA.

Deutsch, Albert. (1949). *The Mentally Ill in America, a History of Their Care and Treatment from Colonial Times.* New York.

Dictionary of Wisconsin Biography. (1960.) Madison, WI..

Donald, David Herbert. (1996). *Lincoln.* New York.

Dorsey, Sarah A. (1866). *Recollections of Henry Watkins Allen.* New York.

Duffy, John. (1962). *History of Medicine in Louisiana.* Vol. 2. Baton Rouge, LA.

East, Charles. (1977). *Baton Rouge: A Civil War Album.* Privately printed. Wisconsin Historical Society.

———, ed. (1991). *The Civil War Diary of Sarah Morgan.* Athens, GA.

Easum, Chester Verne. (1929). *The Americanization of Carl Schurz.* Chicago.

Eisenhower, John S. D. (1997). *Agent of Destiny—The Life and Times of General Winfield Scott.* New York.

Encyclopedia Britannica. (1771 and 1902).

Flinn, Frank M. (1887). *Campaigning with Banks.* Lynn, MA.

Flint, Austin. (1867). *Contributions Relating to the Causation and Prevention of Disease.* New York.

Foote, Shelby. (1958). *The Civil War, A Narrative: Fort Sumter to Perryville.* New York.

Gara, Larry. (1952). *Westernized Yankee—The Story of Cyrus Woodman.* Madison, WI.

Gess, Denise, and William Lutz. (2002). *Firestorm at Peshtigo.* New York.

Glazer, Walter. (1963). "Wisconsin Goes to War." M.S. thesis, University of Wisconsin.

Goc, Michael J. (1999). *"The Dells," An Illustrated History of Wisconsin Dells.* Friendship, WI.

Grob, Gerald. (1973). *Mental Institutions in America.* New York.

Hall, J. K., ed. (1944). *One Hundred Years of American Psychiatry.* New York.

Hamilton, Frank Hastings. (1861). *A Practical Treatise on Military Surgery.* New York.

Harstad, Peter T. (1963). "Health in the Upper Mississippi River Valley, 1820–1861." Ph.D. thesis, University of Wisconsin.

Harrington, Fred Harvey. (1948). *Fighting Politician, Major General N. P. Banks.* Philadelphia.

History and Catalogue of the Fourth Regiment Wisconsin Volunteers from June 1861 to March 1864. (1864). Baton Rouge, LA.

History of Dane County. (1880). Chicago.

History of Jefferson County, Wisconsin. (1879). Chicago.

History of Rock County, Wisconsin. (1879). Chicago.

Hoffman, Wickham. (1877). *Camp, Court and Siege.* New York.

Holbrook, Stewart H. (1950). *The Yankee Exodus.* New York.

Holubetz, Sylvia Hall, and George Nau Burridge. (1981). *The Astor Historic District, Its History and Houses.* Green Bay, WI.

Johns, Henry T. (1890). *Life with the Forty-Ninth Massachusetts.* Washington, DC

Johnson, Charles Beneulyn. (1917). *Muskets and Medicine.* Philadelphia.

Kaufman, Martin. (1979). *The University of Vermont College of Medicine.* Hanover, NH.

Keyes, Elisha. (1906). *History of Dane County.* Madison, WI.

King, Charles. (1891). *Kitty's Conquest.* Philadelphia.

LeSuer, Meridel. (1998). *North Star Country.* Minneapolis, MN.

Love, William DeLoss. (1866). *Wisconsin in the War of the Rebellion; a History of All Regiments and Batteries the State Has Sent to the Field.* Chicago.

McHatton-Ripley, Eliza. (1889). *From Flag to Flag.* New York.

Medical and Surgical History of the War of Rebellion. (Reprint, 1991). Wilmington, NC.

Menn, Joseph Karl. (1964). *The Large Slaveholders of Louisiana—1860.* New Orleans.

Merk, Frederick. (1916). *Economic History of Wisconsin During the Civil War Decade.* Madison, WI.

Mollenhoff, David V. (1982). *Madison, A History of the Formative Years.* Dubuque, IA.

Morison, Samuel Eliot. (1967). *"Old Bruin" Commodore Matthew C. Perry, 1794–1858.* Boston.

Morris, Roy Jr. (1998). *Ambrose Bierce, Alone in Bad Company.* New York.

National Cyclopedia of American Biography. (1900). New York.

Nesbit, Robert C. (1985). *The History of Wisconsin.* Vol. 3, *Urbanization and Industrialization, 1873–1893.* Madison, WI.

Norwood, Frederick A. (1974). *The Story of American Methodism.* Nashville, TN.

Noyes, George H., George C. Markham, and Frederick C. Winkler. (1908). *Semi-Centennial History of The Northwestern Mutual Life Insurance Company.* Milwaukee, WI.

Numbers, Ronald L., and Judith Walzer Leavitt. (1981). *Wisconsin Medicine Historical Perspectives.* Madison, WI.

Official Army Register of the Volunteer Force of the United States Army. (1865). Washington, DC.

Ott, John Henry. (1917). *Jefferson County and its People.* Chicago.

Peck, George W. (1883). *Peck's Bad Boy.* Chicago.

Perry, Matthew C. (1856). *Narrative of the Expedition of an American Squadron to the China Seas and Japan.* Vol. 2. Washington, DC.

Piersol, George Morris, ed. (1935). *Cyclopedia of Medicine.* Philadelphia.

Portrait and Biographical Album of Green Lake, Marquette and Waushara Counties. (1890). Chicago.

Quiner. E. B. (1866). *Military History of Wisconsin: A Record of the Civil and Military Patriotism of the State in the War for the Union.* Chicago.

Robison, Dale. (1976). "Wisconsin and the Mentally Ill: A History of the 'Wisconsin Plan' of State and County Care." Ph.D. dissertation, Marquette University.

Roland, Charles P. (1997). *Louisiana Sugar Plantations During the Civil War.* Baton Rouge, LA.

Rothstein, William G. (1992). *American Physicians in the Nineteenth Century.* Baltimore, MD.

Russell, William Howard. (1988). *My Diary, North and South.* Philadelphia.

Rush, Benjamin. (1812). *Medical Inquiries and Observations upon The Diseases of the Mind.* Philadelphia.

Sanford, Albert H., and J. J. Hershheimer. (1951). *A History of LaCrosse, Wisconsin, 1841–1900.* LaCrosse, WI.

Schaadt, Mark J., M.D. (1998). *Civil War Medicine.* Quincy, IL.

Schlesinger, Arthur M. Sr., and Dixon Ryan Fox. (1996). *A History of American Life.* New York.

Sifakis, Stewart. (1988). *Who Was Who in the Union.* New York.

Sperret, Betty. (2001) *Scenes from the Past.* Vernon County, MO.

Stevens, William B. (1907). *History of the Fiftieth Regiment of Infantry.* Boston.

Steiner, Paul E. (1968). *Disease in the Civil War.* Springfield, IL.

Swart, Hannah. (1975). *Koshkonong Country.* Fort Atkinson, WI.

———. (1981). *Koshkonong Country Revisited.* Vol. 1. Muskego, WI.

Tomes, Nancy. (1994). *The Art of Asylum-Keeping, Thomas Story Kirkbride and the Origins of American Psychiatry.* Philadelphia.

Travelers Official Railway Guide of the United States and Canada. (June, 1868).

Tripler, Charles S., M.D., and George C. Blackman, M.D. (1861) *Hand-Book for the Military Surgeon.* Cincinnati, OH.

Trautman, Rose, and Trautman, Barbara. (undated; early 1890s). *Our Experiences as the Victims of a Foul and Cruel Wrong.* Privately printed. Wisconsin Historical Society.

Tucker, George A. (1887). *Lunacy in Many Lands.* Sydney, Australia.

Twain, Mark. (1991). *Life on the Mississippi.* New York.

United States Biographical Dictionary (Wisconsin edition). (1877). Chicago.

Van Norstrand, Jacqueline. (1995). *The Ancestors and Descendants of Frederick van Norstrand & Elisabeth Harris of Cayuga County, New York.*.

Waite, Frederick Clayton. (1945). *The Story of a Country Medical College.* Montpelier, VT.

Warner, Ezra J. (1964). *Generals in Blue, Lives of Union Commanders.* Baton Rouge, LA.

Warner, John Harley. (1986). *The Therapeutic Perspective: Medical Practice, Knowledge, and Identity in America, 1820–1885.* Cambridge, MA.

Welsh, Jack D., M. D. (1996). *Medical Histories of Union Generals.* Kent, OH.

West, Richard S. Jr. (1965). *Lincoln's Scapegoat General—A Life of General Benjamin F. Butler.* Boston.

Whitaker, Robert. (2002). *Mad in America.* Cambridge, MA.

Williamson, Harold F., and Orange Smalley. (1976). *Northwestern Mutual Life—A Century of Trusteeship.* New York.

Wilson, Edmund. (1962). *Patriotic Gore.* New York.

Winters, John D. (1963). *The Civil War in Louisiana.* Baton Rouge, LA.

Wisconsin Losses in the Civil War. (1915). Madison, WI.

Wesley, John. *The Works of John Wesley.* Vol. 11. (1958). Grand Rapids, MI.

Government Documents

The Acts to Provide for the Government of the Wisconsin State Hospital for the Insane; also the By-Laws of the Board of Trustees, as Adopted by Said Board, and Approved by the Governor. (1863). Janesville, WI.

Annual Reports of the Adjutant General of the State of Wisconsin.

Annual Reports of the Trustees of the Wisconsin State Hospital for the Insane, 1859–1906. (Biennial after 1882.) Madison, WI.

Appendix to Annual Report of the State Hospital for the Insane for the Year 1868. Madison, WI.

Elliott, Thomas B., M.D. "An Address to the Legislature in Behalf of the Insane of the State of Wisconsin," delivered February 6, 1856. Madison, WI.

Journal of the Assembly, 1852, 1867, and 1868. (Wisconsin legislature.)

Journal of the Senate, 1865. (Wisconsin legislature.)

The Legislative Manual, of the State of Wisconsin; comprising Jefferson's

Manual, Rules, Forms and Laws, for the Regulation of Business. (1868). Madison, WI.

Madison City Directory. (1866).

Records of pre-1907 marriages, Columbia County. WHS.

"Remarks of Hon. S. D. Hastings, Chairman of the Committee Appointed to Investigate the Affairs of the State Hospital for the Insane." (1868). Madison, WI.

"Report of the Investigating Committee, State Hospital for the Insane." (1880). Madison, WI.

"Rules for the Regulation of the Wisconsin State Hospital for the Insane," October, 1860.

"Semi-annual Report of Bank of Commerce of Green Bay," Brown County Register of Deeds, Bank Records, 1854–1903.

"Special Report of the Commissioners of the Lunatic Asylum," Madison, WI, 1855.

"State of Wisconsin vs. Harshaw, et al." (transcript). Dane County, WI.

Transcript of testimony, State of Wisconsin vs. Harshaw, et al.

The War of Rebellion: A Compilation of the Official Records of the Union and Confederate Armies. War Department. Washington, DC (referred to in end notes as Official Records).

Wisconsin Necrology. Wisconsin Historical Society.

Periodical Articles

American Journal of Insanity.

The Century Magazine. February, 1885.

"Civil War Letters of Knute Nelson." *Norwegian-American Studies*. 23, 1967.

Cross, Henry Martyn. "A Yankee Soldier Looks at the Negro," edited by William Cullen Bryant II. *Civil War History*, June, 1961.

Davis, L. Clark. "A Modern Lettre de Cachet." *Atlantic Monthly*, May, 1868.

Eaton, Dorman B. "Despotism in Lunatic Asylums." *North American Review* 134, 1881.

Dixon, E. C. "Newport, Its Rise and Fall." *Wisconsin Magazine of History*, June, 1942.

Harstad, Peter T. "Sickness and Disease on the Wisconsin Frontier: Malaria, 1812–1850." *Wisconsin Magazine of History*, winter, 1959–1960.

———. "Sickness and Disease on the Wisconsin Frontier: Smallpox and other Diseases." *Wisconsin Magazine of History*, summer, 1960.

Helgeson, Arian. "The Wisconsin Treasury Cases." *Wisconsin Magazine of History*, Winter, 1951.

Hetter, George P. "An Examination of the Pheno-Croton Oil Peel," parts 1 and 2. *Plastic Reconstructive Surgery*. January and February, 2000.

Hewitt, Lawrence Less, and R. Christopher Goodwin. "The Battle of Bisland, Louisiana." *North and South* 1, no. 7.

Kellogg, Amherst Willoughby. "Recollections of Life in Early Wisconsin." *Wisconsin Magazine of History*, December, 1924.

Kinnett, David. "Miss Kellogg's Quiet Passion." *Wisconsin Magazine of History*, summer, 1979.

Kraus, Robert F., M.D. "J. Edward Lee, M.D., and the Founding of the Wisconsin State Hospital." *Transactions and Studies of the College of Physicians of Philadelphia* 40, no. 2, October, 1972.

"Letters of General Thomas Williams." *American Historical Review* 14, 1909.

McNeil, Donald R. "Dr. Alfred J. Castleman, Agitator and Critic." *The Wisconsin Medical Journal*, March, 1952.

Middleton, William S. "The First Medical Faculty of the University of Wisconsin." *The Wisconsin Medical Journal*, August, 1955.

"Proceedings of the Medical Society of Wisconsin," 1868, pp. 37–42. *Wisconsin Union*, January 31, 1868.

Towle, S. K. "Note of Practice in the U.S.A. General Hospital, Baton Rouge, La., During the Year 1863." *The Boston Medical and Surgical Journal* 70, no. 3, February 18, 1864.

Newspapers

Chicago Times
Chicago Tribune
Daily Mail (Nevada, MO)
Daily Milwaukee News
Gazette and Comet (Baton Rouge, LA)
Green Bay Advocate
Green Bay Press-Gazette

Jefferson Banner
Jeffersonian
Madison Daily Union
Madison Democrat
Milwaukee Evening Wisconsin
Milwaukee Journal
Milwaukee Sentinel
Racine Weekly Journal
Watertown Chronicle
Watertown Democrat
Wisconsin Chief
Wisconsin State Journal
Wisconsin Union

INDEX